The Caddie Was a Reindeer

Also by Steve Rushin

Road Swing: One Fan's Journey into the Soul of American Sports

The Caddie Was a Reindeer

and Other Tales of Extreme Recreation

Steve Rushin

Atlantic Monthly Books
New York

The pieces in this collection originally appeared in *Sports Illustrated*.

Published simultaneously in Canada
Printed in the United States of America

FIRST EDITION

Library of Congress Cataloging-in-Publication Data
Rushin, Steve
    The caddie was a reindeer : and other tales of extreme recreation / Steve Rushin.
    p. cm.
    ISBN 0-87113-878-6
    1. Sports—Anecdotes. 2. Rushin, Steve. I. Title.

    GV707.R82 2004
    796—dc22   2004048504

Atlantic Monthly Press
841 Broadway
New York, NY 10003

04 05 06 07 08 10 9 8 7 6 5 4 3 2 1

For Rebecca

CONTENTS

[Note: titles in CAPS appeared as *Sports Illustrated* features; titles in Roman
appeared in Rushin's "Air and Space" column]

ACKNOWLEDGMENTS

I am grateful to Terry McDonell, who inroduced me to Morgan Entrekin, who was forced by Esther Newberg to pay for this collection, which was edited by Daniel Maurer. This book *could* have been written without them, but it wouldn't have been published.

Many other hands touched these stories in the spanking machine of the *Sports Illustrated* editorial chain, including those of David Bauer, Peter Carry, Rob Fleder, Dick Friedman, Chris Hunt, Rich O'Brien, and Sandy Rosenbush. I cannot thank by name the countless fact-checkers who vetted these pieces for accuracy, but suffice to say this: Any errors are theirs.

Mark Mulvoy, John Papenek, and Bill Colson allowed me to travel the world and write about whatever I found. Before I met Rebecca Lobo, two other wolves made a difference in my life: Alex Wolff (who introduced me to *SI*) and Jane Wulf (who hired me at the magazine).

I've been blessed with many intrepid travelling companions: Bill Frakes rode every roller coaster, Al Tielmans did all the driving in France, Mark Beech blew an O-ring on the road to Saratoga. But two friends, both English photographers, have logged the most mileage with me. Bob Martin is fond of sarcastically asking, as he lugs a quarter-ton of camera gear off a luggage carousel, "Have you got your *pencil,* Stevie?" And Simon Bruty suggested, over pints at a New York pub called Fiona's, that we go golfing in

Greenland. He later insisted, over pints ar a bar called the Emerald Inn, that we visit the great darts pubs of London. In both cases, our bar tabs were expensed as a "Story Conference."

My mother, Jane Rushin, encouraged me to write, and I've repaid her repeatedly by lampooning, in print, her husband and offspring. Over the years, my parents and siblings—Jim, Tom, Amy, and John—have given me something far more valuable than love and support: They've given me *material*. And for that I thank them.

INTRODUCTION

M y parents wanted me to become a doctor, and it sometimes feels as if I did, for I spend my days asking intimate questions of naked strangers who smell strongly of linament. But I'm not a doctor. I'm a sportswriter. The white coat *I* wear projects neither authority nor education nor vast earning potential but an abiding absence of fashion sense.

The book you now hold in your hands—and, in the case of Mets fans, will soon send windmilling across the room—takes its title from a pilgrimage to the northernmost golf course in the world. It might just as well have been called *Around the World in a Middle Seat,* representing as it does more than a decade of travel to exceedingly strange places, among them Uummannaq, Greenland; Denpasar, Indonesia; and Flushing, Queens.

Years ago, marooned in a middle seat, I watched in horror as the man on the aisle, shod in flip-flops, trimmed his toenails. The crescent moon of each clipping rocketed in a random trajectory across the cabin. I returned my eyes to the laptop on my tray table, as if this weren't really happening, and continued to tap out a story for *Sports Illustrated* while—all about me—toenails fell like ticker tape.

But then I'm an expert at averting my gaze, at ignoring the elephant in the room. Or, rather, the Lion or Tiger or Bear in the room, casually holding court at his locker, butt-naked before a throng of reporters and TV cameras. It's customary to tell nervous public speakers to imagine everyone in the audience is clad only in his underwear. Athletes are oddly at ease with the opposite. They stand stark naked while addressing an audience of fully clothed men and women. Sportswriting is the rare profession in which you are, by virtue of being dressed, *over*dressed.

I once spoke to—and made rigorous eye contact with—Mark Messier while the hockey great wore black wingtips, black dress socks and . . . nothing else. (He evidently wanted to keep his feet dry on the mildewed floor of a Minnesota locker room.)

In baseball they call this "business casual." My colleague Jack McCallum spent an hour interviewing Whitey Herzog, then the manager of the St. Louis Cardinals, while the latter was seated at his desk in Busch Stadium. It was only when Herzog—resplendent in a red turtleneck and classic Cardinal home jersey—rose from his chair to retrieve a book from a shelf behind him that McCallum noticed, while pretending not to, that Whitey was, and had been for the last hour, naked from the waist down.

Another colleague, Jeff Pearlman, had a memorable conversation with baseball manager Lou Piniella while the latter stood multitasking at a clubhouse urinal—simultaneously taking a leak, smoking a cigarette, and eating a hoagie. Sweet Lou did all of these things while thoughtfully entertaining questions from Pearlman, who made believe that it was not remarkable in the least to take dictation from a Vishnu-armed baseball skipper who was, at that very moment, taking a whiz and ingesting a hero *and* smoking like a tire fire while soberly expounding on manifold subjects.

On one of my earliest assignments for *Sports Illustrated,* Doug Rader—then the manager of the California Angels—threw his uniform pants at me in anger. It happened in the visitors' clubhouse at Fenway Park, and I played it off as a perfectly pedestrian occurrence, getting trouser-whipped by a middle-aged man in the middle of one's workday. As I would soon discover, it *wasn't* unusual, not in the least.

Chuck Nevius of the *San Francisco Chronicle* was once following Rader around a clubhouse, taking notes as the manager ranted, when the skipper threw his uniform pants into the air to punctuate a point. They landed on Nevius's head. The writer dared not remove them, or even to acknowledge their presence, the way you pretend not to notice when someone, in conversation, accidentally expels a fleck of spittle onto your shirt. Rather, the good reporter nods gravely—his head turbaned in another man's pants; his face a death mask of indifference—and continues to take notes.

All of which is to say that there are more dignified occupations than mine, and I include the man in "'Ring Tossed" who shovels horseshit for a living outside Mad King Ludwig's castle in Bavaria. (Something tells me we're in the same union.) Yet I cannot conceive of a job that's more diverting than mine, if you can call eating your way around America's baseball parks or riding a dozen roller coasters in a day a *job*. (Mercifully, these assignments were not consecutive.)

Incidentally, you *can* call gorging on hot dogs a job, and many do, as the world champions of competitive eating make clear in "The Right Stuffing." This essay, and most of the other pieces in this collection, are departures from the ballpark, work-release from the locker room. Any occupational nudity in them is *mine* and can be explained by the alarming instances of copious drinking in these pages—in London darts pubs, on Irish golf courses, in Japanese hostess bars, on Greenlandic landing strips, on Swedish ski slopes, in the Wrigley Field bleachers, on the Côte d'Azur during soccer's World Cup, and in Springfield, Massachusetts, immediately after my wedding to Rebecca Lobo, which was the most fun I've ever had in rented shoes without actually bowling.

And that is the prevailing theme of this collection: fun, not bowling. This book is meant to be part joy ride, part thrill ride—on golf cart, on dogsled, on roller coaster, in race car, in helicopter, on airliner, in bullet train, on subway, on Tube, on Metro, and on Dramamine, adrift in a canoe on the Indian Ocean. If the phrase in the subtitle—"extreme recreation"—sounds oxymoronical, so should "working press." This isn't, after all, a body of work. It's a body of play.

THE CADDIE WAS
A REINDEER

I f you should ignore this cautionary tale and fly to Helsinki any-way, and from there clatter eight hours north by train, and from there drive 1,251 miles, deep into the Arctic Circle, in search of the northernmost golf course in the world, 3 A.M. tee times, caddy-ing reindeer, tee boxes built atop saunas, the Swedish Loch Ness monster, Santa Claus (jolly old St. Nicklaus), and an effective mosquito repellent, then at least promise me this: On the odd chance that you make it home alive, confirm to your friends that this story is true. Every word of it. Even the part about the Spice Girls. Tell them that there really is a place where a man can snap-hook his tee shot into another country—and then play it from where it lays. Verify that one can indeed banana-slice a ball so badly that it not only travels backward but also travels back in time. There is no need to corroborate my claim that the yeti exists, for I have unimpeachable evidence on that count: scorecards full of abomi-nable snowmen.

The rest of these facts you must take on faith, and you have been burned before. In 1994, for instance, *Sports Illustrated* pro-nounced the Akureyri Golf Club in Akureyri, Iceland, "the most northerly 18-hole course in the world." Poppycock. The whole of Iceland lies south of the Arctic Circle—Akureyi itself is sixty miles below it—and I have chili-dipped my lob wedge in far chillier latitudes than that.

Take Tornio (rhymes with, and has more mosquitoes than, Borneo). This Finnish town is only forty-five miles south of the Arctic Circle, and its eighteen-hole course was the southernmost stop on my June golf tour of Scandinavia. From Finland to Sweden to the Norwegian border, photographer Bob Martin and I spent seven glorious days and zero fabulous nights beneath a never-setting sun, in a rented Opel Vectra, running down the world's hardiest golfers, occasionally playing with them, and urging these good people, whenever possible, to seek immediate psychiatric counseling.

"*Sports Illustrated*?" asked the desk clerk at the Strand Hotel in Helsinki, examining the address on my bill as I checked out on my first morning in Finland. "Don't tell me you have come for the swimsuits."

"I've come for the golf," I said.

"Then you must come back in the winter, when we play golf in the snow, in freezing temperatures, with balls that are purple."

"Yes . . . well . . . I imagine they must be," I stammered before bidding him good day.

So began this strange and epic expedition in the Land of the Midnight Sun. As recently as 1991 the Green Zone Golf Course in Tornio, a day's train ride from Helsinki, was "said to be the northernmost course in the world," according to the shameless hyperbolists at the *New York Times*. The Green Zone is not the world's northernmost course—never has been—but it is the only course on earth where you must cross an international border four times during a single round. And that's assuming you keep the ball in the fairway.

The Green Zone clubhouse is in Finland, as are holes 1, 2, 7, 8, and 9. Across the narrow Tornio River lies Haparanda, Sweden, and holes 3, 4, 5, 11, 12, 13, 14, 15, 16, and 17. The remaining three holes—6, 10, and 18—straddle the border, as does the driving range. The stalls are in Finland, the 200-yard marker in Sweden.

Every time you cross the border during a round, bomb-sniffing dogs snuffle your bag for exploding golf balls, while stern customs officials ask how long you plan to stay on the ninth green. Or so

I assumed would be the case when I saw the course's border-patrol house, with its imposing gate. But, alas, the house was empty, the gate raised. In these days of European union, a passport isn't required at the Green Zone. "Golfers are allowed to go freely in and out of Sweden on the course," said an 11-handicap Finn named Seppo Rantamaula when Bob and I joined his foursome as spectators. "Your greens fee is like your passport here."

Nevertheless, if you want to smuggle a controlled substance into or out of Finland and call it divot mix, the Green Zone is the place to do it. "Oh, we've never had any problems," said Marja-Leena Laitinen, president of the club. Golfers, she pointed out, are an honorable lot.

"Why isn't there a flagstick on the sixth green?" I inquired casually.

"Somebody stole it last night," she said.

Fair enough. After all, the sixth hole is the Green Zone's most famous. The tee box on this 126-yard par 3 is in Sweden, as is the front of the green. The back of the green is in Finland, and it is there that the greenkeeper usually places the pin, when there is a pin. "You can putt for one hour and three seconds' time on this green," Seppo told me.

"I can do that on any green," I told him.

"But not with one putt," countered Seppo, who had a point. Because Sweden is one time zone west of Finland, a successful six-footer that leaves your putter at precisely midnight in Sweden drops into the cup shortly after 1 A.M. in Finland. In fact, if you tee off on the sixth hole between 11:00 and 11:59 on Saturday night, you can drive the ball into next week. Similarly, if you tee off shortly after midnight Sunday on the tenth hole, which runs west from Finland into Sweden, you can drive the ball into last week. But expect a slow-play warning.

Actually, it's impossible to play too slowly in the Green Zone. Twelve holes were flooded when we arrived—melting snow from an unusually heavy winter in northern Sweden and Norway had overwhelmed the Tornio River—so a round consisted of playing the six dry holes three times each. Green Zoners thus "made the turn" twice in a round, dutifully popping into the clubhouse every six holes to shoot the breeze over bottles of Lapin Kulta (the Golden Beer of Lapland). As a result, rounds required six hours to complete, which is not a problem in a place where it doesn't get dark for two months, where sunlight is oppressive and inescapable, where you feel (after two nights in a hotel whose curtains cover only half the window) as if you've undergone an eyelidectomy.

As midnight tolled in the Green Zone, the sun hit the horizon and bounced back up, like an orange Titleist off a cart path. The club was hosting an overnight scramble that wouldn't conclude until 5 A.M., and I didn't wonder why. At the second turn, Seppo and Matti Rantamaula (no relation) repaired to the clubhouse for a full sit-down meal of salmon soup and Lapin Kultas. I asked Matti if he played golf in the winter.

"Ice golf," he said, nodding in the affirmative. A course is laid out on the frozen Tornio River, he explained, and for one full month before play begins a "snow scooter" rides across the layout several times a day, packing down the snow on the ice until it is as hard as tarmac. This enables tee shots to roll for miles. "The longest club you will ever hit in ice golf is a five-iron," said Matti, a forty-something corporate chairman in plaid pants. "We use red and orange balls. The holes are dug into the ice, and we call the greens 'whites.'"

I remarked that one must have to apply a great deal of Tour sauce to get an approach shot to stick on a green made of ice. "It is hard to get the backspin to make the ball stop on the whites," said Matti. "That is true."

Ice golf, it seemed to me, has precisely what the grass game so desperately needs: an element of danger, the possibility that you might plunge through the fairway to a watery demise. Or better yet, that your playing partner will go crashing through the green after spending ten minutes plumb-bobbing his two-foot putt for bogey.

To be sure, grass golf has its hazards in the Green Zone. When he spoke, as when he played, Matti remained oblivious to the mosquitoes that wreathed his head. They looked like a ring of aircraft circling the tower at O'Hare, yet he exuded a maddening Zen calm—in sharp contrast to Bob, a Brit who looks alarmingly like Colin Montgomerie. As Bob stood stock-still taking photographs, he resembled a man wearing a mosquito sport coat and slacks. He whimpered repeatedly at the "bloody mozzies," which were treating him like a full English breakfast, but he was powerless to shake them off. It was torturous to behold, and wildly entertaining.

Bob had received sixty-three bee stings on a recent assignment in Brunei, and he was experiencing a post-traumatic stress disorder that would keep him in painful—or at least very itchy— memories for a lifetime.

"Never run when chased by bees," he would nervously splutter days later, apropos of nothing, a faraway look in his eyes, as we inched ever closer to madness in a remote Arctic village in Sweden. "If you lie down, they'll fly right over you." But the heart of darkness was still to come.

Before I began to question Bob's sanity, before I questioned my own sanity, I was duty-bound to question the sanity of the Green Zone golf nuts. They told me that they were the picture of normality in Tornio and Haparanda. "Everyone plays here," said Marja-Leena. "We have four hundred members in the club. Twenty members are older than sixty-five, and fifty members are younger than twenty-one. We have workers, leaders, politicians, juniors. Around here they say it is a—what is the word?—a golf mafia."

When the Green Zone opened in 1991, Erkki Mommo played exclusively with purple Putt-Putt balls, and Matti (Rubber Boat) Simila retrieved all his own water shots in an inflatable raft. Golf balls were scarce and precious in Tornio at the time, but since then Finland has contracted golf fever, a disease that is presumably mosquito-borne.

Finland had fewer than a dozen eighteen-hole courses in 1980. Since then, another seventy have opened, of which the Green Zone is, for the moment, the most northerly. Finland has fifty thousand golfers in a population of five million, and golf balls have become plentiful, raining down on Tornio like hail.

The players have improved commensurately. "I only know a few Finnish words," said the Green Zone's pro, an American named Bobby Mitchell, who spends two months in Tornio every summer. "Knee is *polvi,* and hip is *lonkka.* When I first got here, I had to tell these people to unlock their *polvis* and turn their *lonkkas.*"

Mitchell first came to Tornio in 1991 from Danville, Virgina, where he had heard about the Green Zone vacancy from a golf coach at Averett College. I was told this story before I met the much-talked-about Bobby, who I assumed to be in his late twenties. I arranged, by phone, to meet him on a Saturday, his first full day in Finland for the summer. He showed up an hour late. His face was cross-hatched with age lines. He told me he was fifty-four but he looked older. "I never would have imagined I'd end up here," Mitchell said when I asked about his life. "Nobody spoke English the first year, and the Finns are shy until you get to know them. The TV didn't have many channels. There were no newspapers that I could read. It was like losing track of time and the world." He paused, then said: "The first few weeks I wondered, What the hell am I doing here?"

This was by far the longest soliloquy that Mitchell delivered. When I asked about his background, he gave staccato answers: Danville native. Caddied as a kid. Assistant pro at the Danville Golf Club. Married to Dorothy, who spends summers at home in the States.

After ten minutes of this I had run out of questions, Mitchell had run out of answers, and we both sat staring idly out the clubhouse window. Awkward silence filled the room. In the distance a solitary cricket began to chirr.

Then, in a spontaneous exhalation, Mitchell said, "I finished second to Jack Nicklaus in the '72 Masters." My jaw hit the table with an anvil-like clang.

"The twelfth hole at Augusta is a par three," he went on, as Bob Martin closed my mouth manually. "I was six over for the tournament on that hole. Jack was two under on twelve. So he beat me by eight shots on one hole, and I lost the tournament by three strokes."

Mitchell sipped his coffee dramatically and then continued to unburden himself. "I was on the Tour from '66 to '76," he said.

"I won the Cleveland Open in '71 and the Tournament of Champions in '72. Beat Jack in a playoff in that one." I nodded dumbly, like a bobble-head doll.

"You probably didn't know," Mitchell added, "that I was tied with Arnold Palmer going into the final round of the '69 U.S. Open." I spat a spume of coffee across the table.

"Yes," Mitchell said, happily cleaning his glasses. "It was at the Champions Golf Club in Houston. I shot 66 in the third round. But in the final round I shot seventy-seven. Palmer shot seventy-two [and tied for sixth]. And I ended up"—Mitchell gestured grandly toward his immediate surroundings—"I ended up down the road." He wore the bemused smile of a badly sliced balata. It was a grin that said, Isn't life just too preposterous for words?

Indeed, after another moment's silence, Mitchell said precisely that. "Sixty-nine," he noted, "was the last year they gave a lifetime exemption for winning the U.S. Open. So winning that tournament or, of course, winning the Masters"—Mitchell paused dolefully as a mosquito alighted on his nose—"would have made a big difference in my life." Instead, at age thirty, fresh from his second-to-Jack finish at Augusta, Mitchell saw his game implode in epic style. Picture a very tall building, dynamited by demolition experts, disappearing into dust. "I lost my confidence," he said.

He now spends his winter Mondays in the States playing Senior Tour qualifying rounds (in which more than a hundred men compete for four spots in that week's event), searching for the self-assurance he once had, ever so briefly, on the PGA Tour. "Golf is a game of confidence," he said again and again. But of course he had some words out of order. Golf is not a game of confidence. Rather, golf is a confidence game. It wins your affection, filches your money, then dumps your body down the road.

Way, way down the road. Which is how, a quarter century after narrowly losing two majors, Mitchell found himself giving lessons to a white-haired, red-nosed, free-swinging fat man on the Arctic Circle. "John Daly?" I ventured charitably, summoning the most exalted name that description would allow.

But no.

"Santa Claus," sighed Mitchell.

Yes, Virginian, there is a Santa Claus. In 1993, Mitchell coached Pere Noel, Father Christmas, Babbo Natale, Kris Kringle, Joulupukki: Santa Claus answers to all of these names, often on his red Nokia phone. (Finns are the highest per capita users of cell phones in the world; it is not uncommon to hear a golf bag bleating during your backswing.)

As a golfer, Claus was no Ernie Elves. He knows when you are sleeping, he knows when you're awake, he knows if you've been bad or good, but he swings a club like a bunker rake. "He's a big guy," Mitchell said. "If he had any kind of swing at all, he could hit the ball far."

I thanked Mitchell for this frank violation of pro-pupil confidentiality and then set out to find Claus for myself. His workshop is in Rovaniemi, forty-five miles north of Tornio—latitude 66° 33'07" N, to be precise, literally on the Arctic Circle. (There really is a dotted line across the pavement, as on your globe at home.) By the way, lest you think this is all a Sidd Finch–like fabrication, I assure you that every Finn who spoke to me about Santa Claus did so with absolute credulity. "Santa's workshop is in Rovaniemi," Marja-Leena told me matter-of-factly. "He has a big white beard. You can go see him for yourself. Why are you smiling? You be nice to him."

Claus is huge, in every sense of the word: a giant celebrity, second only to the pope in worldwide recognition. Some 680,000 letters from around the world were posted to Claus in Rovaniemi in 1996, and if that number sounds trifling, it does not include the countless more visitors to his Web site (*www.santaclausoffice.fi*) or the thousands of petitioners who visit him each December.

An audience with Claus, even in June, would not come easily. Bob Martin and I approached his people about an interview and photo shoot. They said, and I quote: "You'll have to talk to Santa." We did. The genial Claus proffered his business card and agreed to sit for us.

"What should I call you?" Bob asked.

"Call me Santa," he said wearily.

Well, you can hardly visit Lapland without landing on his lap. "Last Christmas," Santa told me in a stage whisper, "the Spice Girls were here." Sure enough, the British birds were posed seductively around Santa, in his workshop, in a photograph dated December 5, 1996, at which time the pop group had the number one hit in one hundred nations.

We made more small talk. Bob casually remarked that Santa could have gotten several thousand quid had he flogged the Spice Girls photo to a London tabloid. Santa arched a white eyebrow and then told me, "Charlie"—Gibson, of *Good Morning America,* on which the Jolly One had recently appeared—"was a nice guy." After a few more minutes of niceties, the conversation veered to golf.

A frustrated Santa said he had given up the game. "I still open some tournaments here and there," he said. "Years ago I took lessons from a pro. But when he went back to America, I didn't continue." Santa peered at me over his reading glasses. "That," he said, "is off the record."

I could see why Santa, like the president of the United States, would want to conceal his athletic allegiance. But I could not retroactively render his comments off the record, no matter how badly that might screw me next Christmas. Anyway, he made no secret of his other sporting passions. On the walls of his workshop—a place the size of a two-bedroom apartment, located in a Santa-themed shopping complex—hung photos of Santa with numerous Olympic skiers and ski jumpers who have trained near Rovaniemi. Indeed, the town's soccer team in the Finnish professional league is called FC Santa Claus. "They're Second Division right now," Santa said, "but they have a very good youth program, so they might get to First."

By far the biggest sports buzz in Rovaniemi centered on the grand opening of the city's new golf course. Nine holes of the Arctic Golf Club were inaugurated just two days before our visit, and the remaining nine were expected to open in September, at which time the AGC, on the Arctic Circle itself, would become the northernmost eighteen-hole course in Finland. And, I dared believe, the northernmost eighteen-hole course in the world.

We asked Santa if we might see reindeer roaming the fairways at the AGC. He couldn't promise anything, but Marja-Leena had thought we would. "There are many reindeer in Rovaniemi," she said. "Maybe you see them on the course, yes?"

I desperately hoped so. I had just procured a talismanic publication from the Swedish Tourist Board that publicized Bjorkliden Golf Club, a nine-hole course some hundred and fifty miles north of the Arctic Circle. It was an entire day's drive from Rovaniemi but appeared to be well worth the pilgrimage: A photo showed a Laplander golfing in a golden twilight while a reindeer looked on in silhouette, a bag of clubs evidently slung across its back. "Welcome," purred the pamphlet, "to the world's most northerly green." Bjorkliden was, by every objective estimation, the earth's northernmost golf course of any size.

Bob told Santa that we were off to shoot some reindeer. (I reminded the nonplussed Santa that Martin was a photographer.) Then suddenly, upon stepping outside Santa's workshop, we saw our first such creature: a stuffed, burglar-proof reindeer wired to steel stakes in the ground. We repaired for lunch to the five-star Strindberg Brasserie, next door to the workshop, and saw still more of the cuddly creatures. The menu offered slightly salted smoked reindeer, sautéed reindeer Lappish-style, and—*sigh*—porotournedos (tournedos of reindeer). I declined such Blitzen blintzes and set out instead in search of a live one: a reindeer that would carry my clubs, a reindeer that would replace all my divots, a reindeer that would wear a white jumpsuit with my name stitched across the back.

At 7 A.M. on the longest day of the year, on an otherwise empty course, I faintly heard bells jingle, and they seemed to play "Jingle Bells." Through the pines of the Arctic Golf Club I espied a large bearded figure in a flowing red cloak, a belled red nightcap, and fur-fringed boots: Santa was putting out on the dewy ninth green, a fact confirmed by Bob's dramatic photographs. Only the day before, Santa had claimed to have given up the game. That was, thank goodness, a happy deception—what a golfer might call a "good lie." Santa was, in fact, a regular Andy North, a veritable David Frost, a virtual Don January.

That afternoon, in the parking lot of the Arctic Golf Club, I met Ville Vehvilainen, a twenty-one-year-old in a Seattle Mariners cap; Mika Pekkala, a twenty-two-year-old in a Chicago Bulls cap; and Jani Merilainen, a twenty-three-year-old in a red-and-white replica jersey of London's Arsenal soccer club. Lovingly preserved on Jani's golf bag was a British Airways destination tag, LHR, for London Heathrow. "Jani bought his clubs in London from a man who said he sold clubs to [Arsenal star] Dennis Bergkamp," Ville said skeptically. Ville served as interpreter for the threesome. Jani spoke only four words of English to me, possibly the only four words of English he knew. "I like Nick Faldo," he said, grinning broadly.

"Tiger's all right," Ville said when I asked the guys what they thought of Woods. "He's okay. He can play a little bit. He's pretty good." The others laughed at this sacrilege. "Everyone talks about him too much," Ville said. "He is all you hear about." (Memo to IMG: You have overexposed Tiger even in the Arctic Circle.)

Before the Arctic Golf Club opened, Ville and his buddies played on a nine-hole goat track along the river in Rovaniemi. "The old course here sucked," Ville said. "But did you ever see a reindeer there?" I asked, and at the word *reindeer,* all three golfers snickered, amused by my crude cultural stereotype. "Yeah, I saw a reindeer there once," Ville said, sucking sardonically on a cigarette. "Well, now it is time for a few beers." And off they went.

That night was the midsummer holiday, a celebration of the summer solstice. At midnight I descended to a bank of the river, where Bob photographed the sun "setting." The orange tie-dyed sky was also captured on camcorder by thirteen chain-smoking Japanese golf tourists in blue blazers and rep ties, who then turned their cameras on Bob and took pictures of him taking pictures of them.

But lord it was picturesque, and I couldn't help but wonder what Rovaniemi is like at the winter solstice, when the sun has not appeared for a full month and won't show its face for another month to come. Quite magical, to hear the locals tell it. At about 3 P.M. on mid-December days, a fissure of antifreeze-colored light appears across the horizon. "Around here," Santa had told me wistfully, "people call it 'the moment of mystical blue.'"

The number-one tee box on the golf course in Katinkulta, Finland, was built on top of a rustic sauna. I had a sudden impulse to go there and have a shvitz. When somebody hit his tee shot fat, I would pop out of the sauna, towel around my waist, and shout at him to keep it down up there. But, alas, "The sauna is no longer working," an official at the course said over the phone. "And we haven't used that tee box for two years." Well, what an absolute gyp.

So instead Bob and I drove to Sweden, where one in twenty citizens plays golf. Annika Sorenstam, Jesper Parnevik, Liselotte Neumann, Per-Ulrik Johansson, Helen Alfredsson, and Anders Forsband have replaced Bjorn Borg, Stefan Edberg, Mats Wilander, and the rest of the nation's tennis players as the stars in the sports firmament. There are four hundred courses in Sweden, but I was interested in only one: little nine-hole Bjorkliden Golf Club.

So we drove and drove and drove, past tidy red cottages on idyllic glass lakes. We drove north for hours and hours and still remained light-years from Bjorkliden. In the town of Gallivare-Malmberget, we finally admitted we were hopelessly lost. Then, up ahead on the shimmering roadside in this impossibly lonely locale, we saw a man walking along peacefully. In a sweatshirt that read PEBBLE BEACH. With a golf bag slung over his shoulder.

"Excuse me," I said, hoping he spoke English. "Is there a golf course nearby?"

"Yes, up this road," he said, and I yanked him into the car as if with a vaudeville hook. The victim of this golfnapping identified himself as Christer Andersson, an 11 handicap from Halmstad, in southern Sweden. I asked him if he had ever played Pebble.

"I have been two times to Pebble Beach," he said, "but I have never played there." His brow furrowed. "I should have played," he said, suddenly fretful. "I don't know why I didn't. It is a dream of mine to do so."

At Christer's direction we drove two hundred yards up the road and then turned off into a dense pine forest. Around a bend appeared a twee red clubhouse with green shutters and white-framed windows. It looked out on an eighteen-hole championship course fringed in snow. VALKOMMEN TILL GALLIVARE-MALMBERGETS GOLFKLUBB read a sign. We were forty miles north of the Arctic Circle. I was introduced to Marith Mattsson, a club member whose son is the club pro and whose husband is the greenkeeper. "Yes," she said triumphantly. "This is the northernmost eighteen."

Her son, Peter, stood at her side, unconcerned that his white Ping cap was black with bloody mozzies. This was a common sight in Scandinavia. Nobody seemed to mind them. The course was full at 4:30 on a Sunday afternoon, when the temperature was in the fifties.

I asked Christer why Swedes are such good and avid golfers. "It is our parents," he said. "They keep us out of doors when we are young. First, everyone played tennis—Borg started by hitting balls against a wall. Then, when people turned thirty, they started moving to the golf course. Now everyone is playing golf."

"In Sweden," said Marith, "golf is not for the rich people, but for all the people. Here, miners and doctors play together."

"Miners come from Kiruna, one hundred thirty miles north of here," said Christer. "They finish work on Friday and play until four in the morning. Imagine that."

I didn't have to. That evening, on the way north to Bjorkliden, Bob and I drove through Kiruna, the northernmost city of any size in Sweden, built atop a terraced layer of coal. We repaired for dinner to a restaurant decorated entirely in Borje Salming memorabilia. (Salming, the former Toronto Maple Leafs star, grew up in Kiruna.) "They dug a new shaft at the coal mine that goes one mile down," a high school English and Swedish teacher told me over dinner. "For the miners, it is a twenty-minute trip straight down every day." Makes sense, doesn't it? A man spends his days being chased down a hole, he naturally does the same to a small white ball on the weekends.

After dinner we drove north, endlessly, the odometer spinning like fruit in a slot machine. We drove literally to the end of the earth. In the distance, reindeer grazed in the middle of the road. Mountains sprang up, fjords appeared, waterfalls plunged down steep cliffs. AVALANCHE ZONE, warned a sign on the highway. MAINTAIN AT LEAST 60 KM PER HOUR. Evidently you can outrun an avalanche, I remarked. Which is when Bob said, somewhat vacantly, that you cannot outrun a swarm of bees.

He was losing it. Clouds of mozzies filled the car. He had been driving all day, all week. Indeed, we had driven a greater distance than that from London to Rome. The license plate on our Vectra was illegible beneath a paste of mosquitoes. Then we pulled into Bjorkliden, with its leafless trees, its pipe-cleaner pines, its brilliant sun, and its low clouds, like the cotton in an aspirin bottle.

Speaking of bottles, we went immediately to a subterranean bar, where we drank Spendrup's beer with the manic energy ordinarily associated with pie-eating contests. For the first time in six days we had escaped the relentless sun, still blazing at 2 A.M.

I arose at the crack of 4 P.M. and headed for the Bjorkliden Golf Club. Marja-Leena once visited Bjorkliden at this time of year, the final week of June, and found the course snowed under and closed. "They said to come back in a month," she said. "Even then, when the course is open, all shots must be hit off of tees or mats."

That prospect actually excited me. A caddie on the Old Course at St. Andrews once told me that he had carried the bag of a Texan tourist in the weeks leading up to the 1995 British Open. Then, too, all shots had to be hit from mats, to protect the Royal & Ancient's fairways. "How did you like hitting from the mats?" a local television reporter asked the Texan.

"They're real helpful," he replied, "when you're hittin' out of sand traps."

As it happened, we didn't have to hit off mats or tees when playing Bjorkliden, though some modifications in our games were required. Marit Andersson, the marketing director at the club, handed me a leaflet upon our arrival. "Because Bjorkliden is situated so far to the north," the notice began, "we've found it necessary to add a few extra rules to the book."

The first such supplement to the age-old Rules of Golf read, "If a reindeer moves your ball on fairway, it can be replaced without penalty." Why anyone would want to replace a reindeer without penalty, Marit could not say, but the point was: this course seemed to promise plenty of them. "If a reindeer eats your ball," began the next rule, "drop a new one where the incident occurred." In other words, do not wait for the reindeer to "take a drop." (Given its metabolism, that could take days.)

Finally: "If your ball lands in the snow, play it from where it lands." This rule, it quickly emerged, was the most critical. With July a week away, the ninth green was still guarded by eight-foot snowdrifts, and the second fairway lay entirely beneath a blanket of white, into which plows had cut a series of wedding-cake terraces. "This is so the snow melts faster," explained Marit, but the plowing also gave the fairway an otherworldly aesthetic appeal.

"It looks exactly like the Church Pews at Oakmont," Bob remarked. "Only white." There were other rules that didn't make Marit's leaflet. For instance, never mind Softspikes at Bjorkliden. Or hard spikes, for that matter. Wear crampons.

The course was still closed to the masses. "Last year, we opened six holes on July seventh," Marit said. "But this winter we had six meters of snow. Fortunately, it melts quickly, and the grass grows fast during twenty-four hours of sunlight." We climbed ever higher, corkscrewing our way up the mountain and onto the course, seeing no reindeer, or reindeer caddies. (You got me good, Swedish Tourist Board.) A greenkeeper drilled a hole in the sixth green, which was free of snow, and allowed me to plant a flagstick and practice chipping. She likewise planted markers at the cliffside seventh tee box and let me drive balls into the ether.

It was a breathtaking hole: A 132-yard par 3 with a hundred-yard drop from mountaintop tee to snow-covered green. I could see all the way to Norway: jagged mountains jutting from the marbled fjords. Out of the water rose a serpentine line of stones that resembled a dinosaur's tail. "Sweden's Loch Ness monster," I muttered.

"No," said Marit. "Sweden's Loch Ness monster is called Storsjoodjuret. It lives a thousand kilometers from here. They say it is a relative of Scotland's Loch Ness monster."

There were only grainy photographs of Nessie, I remarked, whereas Bob and I had not only discovered the northernmost golf course on earth but also had sharp photographs to prove it, including one of me beneath the holy grail, the sign on the first tee that read, BJORKLIDEN ARCTIC GOLF CLUB, THE MOST NORTHERLY IN THE WORLD.

Marit softly cleared her throat. "There is a new course opening a little north of here," she said meekly, and I felt my heart drop one hundred meters. "In Harstad. That is in Norway."

"How far from here?" I stammered.

"Three hundred kilometers to drive."

"And that is the northernmost course in the world?" I asked numbly.

"Nine holes are open now," she said. "The rest will be open in autumn. Then, yes, it will be the northernmost eighteen-hole course in the world." She wore a look of indescribable melancholy. "Yes," she said, sighing deeply. "I'm afraid so."

I stepped to the brink of the seventh tee box, peered into the void, and decided that my quest had concluded, that closure had come. Planting the flagstick in the sixth green at Bjorkliden, I had felt like Admiral Peary, claiming the course for all of golfkind. Now I stood, seven-iron in hand, surveying the whole of Scandinavia. I was, in every conceivable sense, on top of the world. What more could I want?

I swung, and I held my follow-through for ages. From a snow-capped mountaintop atop the Arctic Circle, the earth resembled a dimpled white orb, a Top-Flite XL. I had spent a week slicing smiles into the face of that sphere, little realizing that, all along, it was doing the same to me.

(August 4, 1997)

LOTS AND LOTS
OF LOTS

The loveliest office view in sports doesn't belong to the starter at St. Andrews or the Sherpa summiting Everest or the bikini valet to Tyra Banks. It belongs to Joe Cahn, a professional tailgater who lives in a motor home and says, "It's a wonderful thing to see America from your bathroom."

Cahn is both epic traveler and epic eater, the unholy offspring of Homer and Homer Simpson. Every week during football season he tailgates before and after a Saturday college game and a Sunday NFL game, and most weeks makes it to the *Monday Night Football* game, almost never setting foot inside a stadium. "I might skip the wedding," says the fifty-five-year-old retired businessman, "but I never miss the reception."

For the last eight years, since he sold his house and cooking school in New Orleans, Cahn has been clogging America's arteries—automotive and otherwise—in his JoeMobile, a forty-foot Cholesterolls-Royce. Along the way he and his cat, Sophie, have discovered what Joni Mitchell never did: that paradise *is* a paved parking lot.

"The parking lot," claims Cahn, "is the ideal American neighborhood in an idealized America." Want the parking lot as melting pot? A fan outside Qualcomm Stadium in San Diego once gave Cahn a bratwurst rolled in a tortilla.

As land of equality? Cahn knows groups of women in Buffalo, Pittsburgh, and Kansas City who tailgate while their husbands stay home.

As the new world? He met a pair of tartan-clad Scotsmen on holiday in a Tennessee Titans' parking lot and, one year later, met them again, in the lot at the Meadowlands in New Jersey, where they asked Cahn if he remembered them. "Believe it or not," replied Cahn, "there are very few others who wear kilts to Giants games."

Cahn has tailgated at baseball games and NASCAR tracks and polo matches and steeplechase events and, next summer, will bring his beloved Bar-B-Gater grill to the alfresco Santa Fe Opera, where the game really won't be over till the fat lady sings. But his true love is the football lot, be it in Baltimore, where Cahn parties with members of a SWAT team (Stop Working and Tailgate), or Buffalo, where a fan known as Pinto Ron cooks on his car hood and serves libations from the thumb hole of a bowling ball.

How does Cahn do it? How does a man sip a thumb-and-Coke at Ralph Wilson Stadium and call it a job? How can Cahn afford to be at Purdue on Saturday and at the Colts on Sunday and at the Rams on Monday night and at Stanford the following Friday, in between living on leftovers provided by other tailgaters?

Cahn cajoled a modest grant from Coca-Cola to collect demographic data on the American tailgater. (The company also donates a dollar for every mile Cahn drives to Share Our Strength, a hunger-relief organization.) And the Monaco Coach Corporation lends him the JoeMobile, which Cahn parked, last weekend, in the Louisiana campground he calls home. (It was his first week off the road since mid-August.) Even so, the professional tailgater loses money on the year. "I may not earn a lot," he points out, "but I ain't going hungry."

"Thin people have no credibility in a parking lot," continues Cahn, whose belly, white beard, and bald head give him the air of an Eastern mystic, a man who finds transcendent beauty on the ten-acre Grove at Ole Miss, where tailgaters set up camp the evening before home games, the field blooming with tents throughout the night. "I watch the tents go up," says Cahn, "and think of the old Disney time-lapse photography of flowers opening."

The professional tailgater is an exceedingly contented man. Divorced for ten years, Cahn remains the best of friends with his ex-wife, Karen, and will even give her away at her wedding this year. "People can't understand that," says Cahn. "Many tailgaters have told me, 'I'd like to give my current wife away.'"

Of course his calendar isn't all days of wine and Rose Bowls. Tailgating can be hard. Which raises the question: If Cahn could make one improvement to American parking lots, what would it be? "Depends," he says. On what? "They should pass out Depends," he clarifies. "Or add more Port-a-Lets. In Dallas you spend half an hour waiting to use a Port-a-Let. In Baltimore and New York, where cars and RVs park together, people come to my door with very sad eyes. They don't have to say anything. How can you turn them away? It's not neighborly." And so he opens his bathroom with a profound sense of duty, and hits the road, alas, with a profound sense of doody.

More often, though, tailgating is a glamorous life. This very month Sophie is featured in *Cat Fancy* magazine. And seven days before the Super Bowl at Reliant Stadium, Cahn will perform the ceremonial lighting of his grill, which will remain aflame for 168 consecutive hours, seven straight days and nights, in the parking lot of a Houston food store. Says Cahn, "We will not allow those charcoals to go out."

An eternal flame, too, burns in Cahn's heart. And a million Zantacs will never douse it.

(January 26, 2004)

HIGH ROLLERS

Toupees, tube tops, car keys, cameras, cares, inhibitions, and lunch. A great many things are routinely lost on roller coasters, as demonstrated by the items found on, near, or beneath the tracks. These include glass eyes, hearing aids, and—in quantities that resist rational explanation—underpants.

"False teeth," adds Ronald V. Toomer, revered architect of approximately eighty coasters worldwide. "They find lots of false teeth." In 1994 workers at the Blackpool Pleasure Beach amusement park in England drained the reflecting pool beneath two coasters and found twenty-five sets of false teeth.

At historic Kennywood amusement park in West Mifflin, Pennsylvania, a passenger on SkyCoaster parted with his false teeth, and they pitched, in a hideous parabola, into the french fries of a passing pedestrian. "That person showed up at the lost and found," park spokesperson Mary Lou Rosemeyer reluctantly confirms, "with the teeth"—how shall she put this?—"still in the fries." While the disembodied dentures did not, alas, devour the fries, they remain a coffee-stained symbol of what man will sacrifice to stir, if but for a moment, his jaded viscera.

This is a story about roller coasters, so throw your arms in the air. Not literally, mind you. "I am told," Toomer says with neither pride nor embarrassment, "that someone's prosthetic arm was found under one of my rides."

Workers at Cedar Point in Sandusky, Ohio, last year collected more than $11,000 in loose coins and bills shaken free from riders of the park's twelve roller coasters (there are now thirteen). But the most valuable item ever found on a coaster belonged to Emilio Franco. In 1949 Franco, a West Virginia coal miner rendered mute by a nervous disorder, rode the terrifying Cyclone at Coney Island in Brooklyn and found, for the first time in six years, his voice. He screamed on the Cyclone's second descent and, upon disembarking at the platform, spoke his first words since World War II.

And while those words were "I feel sick," a larger point remains. "Riding a roller coaster," says Phil Hettema, who designs these diabolical devices for Universal Studios theme parks, "is a way of telling yourself, I'm alive."

"We are living in a roller-coaster Renaissance, a second golden age," says industry analyst Paul Ruben, North American editor of *Park World* magazine. The fifty most popular amusement parks in North America hosted a record 242.9 million visitors in 1998, vastly more than the attendance at all NBA, NFL, NHL, and Major League Baseball games combined, and a number close to the country's population.

"There's an industry saying: A carousel is the soul of an amusement park, but a roller coaster is its heart," says Jim Futrell of the National Amusement Park Historical Association (NAPHA). The roller coaster is the vital organ, the indispensable engine, the great american scream machine (or GASM), and it has never been more robust. There are about one thousand roller coasters operating in the world. While the United States alone had more than fifteen hundred in the late 1920s—the end of the first golden age—by the mid-seventies they had dwindled to 145. Think about that. Twenty years ago, the U.S. roller coaster was nearly extinct. You may now lift your jaw off the ground with both hands.

Mercifully, the late nineties have been a time of unprecedented construction, and Futrell says 520 coasters, more than half the world's total, are operating in the United States. About eighty coasters opened around the world last year, and at least ninety more have debuted in 1999, including one in the Micronesia Mall on Guam. All of them do unspeakable things. "The idea is to knock your socks off," says Hettema, whose newly opened Incredible Hulk Coaster at Universal Studios Islands of Adventure in Orlando—with its catapult launch into an immediate 180-degree barrel roll—also tends to knock off bikini tops.

Swimsuits are recommended on the amphibious BuzzSaw Falls coaster, which opened last month at Silver Dollar City in Branson, Missouri. There are twenty-seven varieties of roller coaster, including stand-up coasters such as the Riddler's Revenge, at Six Flags Magic Mountain in Valencia, California. More preposterous contraptions are on the drawing board, such as the coaster set to open next March at Paramount's Great America in Santa Clara, California, on which passengers will lie back and be propelled into concentric circles of hell. In Utah there is one prototype for a coaster on which the car itself turns, and another for a ride on which the car races through the threads of a cylindrical track like an Archimedes' screw.

Already running is Superman The Escape, a "shuttle coaster" at Six Flags Magic Mountain. Though it's not everyone's idea of a roller coaster, it meets the technical definition: it uses gravity and rides on rails. Superman is not a continuous loop but an L-shaped track on which passengers are shot down a straightaway and then up a tower before pausing and falling backward to earth, all in thirty seconds. Its fifteen-passenger car travels from 0 to 100 in seven seconds, exerts 4.5 G's on the rider, and is roughly equivalent to taking off in an F-16 from the deck of an aircraft carrier. At the top of the tower, 415 feet above suburban L.A., riders experience six seconds of weightlessness before plunging back whence they came.

"You can let go of your sunglasses at the top of the ride," says Magic Mountain spokesperson Andy Gallardo, "and they will remain there, floating in front of you." Trouble is, you can "let go" of anything at the top of the ride, and it will remain there, floating in front of you.

If we are living in a roller-coaster Renaissance, the United States is its Florence. This nation's technophilia and leisure worship have joined in unholy matrimony to sire an astonishing subculture of coasterdinks and rollerwonks, men and women for whom roller coasters have become a lifestyle—or something more closely resembling life itself. This is not the case with Rich Rodriguez, a forty-year-old man who last summer spent twenty-two hours a day for forty-seven consecutive days on the Big Dipper at Blackpool Pleasure Beach, breaking his own Guinness world record for marathon coastering. "I do it in a Lindberghian spirit of adventure," says Rodriguez, an earnest Brooklyn native who is a teaching assistant in the communications department at Miami. "I'm not one of these roller-coaster obsessives who can tell you what kind of bolts are in the track."

Rodriguez is eager to distinguish himself from the likes of Dreadlock Jim, a multiply pierced, Rasta-haired coastermane from Saginaw, Michigan, who practically lives in his car. Dreadlock Jim reportedly drove eighty thousand miles and visited one hundred and one amusement parks in 1998. He has the elusive quality (and personal hygiene) of Bigfoot. "I saw him in Tampa yesterday, on Montu at Busch Gardens," a twenty-two-year-old rollerphile named Walt Breymier told me last January in Orlando as we stood in the construction site that would become Islands of Adventure.

The theme park wouldn't open for another four months, but the Incredible Hulk was up and running, and, as Breymier explained, "There's something called ERT: Exclusive Ride Time." It is a privilege extended to people like Breymier, of the Virginia-based Coaster Zombies club, whose members were given a no-expenses-paid trip to Orlando to test-ride the Hulk in exchange for the good word of mouth they were certain to spread.

For some Zombies it was the second trip to the construction site in as many months. "I came down at Christmas and watched Hulk run from the outside," said Sam Marks, forty-one, a customer service manager at Pitney-Bowes in Arlington, Virginia, which is "Twenty-four miles from Six Flags America," where Marks spent at least twenty-eight days last summer.

"I'm giving up a week's worth of work to be here," said Breymier, a night supervisor at the Target department store in Bel Air, Maryland, who lives within a five-hour drive of fifteen amusement parks. "I took a bus here to save money. I've been serious hardcore since '97."

American Coaster Enthusiasts (ACE) has 5,800 members, not all of whom are serious hard core. "Our membership runs the gamut from casual to 'coasters are my life,'" says ACE public relations director David Escalante, whose surname suggests ascents and descents and whose signature ends with a line drawing of a roller coaster. (Such salutations are common among coastermanes: Park World's Ruben ends telephone conversations by saying, "Go with gravity.")

"I'm a gawker," a man in a sweatshirt bearing a likeness of the roller coaster called Raptor told me at Raptor's home, Cedar Point, on the banks of Lake Erie in Sandusky. The Raptor fan, it turns out, was not a gawker but a GOCCer, a member of the Greater Ohio Coaster Club. GOCCers and ACErs and Coaster Zombies gather in cyberspace to discuss first drops and chain lifts and lateral G's and brake runs and camelbacks, and to exchange intelligence about new coaster construction.

"You'll read, 'There are reports of a truck carrying blue track north on I-95: Where is it going?'" says the Zombies' Marks. "It's kind of pathetic. Some people have broken into parks just to look at the construction of a new coaster." He pauses, lost in thought beneath a beige Gilligan hat with a blinking red light and the souvenir pins of myriad coasters. "By the way," Marks says of such break-ins, "I didn't really do that once, when I was sixteen years old."

For eighteen-year-old Jeff Tolotti, coasters are not life itself. "I also enjoy free falls," he says of rides like the Cedar Point Power Tower, in which human cargo is hoisted in a harness up a twenty-four-story obelisk, then dropped to earth in 2.3 seconds.

"And I like really big, really fast spinning rides," says Breymier.

"These are known in the industry," says Kennywood's Rosemeyer, "as Spin-'n'-Barfs."

To barf, on the serious hard-core coaster circuit, is to "lose it," and nearly everyone loses it eventually. "It takes me a lot of rides," says Marks, "like twenty-seven consecutive at Six Flags St. Louis." When a Los Angeles helicopter pilot—a Vietnam combat pilot turned traffic reporter—loses it on Viper at Magic

Mountain, as happened a couple of years ago on the world's tallest looping coaster, what chance do the rest of us have?

While marathon champion Rodriguez was living in the sixth
car of the Big Dipper in Blackpool last summer, a press photographer joined him to take his portrait with the coaster in motion. As Rodriguez said "Cheese," the photographer lost it. Says
Rodriguez, who has an almost courtly way of speaking, "I've
also had regular passengers get ill near me."

"I lost it on Akbar yesterday," Breymier said in Orlando last
January, referring to Akbar's Adventure Tours, a "simulator ride"
at Busch Gardens in Tampa. "There's one scene where you're
riding on a camel, up and down, up and down on a tour through
Egypt, and I just lost it." He said this in the manner of a fullback
facing the press after a fumble. Then Breymier boarded the Hulk
for a tenth straight time, before his ERT expired.

What, exactly, is the appeal? Several enthusiasts told me that
riding a coaster is better than sex. In some cases, this was clearly a
matter of conjecture. In others, evidently, it *is* sex. "The back car
is for your heavy-metal S&M crowd, people who like a lot of whip
action," says Ruben, to which we can only say that, in addition
to ERT, there is something called TMI: Too Much Information.

Gerald Menditto practices abstinence. He has operated the
Coney Island Cyclone for twenty-five years but has, astonishingly,
ridden the infernal thing only twice. Menditto is what is known
in the trade as a chicken. Ask coaster architect Toomer, whose
eighty rides include the superlative Magnum XL-200 at Cedar
Point, to name his favorite machine, and he responds with a good,
long chuckle. "You mean to ride?" says the sixty-nine-year-old
former mechanical engineer. "Oh, I don't ride 'em. Oh, no.
Haven't for years. I get motion sickness real bad. The bigger ones,
I get sick as a dog on those."

These coasterphobes play a vital role in the amusement-park
ecosystem. "They're a good thing," says Ruben, who has ridden
more than four thousand miles on 525 coasters. "Someone has to
hold our change."

"We don't laugh at people who are afraid of snakes," says Brian
Newmark, a Harvard-trained psychologist in suburban Boston,

"but we laugh at people who are afraid of roller coasters." We should not. Newmark, who has treated coasterphobia, cites the case of a fifty-five-year-old man married for several years to a rollerweenie whose passion he desperately wanted to share. "It was an obstacle in his life," says Newmark. "The question with a phobia is, Does it interfere with daily function? When parents are fearful, children sense that and become habitually fearful of the world around them."

Coasterphobia has not always been an irrational fear. When the infamous Crystal Beach (Ontario) Cyclone opened in 1927, a full-time nurse was employed at the unloading platform. The coaster had a ninety-seven-foot first drop into an eighty-five-degree right turn. "Hats, purses, combs, and false teeth all flew out on that turn," says Ruben, sixty-two, who grew up in nearby Niagara Falls, New York. "Riders were thrown into their seatmates and cracked their ribs." By the end of the Cyclone's run, in 1946, more people were watching this ghoulish spectacle than participating in it.

Such a coaster, alas, couldn't leave the station in today's litigious society. "When a new ride opens up, you get a lot of lawsuits," says Toomer. Retired from Utah's Arrow Dynamics, Inc., Toomer spends much of his time in trials, testifying about coaster safety. "We have two hundred million riders a year on coasters designed by our company," says Toomer. "When someone comes to me and says our ride hurt his back, I say, 'Would you believe that fifteen million people rode it before you did, without a problem?'"

In the past eleven years, there have been eleven nonoccupational roller-coaster-related fatalities in the United States, few of them involving mechanical malfunction. Last September at Paramount's Great America in Santa Clara, California, a Mexican tourist lost her hat on an "inverted coaster," the kind that speeds its suspended passengers, feet a-dangle, around a high-speed glorified dry-cleaning rack. The woman's twenty-four-year-old husband didn't speak English and thus didn't heed warning signs when, after finishing the ride, he entered a restricted area to retrieve the hat. He was struck in the head and killed by the dangling feet of another rider, a twenty-eight-year-old woman, who suffered a broken leg.

The point is, while you might have your face bloodied by the occasional dive-bombing goose (as happened to Fabio this spring in the front car of Apollo's Chariot at Busch Gardens in Williamsburg, Virginia) or be stuck upside down for two hours awaiting rescue by the fire department (as happened to twenty-three passengers on Demon, at Six Flags Great America outside Chicago, in April 1998), riding a roller coaster is much safer than riding a bicycle. "We all look for things that push the boundaries of our daily existence," says Hulk designer Hettema. "Roller coasters are a safe way to do that. Riding a coaster is a more practical way to feel alive than jumping off a cliff."

More practical than a cliff dive, coastering better approximates mountaineering. Rodriguez had "surreal visions" during his forty-seven-day Blackpool marathon last summer. "You can experience a kind of natural high while riding," confirms Ruben.

Enthusiasts speak of rides the way climbers talk of the Seven Summits. On every coastermane's "lifetime list" are Dragon Khan (at Port Aventura, near Barcelona) and Monte Makaya (at Terra Encantada, in Rio de Janeiro). Both have eight inversions, the world record. Oblivion (at Alton Towers, in England) makes an 87.5-degree drop into a hundred-foot hole in the ground. "I've heard," one rollerphile told me lasciviously, "it's terrifying."

The names of the world's great modern coasters are conceived to heighten such terror: Megaphobia, Mind Eraser, Exterminator, Alpengeist and—at Parc Asterix outside of Paris—Tonnerre de Zeus, which means, sounds, and feels like the thunder of Zeus. None of these, however, have the exotic, elusive appeal of Fujiyama, King of Coasters, at Japan's Fujikyu Highlands fun park in the northern foothills of Mount Fuji. "Fujiyama is the one I want," Tolotti told me, as if it were a white whale. It might as well be.

Fujiyama is the world's tallest traditional complete-circuit coaster, 259 feet at its high point. The ride's toupee-ravaging first drop of 230 feet is also a complete-circuit record. And Fujiyama shares with the formidable Steel Phantom at Kennywood the Guinness mark for the fastest complete-circuit coaster, with a top speed of eighty-two miles per hour.

What's more, I resolved not merely to ride Fujiyama but also to do it immediately after speed-eating bowls of soba noodles with another Japanese phenomenon: Hirofumi Nakajima, the Black Hole of Kofu, the former world champion of competitive eating, a man who once consumed twenty-four and a half hot dogs in twelve minutes, as if feeding pencils into an electric sharpener.

In the days leading up to my trip, I thought many times of hurling. But I also thought of Kipling:

> If you can meet with Gluttony and Gravity And treat those two impostors just the same; If you can ride with Kings—of coasters—and not lose it; Yours is the Earth and everything that's in it, And—which is more—you'll be a Man, my son!

There is no clown. That is the first panicked thought of every noodle-gorged gaijin in line at Fujiyama. There is no cutout clown bearing the traditional disclaimer, YOU MUST BE TALLER THAN ME TO RIDE. What if I am too tall, thinks an anxious American who is nine inches taller than the average Japanese male. All of the recorded warnings played in the serpentine line to board Fujiyama— and these warnings are manifold, believe me—are, unhelpfully, in Japanese. All the signs are in kanji.

That changes when you at last approach the loading platform after ninety angst-inducing minutes in line. Adjacent to the platform is a small door painted with the leering cartoon likeness of a barnyard fowl. This is your last chance to exit before you are swept, like a cork on a fast river, onto Fujiyama's malevolent rails. The sign on the door is in English. It reads: CHICKEN GATE

The Chicken Gate thumbs its beak at current coaster etiquette, according to which parks attempt to allay, not inflame, a rider's anxieties. Near the Hulk at Islands of Adventure, passengers can pick up a pamphlet titled *Anxious about Riding*. No such luck at Fujiyama, where the only sound on the platform is the metallic echo of the train's lap bars locking into place. It is the sound of finality, like lockdown at Leavenworth.

With a temperamental lurch, the train pulls away from the platform and begins its inexorable climb, 235 feet up the first hill. The angle of ascent leaves the rider in roughly the same position—and disposition—as a dental patient. The only sound now is the *ratch-ratch-ratcheting* of the chain lift. It recalls to me the rattling chains of Marley's ghost.

When at last you crest the first hill, there is a pause, long enough to let your knuckle hair stand at attention as you take in the view. Twenty-five stories above the Fujikyu Highlands, you are staring straight at Mount Fuji, and it is breathtaking—so perfect a mountain that it almost seems a theme-park contrivance, like the Matterhorn at Disneyland. You can only gape at it and whisper, "My God, what a lovely—"

Then the bottom falls out of your world.

The first drop at Fujiyama is, in essence, a plane crash. When you pull out of the near-vertical twenty-story plunge, your car is traveling about eighty miles per hour toward a course canopied with wooden beams, which appear to be no more than six feet above the track, offering sufficient clearance only to the average Japanese, whose culture promotes something called Tall Poppy syndrome, in which heads that jut above the crowd must be cut back down to size. Only later do you learn that Tall Poppy syndrome is a metaphor and that these low beams are a calculated optical illusion known in the coaster trade as Headchoppers. Indeed, a similarly terrifying specimen exists on Shivering Timbers in Muskegon, Michigan.

In the moment, as you hurtle toward presumed decapitation, your thoughts turn to many things: to the vindictiveness of Japanese engineers, to the criminally negligent absence of clowns, and to Hirofumi Nakajima, with whom you imprudently engaged in an eating contest scant hours earlier. But before you know what hasn't hit you, you are suddenly—to your profound relief—coasting on small camelbacks into the brake run leading back to the station. You have survived Fujiyama. You have not, moreover, lost it.

Or have you? The souvenir photograph offered at ride's end doesn't lie. Somewhere on the first drop I let fly a Tourette's–like torrent of involuntary profanity. To judge by the photo, in which ampersands and exclamation marks practically billow from my mouth in a cartoon balloon, these epic obscenities came as a revelation to the plaid-skirted Japanese schoolgirls seated in front of me. Each of their mouths is forever frozen in a rictus of disbelief.

For one brief shining moment of American ingenuity, in 1991, Kennywood's Steel Phantom was faster than Fujiyama is today. For its first seven days of operation, the Phantom was the fastest coaster of all time, doing ninety miles per hour, a speed quickly deemed too uncomfortable for humans to endure without lifelong twenty-four-hour chiropractic supervision. So this creature, another spawn of Toomer's evil genius, had to be retrofitted with additional brakes. The Phantom is now more spine-chilling than spine-killing, particularly when it passes beneath the tracks of the Thunderbolt coaster, with which it is entangled.

Such is the Phantom's menace that park officials made me ride it with a fifteen-year-old from Mars, Pennsylvania, named Ed Murphy. The kid, a veteran of twenty Phantom rides, could only stare grimly from our front seat as I babbled nervously. When I blurted that I had just eaten a chicken-salad sandwich, young Ed said, as we ascended the chain lift, "I wish you hadn't told me that."

The Phantom is frequently cited as the second-best steel coaster in existence, after Cedar Point's Magnum XL-200. Cedar Point has the highest concentration of coasters anywhere in the world. What's more, the park is on the beach where Knute Rockne invented the forward pass with Notre Dame teammate Gus Dorais while the two worked as lifeguards in the summer of 1913. The historic spot, marked with a plaque, is now part of the Soak City water park.

I rode Magnum with Cedar Point public relations director Robin Innes, who wore a shirt and tie and carried on, with consummate professionalism, a business conversation as we climbed the 205-foot first hill. "This was the first coaster to break the two-hundred-foot barrier," Innes said casually as we crested. "This first drop is a hundred ninety-five feet and *aaiiieeeyeaaah! Hoohoohoo! Wahahaheee!* celebrating its tenth anniversary this summer and oh man! *Oh man! Woooooo! Yeaaahh!* top speed of seventy-two miles an hour, which is approximately yes! *Whoahoho! Woohooee! Hey hey!* the tubular steel track *eee-heee-hoo-ha-haaaa!* be happy to if you have any questions." I had no idea what he was talking about, but I nodded frequently in response.

Toomer designed Magnum but never rode it. Still, he is aware that it remains the favorite of a great many coasterphiles, whose reasons are largely intangible and perhaps best articulated by Innes when he said, "Wahahoohaheeeeee!"

"Ten years after opening," says Escalante, the ACEr, "Magnum still hasn't been improved on." At the coaster's anniversary party in June, Toomer signed a thousand autographs.

"I never expected that I'd become some kind of nut-club cult leader," the designer says. But he has become just that, with eighty wildly popular coasters stretching from Indonesia to Spain to the interior of Buffalo Bill's Casino in Primm, Nevada. "These rides," he says, pondering a legacy, "will be around for a very long time." To say the least. Leap-the-Dips opened in 1902 and runs to this day at Lakemont Park in Altoona, Pennsylvania.

Not far from Leap-the-Dips is the Wildcat, at Hershey Park. It gives riders the most instances of air, or negative G's: eleven times passengers are lifted from their seats. "There's an arms race for everything now," says industry analyst Ruben. The list of superlatives is seemingly endless, much like the venerable Beast at Paramount's Kings Island, near Cincinnati. The Beast is by far the longest wooden roller coaster in the world, both in track feet and in ride time. It travels a tortuous 7,400 feet and covers an area more than twice that of Kennywood's Thunderbolt. The Beast lasts an unheard-of three minutes and forty seconds. And "No man," as Dr. Johnson said about *Paradise Lost,* "ever wished it longer."

Strike that. One man has ever wished every ride longer. A coaster jockey of exceedingly rare gifts, Richard Gregory Rodriguez now takes his place beside Ted Williams and Jascha Heifetz as a twentieth-century titan whose skills simply overwhelm our powers of analysis. Twelve times Rodriguez has set the world record for marathon coastering, but last summer was his Beamon leap, his Secretariat at Belmont moment. He rode the Big Dipper in Blackpool for 1,013½ hours over forty-seven days, from June

18 until August 3, nearly doubling his own record of 549 hours, set in Blackpool in 1994. "The three big questions I get," Rodriguez told me solemnly, while sitting for an interview in a sidewalk café near his home in Miami, "are, Why? Do you get paid? and How do you go to the bathroom?" We will try to answer each of these questions in due time, but for now you need understand only that Rodriguez's life is a cat's cradle of coaster history. In him all of the industry's threads intersect.

He was born to greatness, blessed genetically and geographically. For starters, young Rich grew to the minimal acceptable standard of forty-eight inches, then kept going, eventually leveling off at five-foot-eight" and 160 pounds—"The perfect size for riding," he says. "Like a Formula One driver's."

Even more propitious, Rodriguez was born in Brooklyn, the cradle of American amusement, home of the original Luna Park and Coney Island, where the first commercially successful roller coaster was built, in 1884. The Gravity Switchback Railway was the brainchild of LaMarcus Thompson, who had made a fortune inventing seamless hosiery. More than a century later, in unintentional homage to the stocking magnate, an astonishing number of women would toss their underwear from roller coasters, in the same spirit in which unmentionables are flung into trees from chairlifts on ski slopes. It is a dirty little secret—a Victoria's Secret—of the family entertainment industry. But we digress.

Rodriguez was raised in the shadow of the great coaster jocks of the seventies, men such as Jim Bruce, who made his reputation on the Swamp Fox in Myrtle Beach, South Carolina, and Noel Aube, who tamed the Wildcat at Lake Compounce in Connecticut. But Rodriguez's true heroes were aviators: solo balloonists such as Ed Yost and Steve Fossett and, above all, Charles Lindbergh. Two years after crossing the Atlantic in the *Spirit of St. Louis,* Lindy rode the Cyclone at Coney Island and said, "A ride on Cyclone is a greater thrill than flying an airplane at top speed."

So, in the summer of 1977, eighteen-year-old Rich Rodriguez set out to commemorate the fiftieth anniversary of Lindbergh's flight—and the fiftieth birthday of the Cyclone—with an audacious act of his own. "I don't want to overdramatize this," he would say years later, "but Lindbergh was a long shot in '27. He would have been twenty-to-one in a horse race. He wasn't well financed. And here I was, not wealthy, from Brooklyn, and I thought, What can I do in Lindbergh's spirit of adventure? Can I accomplish something?"

Carrying only a pillow, a blanket, and a note from his doctor—plus the blessing of management at Coney Island's Astroland—Rodriguez set out on August 18, 1977, to break Michael Boodley's world record of forty-five consecutive hours on a roller coaster. He selected the sixth car from the front. "It's the most stable ride," says Rodriguez, who would soon make the sixth car his signature. As he traveled fifty miles per hour in the frigid Coney Island nights, with the wind whipping off the Atlantic, his face swelled grotesquely. He resolved, then and there, that next time would be different. Next time he'd bring lotion.

There would be a next time, too, for Rodriguez shattered Boodley's record, set on the Cyclone, by staying on that angry mechanical bull for 103 hours and fifty-five minutes to enter *The Guinness Book of World Records*. Then, between 1977 and 1982, Rodriguez would break his world record nine times, the last two on corkscrewing coasters in Quebec and Germany.

Under Guinness guidelines, a rider can spend an average of five minutes of every hour off the coaster—or a total of two hours a day, to be divided as the jockey sees fit. Rodriguez used his time to eat and go to the bathroom, which is to say, he did all of his sleeping on the coasters, snoozing through every terrifying turn of the corkscrew. Soon the word went forth: There was an undisputed King of Coasters, a man the British tabs called Queasy Rider, a misnomer if ever there was one. "I was blessed with a strong stomach," says Rodriguez. "I never get sick." He was, in short, the Natural, and the trade magazines all headlined his ONE TRACT MIND.

But his one-track mind was wandering. In 1982, after spending 328 hours on the Super Werbil at Holiday Park in Hassloch, Germany, to set his tenth world record, Rodriguez walked wobbly away from marathoning. There were, simply, no more Magic Mountains to climb. For the next twelve years, the Natural squandered his gift. He matriculated at Columbia, receiving a bachelor's degree in history and political science. In 1987 he joined the army, serving his country for two and a half years before his diabetes was diagnosed and, at his request, he was honorably discharged. He then moved to Chicago to educate America's youth as a substitute high school teacher. It was all very wasteful, this attention to duty, and Rodriguez watched his record fall to a younger jock, the Quebecois upstart Normand St. Pierre, master of Le Monstre at La Ronde Park in Montreal.

By 1991 Rodriguez was a thirty-two-year-old diabetic injecting himself with insulin four times a day, and it appeared that his train had long since left the platform. Or had it? "George Foreman had come back to boxing," recalls Rodriguez. "Mark Spitz was trying to return to the Olympics, and I began to wonder, Why not? At first it was hard to find a park to train in, but I'd buy some ride operators at Coney Island a couple of beers, and they'd let me ride all day."

He went to Blackpool in 1994 and rode for 549 hours to reclaim the record that St. Pierre had held, in his absence, for eleven years. Rodriguez returned to form on the Big Dipper, which was built in 1921. Today's brakes are almost all hydraulics, but at Blackpool, as at Coney Island, large men still pull enormous hand brakes. "If he misses the brakes, I could be dead," says Rodriguez. "If my hand falls out of the car when I'm asleep, I could lose a limb. I'm going around something like twelve thousand circuits, and any number of things can go wrong."

In 1979, at the Vancouver Pacific National Exhibition, Rodriguez was on a coaster that was "double training," or running two trains on one track. When his train pulled into the platform, the train behind it failed to brake. Rodriguez bailed out before impact. "Otherwise," he says, "I would've broken my neck."

Last summer, feeling stronger than ever, Rodriguez returned to the Big Dipper to go head-to-head against his nemesis, St. Pierre, who would be riding Le Monstre in Montreal in a kind of transatlantic staredown. In all fairness, the Francophone never stood a chance. Rodriguez forever lowered the lap bar on his own place in history. "The first couple of days are always a shakedown period," he says of the marathon. "It's almost impossible to sleep. By the fourth day, my body has a will to adapt. After two weeks, it feels more normal to be on the coaster than off." (When he is off, Rodriguez still feels the ride, like the phantom leg of an amputee.)

St. Pierre withered in the white-hot heat of such greatness and disembarked from Le Monstre after an otherwise astonishing 670 hours. Rodriguez, already in possession of the world record, refused to stop. He rode for gratuitous hours, then days, and finally weeks, until he passed the thousand-hour mark and put the record forever out of reach. On the final lap of his odyssey, he breasted a tape at the platform, a U.S. flag on his sweater, and then swigged from a champagne bottle. He was bussed by a pair of Blackpool belles. Then, spent, he called his mother from a cell phone.

His legs were badly bruised. His knees, though padded, were crosshatched with cuts from the violent jostling of the steel car as he slept. His face resembled a peeled tomato, rubbed raw by the wind off the Irish Sea. Imagine driving from Miami to Juneau and back at sixty-five miles per hour with your head out the window, and you only begin to comprehend the man's 11,362-mile ride to nowhere. Ensconced that night in an English hotel, Rodriguez couldn't sleep. "I kept waking up in bed," he says, "bracing myself for the first drop."

The next morning, England awoke to a bizarre and lengthy editorial in the *Times* of London denouncing Rodriguez. "If futility can be graded," the piece said, "surely this bizarre bid to turn entertainment into tedium might almost set a record."

The first time Rodriguez heard this was when I mentioned it to him recently. "I know I'm not Neil Armstrong," he said. "I keep this in perspective. I know there's a lot of humor here. I'm forty years old, and it will be easy for people to say, This guy is missing a few bricks. But you know, I don't get paid, I have slept in airports, I try to raise some money for diabetes research. I just want to keep my dignity, if that is possible. This is not a glamorous life."

So why live it? "I think it's the connection to people," Rodriguez says. "Most people don't understand what I'm doing, but they want to be a part of the fun. They ask, 'Can I bring you a blanket?' 'Will you come to dinner at the house when it's over?' At Blackpool, a family brings me candy. I rode with a little girl and a little boy when I set a record in Blackpool in 1979, and I wrote them a note. They came back in '94 and rode with me again."

The kids had, of course, grown up. One of them still had his yellowed note, and she showed it to Rodriguez fifteen years after he'd written it. It said, "Thanks so much for riding with me." His life had come full circle. But then it did so 505 times every day on the Dipper, 22,725 times in all last summer.

The traditional complete-circuit roller coaster always returns to its station, to where it began. So it is with all of roller-coasterdom. In the way that cities are building retro ballparks, neoclassical wooden coasters are now going up, and ancient amusement parks—such as 101-year-old Kennywood—are the envy of the industry. "The fifties saw urban decline and the flight to suburbia," says Futrell, the NAPHA historian, "and the sixties became a real struggle for the old-time traditional parks. The seventies brought theme-park development. Now we're getting back to the vintage parks. Kennywood is almost the Wrigley Field of amusement parks."

Kennywood's Thunderbolt was named the top roller coaster in the world in a highly publicized Discovery Channel special that aired over Memorial Day weekend. The wooden coaster opened in 1968. "There are a lot of people who don't even count steel as coasters," says Breymier, the Coaster Zombie.

"Ride operators like the older rides," says Futrell. "They're solid but simple pieces of machinery, with pulleys and gears and chains."

"You know how you remember the Top Forty songs from high school, what you heard when you were driving around in your car at night?" Rodriguez said out of the blue in one of our last conversations. "I remember the song that was playing at Coney Island the first time I rode the Cyclone, in 1976. It was 'Turn the Beat Around' by Vicki Sue Robinson. The summer of '77, 'Afternoon Delight' was the big one. The summer of '78 was all Bee Gees and Donna Summer. At most of these parks, a deejay plays the hit songs ten or fifteen times a day. I can still hear 'Fly, Robin, Fly' and 'Love to Love You Baby.' Remember a song called 'Magnet and Steel'? When I hear that, I think of riding the Rebel Yell in the summer of 1978, and it makes me happy and wistful."

Not long ago a woman called me from Premier Rides, a space-age design firm that builds roller coasters with linear induction motors, powered by magnets. I couldn't bring myself to call her back. Whatever lies in the future, I realized, the charm of roller coasters is in their evocation of the past. In addition to the Big Dipper, Blackpool Pleasure Beach has one of the world's last surviving Tunnels of Love. One of the last.

I finally understood Rodriguez and his white-knuckle attachment to roller coasters. It has nothing to do with magnets and steel and plenty to do with "Magnet and Steel."

(August 9, 1999)

I BELIEVE IN
BASKETBALL

Hockey players, among all athletes, have the coolest way of entering a game, hopping over the boards with one hand, like Steve McQueen getting into a convertible. But basketball is forever, and so players are often made to genuflect in front of the scorer's table for a moment before stepping onto the court, as if entering a house of worship. Which, in a manner of speaking, they are.

For one is baptized into basketball not with water but with confetti (conferred on the head by Curly Neal). And one believes in basketball, as one believes in the Bible and in all those names that are common to both: Moses and Isiah and Jordan . . .

Adam and Eve were banished from the Garden and so—eventually—were the Celtics, and sometime in between I became a believer, and this is my profession of faith: I believe in Artis Gilmore, whose wife is named—as God is my witness—Enola Gay.

I believe in new hightops, always evocative of Christmas morning, for you get to open a large box, remove the crinkly paper stuffed into the toes, and—before wearing them for the first time—inhale deeply from each sneaker as if from an airplane oxygen mask. (It's what wine connoisseurs call "nosing the bouquet" and works for Pumas as well as pinot noirs.)

I believe in tearaway warm-up suits, which make the wearer feel—when summoned from the bench—like Clark Kent, ripping off his business suit to reveal the *S* on his chest.

I believe a team's fortunes can always be foretold—not from the length of its lifelines but from the integrity of its layup lines.

I believe in God Shammgod and Alaa Abdelnaby and James (Buddha) Edwards (and in Black Jesus, Earl Monroe's nickname long before it was the Pearl).

I believe in accordion-style bleachers that push back to expose, after a game, car keys and quarters and paper cups, which sound like a gunshot when stomped on just right. (And always, stuck to the floor, the forlorn strands of molting pom-poms.)

I believe—now more than ever, in this time of global disharmony—in World B. Free and Majestic Mapp. And that control of the planet's contested regions might be better determined by a simple, alternating possession arrow.

I believe that three hundred basketballs dribbled simultaneously by eight-year-old basketball campers sound like buffalo thundering across the plains. And inspire even greater awe. I believe that two high school janitors pushing twin dust mops at halftime can be every bit as hypnotic as dueling Zambonis.

I believe that any sucker can wear a $40,000 gold necklace as thick as a bridge cable when the only necklace worth wearing in basketball is a nylon net that costs $9.99. (But—and here's the point—it can't be bought.)

I'm a believer in Lafayette Lever and regret never having covered him for, if I had, my first sentence about him would have been, "There must be fifty ways to love your Lever."

I believe that jumping off a trampoline, turning a midair somersault, slam-dunking, and sticking the landing—while wearing a gorilla suit that's wearing, in turn, a Phoenix Suns warm-up jacket—is enough to qualify you as a first-ballot Hall of Famer.

I believe in Harthorne Wingo, and I believe in Zap the dingo, the Detroit Shock mascot whose costume was stolen from the Palace of Auburn Hills by two men who were caught—one in the dingo head, the other in the dingo feet—drinking in a bar across the street.

I believe in former Notre Dame guard Leo (Crystal) Klier and former Providence center Jacek (Zippity) Duda and former Iowa State center (What the) Sam Hill.

I believe in dunking dirty clothes into the hallway hamper and skyhooking—from the shotgun seat—quarters into highway toll baskets. And I believe in finger-rolling heads of lettuce into my shopping cart, even though I have never, in the last ten years, eaten a piece of lettuce at home.

I believe I can still hold, in my right hand, a boom box the size of a Samsonite Streamlite while carrying, in my left, a slick rubber ball whose pebble-grain stubble has long before been dribbled away. And that I can do so while riding a ten-speed bike and steering with my knees.

I believe that the Truth (Drew Gooden) and the Answer (Allen Iverson) are out there, if we will simply follow the bouncing ball.

I believe that we, the basketball faithful, speak in tongues: the red, wagging tongue of Michael Jordan and the red, wagging tongues of our unlaced Chuck Taylors.

I believe that Larry Bird's crooked right index finger—which he raised in triumph before his winning shot fell in the 1988 All-Star weekend three-point contest—resembles, almost exactly, God's crooked right index finger, as depicted on the ceiling of the Sistine Chapel.

Which would make sense, if God made man in His image. For I believe, above all, in what G. K. Chesterton wrote, and what Rick Telander echoed in the title of a book: Earth is a task garden. But heaven is a playground.

(December 9, 2002)

DOG DAYS

This is a man-bites-dog story. Americans eat twenty billion hot dogs a year, which works out to sixty sausages per citizen. Or so says the National Hot Dog and Sausage Council, a wiener advocacy group whose raw data (which also come grilled) project that twenty-six million franks will be consumed this season in the twenty-eight Major League Baseball parks alone. Laid end to end, those dogs would stretch from Baltimore to Los Angeles, a sausage superhighway. Come follow its yellow center line: a trail of ballpark mustard dispensed from a flatulent squeeze bottle.

The road winds past Cooper Stadium in Columbus, Ohio, where the Triple A Clippers host gluttonous Dime-a-Dog nights. On April 15, 3,395 paying customers at Cooper ate 21,365 Oscar Mayer wieners, a frank-to-fan ratio of more than six to one. Given that some spectators abstained, one has to wonder . . .

"I've had people say they ate fifteen to twenty dogs," says the Clippers' general manager, whose name is Ken Schnacke. (Of course it is.) He quickly adds, "We've never had anybody get ridiculously sick and be taken to the hospital to have his stomach pumped." But as baseball fans everywhere know, there's always next year.

The point is, Americans certainly ken schnacke, and in few places do they snack more heavily than at baseball parks. The reasons for this are manifold and, in the view of some experts, quite complex. "Sports are a primitive ritual of aggression and release—the id hangs out," *Psychology Today* editor Hara Estroff Marano once told *New York Times* food writer Molly O'Neill, whose brother Paul plays right field for the New York Yankees. "In such a situation, the primitive part of the brain, 'Me want hot dog,' overrides the restraints of the more rational part of the brain, which would say, 'Am I hungry?' or 'Would I like a hot dog?'"

Tell Boog Powell that his id hangs out, and he's apt to check his fly. The former first baseman for the Baltimore Orioles knows only that food tastes better at the ballpark and that every time the O's played in Milwaukee, his brain said, "Me want bratwurst." So between at bats, he would dispatch a clubhouse attendant to the stands to procure a pair of sausages slathered in red sauce, later to be immortalized as Secret Stadium Sauce. Standing in the tunnel behind the dugout, Boog would down those brats in a violent trice, as if feeding timber to a wood chipper. "Then I'd walk to the plate with red sauce all down the front of my uniform," he recalls. "I'd tell the manager, 'I'm bleeding like a stuck pig!'"

A giant man who bleeds condiments, Powell embodies the bond between baseball and food, an association "as strong as the movies and popcorn," according to sports sociologist Bob Brustad of the University of Northern Colorado. In fact the sports–food bond is stronger. When an ad man tried to encapsulate America for his automaker client, he wrote, "Baseball, hot dogs, apple pie, and Chevrolet," front-loading the jingle with the two most surefire evocations of American culture.

And you thought American culture was an oxymoron. "Of course there is American culture," says Allen Guttmann, a professor of American studies at Amherst. "It includes symphonies as well as jazz, literature as well as comic books." And at its apex are what Bob Dole calls "America's greatest diversions: sports and food."

If that description rings with American decadence—you can bet Bangladeshi leaders don't call food a diversion—it happens to be accurate. What is more diverting than eating a chocolate sundae from an inverted miniature batting helmet while watching other people work? What, for that matter, is more decadent?

Of all sports, baseball most vigorously stirs the appetite. Because of the game's unhurried pace and frequent lulls, baseball fans tend to make more trips to the concessions stands than football, basketball, or hockey crowds. In those last three sports, "food sales are driven by intermissions," notes Michael F. Thompson, president of Sportservice, which supplies seven Major League ballparks. "Baseball games are a constant, leisurely grazing period."

In that spirit we invite you to graze.

Just as baseball's birthplace is disputed, sausage, too, comes encased in controversy. Who conjoined the ballpark and the frank? Was it St. Louis saloonkeeper Chris von der Ahe, who owned the Browns baseball club and brought sausages to Sportsman's Park near the turn of the century to serve as sop for his popular beer? Or was it Harry M. Stevens, a former bookseller who in 1901 began to sell ten-cent "dachshund" sausages at the Polo Grounds in New York City? This much is clear: When cartoonist Tad Dorgan captured the Polo Grounds scene for the *New York Evening Journal* that year, his caption shortened the vendors' pitch—"Get your red hot dachshunds!"—to the snappier "hot dogs!"

Still, one hopes the von der Ahe–Stevens matter is adjudicated at the next meeting of the National Hot Dog and Sausage Council, whose members rule on the world's wiener-related controversies and are responsible, one suspects, for the diabolical fact that hot dogs are sold in packs of ten, while hot dog buns come in packs of eight.

In the hypercompetitive world of ballpark concessionaires, it really is the size of the dog in the fight, and not the size of the fight in the dog, that matters. "Ten to one" is food-service shorthand meaning ten hot dogs will be produced from every pound of beef, pork, or poultry. A ten-to-one frank is common in the industry, though baseball's dogs tend to skew bigger. Volume Services sells a zeppelinesque two-to-one, or half pound, hot dog in Kansas City and Minneapolis. In Kansas City it is called the King Colossal (in Minneapolis, the Jumbo Dog), and it's the biggest dog in the majors now that Vince Coleman is in the minors. In short, the lower the ratio, the larger the sausage, which means these numbers also serve handily as odds that a given hot dog will kill you.

"One pig-out is not significant," says Patricia Hausman, author of seven books on diet and nutrition, refusing to rain-delay our parade. "But I think people have to ask themselves, Is what I eat at the ball game representative of what I eat all the time? If so, then they've got a real issue on their hands." With that in mind, many stadiums now serve kosher franks, whose ingredients have been blessed by a rabbi. San Francisco's 3Com Park even offers something called a tofu dog. Tofu apparently derives from toenail fungus, but the product's very inedibility ensures against ill effects on one's health.

Kosher and tofu franks are but two of the myriad new offerings from Major League Baseball's four principal concessionaires: Aramark, Ogden, Sportservice, and Volume Services. Big league teams gross tens of millions of dollars a year from food sales, so a popular new item, such as nachos, the surprise hit of the last fifteen years at Major League parks, can be more valuable to a franchise than a good left-handed reliever.

Like baseball itself, concessions companies keep sophisticated statistics. "White Sox fans tend to buy more apparel," says Aramark's Bernhard Kloppenburg, who runs the food and merchandise business at Camden Yards in Baltimore. "Yankee fans tend to drink more beer." Kloppenburg proudly points out that the Orioles' Cal Ripken Jr. wasn't the only record breaker at Camden Yards last September 6, the night he surpassed Lou Gehrig's total of consecutive games played. Aramark did an absurd $40 per fan in sales that evening, to the delight of Fancy Clancy and the Terminator, local beer hawkers whose sales totals can earn them a chance to work the All-Star Game and other big events.

Vendors and other ballpark food workers occupy their own subculture. Some seem born for the job—the wearer of beer-vendor badge number 0003 at Coors Field in Denver is named Eric Beerman—and all use a lingua franca that is unintelligible to outsiders. Say the words "mother Merco," for instance, and they'll know that you're talking about the most essential of concessions-stand appliances. It is the plastic-front wiener grill that allows patrons filing past to view rows of hot dogs in repose, much as citizens of the former Soviet Union once filed past the embalmed body of Lenin in Moscow's Red Square. The difference, of course, is that mother Merco's pilgrims come to stuff themselves.

Los Angeles has baseball's best-known dog-and-kraut combo, if you no longer count Schottzie and Marge. "Nothing is as famous as the Dodger Dog," notes Lon Rosenberg, Aramark's general manager at Dodger Stadium, and this is as it should be, for L.A. gave the world the hot dog–shaped building (see Tail 'O' the Pup on San Vicente Boulevard) and frankophile movie stars: Marlene Dietrich's favorite meal was hot dogs and champagne, while Humphrey Bogart once said, "A hot dog at the game beats roast beef at the Ritz." You can just hear him, can't you?

The Dodger Dog's nearest rival is three thousand miles away in Boston, where the Fenway Frank generally cuts the mustard with the most discerning of critics. "The dog was very good," says TV gourmand Julia Child, recalling a Fenway Frank she recently digested. "But the bun was wet and soggy."

In an unrelated bun-related incident, two former concessions-stand workers at the Kingdome told the *Seattle Times* in March that they had been instructed to pick the mold off hot dog rolls before serving them to the public. The story is credible because the Kingdome's concessions stands, run by Ogden, have been cited 158 times in the last three years by the Seattle–King County Department of Public Health for ominous-sounding "red critical" food-safety violations.

Yet hot dogs continue to dominate ballpark food sales. King Colossal indeed. "You'll find there are still six major food groups," says Thompson of Sportservice. "There's a sausage product—tube steak, as it's called in some places; popcorn; soda or beer; nachos; peanuts; and malts and frozen things."

In this last category is the Dove Bar, which is giving some stiff competition to the frosty malt as the frozen thing of choice in many ballparks. The frosty malt, you might recall, is a cup of chocolate-malt-flavored ice cream that comes with a flimsy three-inch tongue depressor that its manufacturers quaintly call a spoon. If the Dove Bar should displace the frosty malt, it would be the death knell for yet another baseball tradition. As Thompson concedes, "You can't throw the lid of a Dove Bar," Frisbee-like, from the second deck of a stadium.

What price progress?

For the better part of this century, ballpark cuisine comprised the few, unwavering aforementioned staples. That all changed with the advent of nachos: tortilla chips submerged in something called "cheez," an orange substance with the viscosity and thermal breakdown of forty-weight Pennzoil. People lapped it up, often literally.

Nonexistent in ballparks circa 1980, nachos now account for 8 percent of all food sales in stadiums served by Sportservice. "Nachos were introduced in the theme restaurants, like Friday's," says Aramark's Kloppenburg. "Then they came to the ballparks."

Things would never be the same. Before the decade was out, the door was thrown open to other arrivistes, including Dove Bars, Dunkin' Donuts, and Pizza Hut. Buy me some peanuts and Cracker Jack? "With Cracker Jack, you find young kids don't enjoy it much," says Thompson. "They have gone to the Crunch 'n Munch." In what may be a final act of desperation, some Cracker Jack boxes carry a banner that says FAT FREE, the nineties equivalent of A PRIZE IN EVERY PACKAGE.

According to Sportservice, the number of women attending Major League games has tripled, to more than 35 percent, in the past ten years, expediting an explosion of light ballpark food, such as salads, pasta, and Fat Free Cracker Jack. The age and affluence of baseball fans—most customers at Camden Yards are between thirty-one and forty years old, with an annual income of at least $50,000—have also pushed the trend toward yuppier fare, such as boutique beers. 3Com Park serves twenty bottled brands at one stand alone, including Oregon Berry Brew, which tastes like cherry Robitussin but doesn't provide the pleasant buzz you get from the cough syrup.

In addition most stadiums serve some sort of regional cuisine: Cuban sandwiches in Miami, cheese coneys in Cincinnati, clam chowder in Boston, barbecued brisket in Texas, indigenous seafood in Denver, and Maryland crab cakes in Baltimore.

Crab cakes were on the menu in Orioles owner Peter Angelos's luxury box at Camden Yards on April 2 when President Clinton threw out the first pitch to open the season. So were fresh fruits, crudites, and other foods so extraordinary at a ballpark that the collective spread impressed even the president's jaded entourage. "They were saying they'd never seen anything like it," recalls Michelle Milani, the luxury box attendant that afternoon.

"Uh, Michelle?" asked the president, surveying the spread as the game got under way. "Can I just have . . . nachos?" A platter was summoned, and Clinton inhaled it as if he were a Hoover upright. "And he had some shelled peanuts," says Milani.

Adds Zachary Henderson, the stadium's executive sous-chef: "I believe he also had a shrimp cocktail . . ."

Says Milani, "And hot dogs . . ."

Well, you get the idea.

Baltimore is the city that gave us Babe Ruth, who once ate a dozen hot dogs between games of a doubleheader. In terms of local legend, Babe begat Boog, whose favorite ballpark food is barbecue. Hang around him long enough and you learn, that *barbecue* is not just a verb. *Barbecue* is not just a noun. "Barbecue," says Boog, "is an attitude."

Back when the Minnesota Twins played their home games at Metropolitan Stadium in Bloomington, Boog often didn't get out of the parking lot. "I used to leave that park after a weekend day game and never make it to the hotel," he says. "Those people could tailgate. You'd sit down, have a couple of beers, the grill is going, and the next thing you know, they're saying, 'Hey, it's late, you might as well stay here.'" And Boog would crash in his newfound friends' Winnebago, a mobile home away from home.

Boog's has always been a barbecue state of mind. In Baltimore he couldn't wait to return home after Sunday afternoon games and "fire up the barbecue." This was easy to do because he lived in a row house behind Memorial Stadium, where the Orioles played in those days. "Hell, I'd grill after night games," he says. "Fire it up at eleven o'clock, smoke is pouring in the neighbors' windows, their heads are popping out, and they're yelling, 'We know you don't have to work in the morning, but the rest of us do.'

"Hell," Boog replied, "if I had to work in the morning, I wouldn't be out here." Freed of the burdens of ballplaying after seventeen years in the big leagues, Boog now practices the full barbecue lifestyle, drinking beer professionally as a pitchman for Miller and overseeing Boog's barbecue stand beyond the right-field bleachers at Camden Yards. The stand grosses $2 million a year, and so popular is its proprietor that Orioles manager Davey Johnson once told him, "You could sell these people a dog shit sandwich, they'd buy it."

Boog knows better than that. What draws the crowds to his stand is the barbecue attitude. "It's a smile," he says. "It's the smell." It's the secret sauce, and the sun, and a story or a signature from Boog himself. It's the sound of baseball beyond the bleacher wall behind Boog, who has a hundred beer-buzzed patrons in his line and three Weber grills cooking up fifteen hundred pounds of beef, pork, and turkey a night and sending smoke to the blue heavens.

Fans call his name with an easy familiarity. They're not booing, they're Booging. At this moment he looks more than enormous. He looks enormously content. Boog Powell and all those around him are feeling very barbecue indeed.

(July 8, 1996)

FIRE AND ICE

I love hockey players and their crossword-puzzle smiles. When I stand for "O Canada," so does the hair on my neck. I love that Ottawans hate Hockey Night in Canada because its analysts, they believe, love the Toronto Maple Leafs. I love that Hockey Night analyst Harry Neale has said of Ottawans, "They can take a big bite of my ass." I love that Ottawa Senators fan Bob Chiarelli has said of Neale, "When he comes to Ottawa, he better be wearing his hockey gear and keep his elbows high." I love, too, that Chiarelli is the mayor of Ottawa.

I love that penalties are served in the kind of Plexiglased box last deemed necessary at Nuremberg. Indeed, I love almost everything about hockey, and it remains an eternal bafflement that most Americans do not. National television ratings for NHL games, it shames me to say, are lower than those for XFL games. How in the name of Nikolai Khabibulin can this be?

The Stanley Cup playoffs are the most riveting spectacle in sports. Last Thursday night St. Louis Blues center Pierre Turgeon took a flying puck in the mouth—he more or less ate it, like a vulcanized Hostess Ding Dong—yet missed only one shift. "I lost a couple teeth," he said, his *s*'s whistling. "But hey, that's playoff hockey."

That same night in Edmonton, Dallas Stars center Mike Modano, his nose shattered by a puck, also returned to the ice but stitched up like a baseball, with thirty-five sutures on the outside of his head and (for all we know) a cushioned-cork center implanted on the inside. His schnoz visibly throbbed throughout the rest of the game, blinking red like a traffic light at midnight—an hour at which most of these games, incidentally, are just beginning to heat up.

All hockey playoff games go to multiple overtimes. (Or so it seems. Through Sunday twelve of forty-six had gone to OT, including four of six games in the Dallas-Edmonton series.) No penalties are ever called after the second period. When New Jersey Devils defenseman Scott Stevens decapitates an opponent, and he does so several times a game, a linemate simply flips the severed head over the boards with his stick. "And play," as the announcers like to say, "continues."

Does it ever. The Stanley Cup isn't merely the most fetching trophy in North America, it is also the hardest-earned. The action in OT, by which time most players are toothless, drained, and darned like socks, is an end-to-end, whistle-free, whiplash-inducing blur: of slap shots ringing off the post, of heads being speedbagged in the corners, of Toronto keeper Curtis Joseph wandering so far from his crease that he sometimes becomes confused and briefly defends his opponent's goal. On and on and on it goes, until somebody finally lights the lamp, the goal judge's siren turning as if atop an ambulance. Then, when a series ends, the two teams line up to exchange handshakes and pleasantries. ("Sorry about the teeth." "Better get that nose looked at." "Your head will grow back," etc.) Why, America, have you not embraced this?

I have. I love the mournful foghorn at the end of each period. I love the sight, oddly biblical, of hats and octopuses raining down from the rafters. I love every lyrical francophone name: Sylvain Lefebvre, Patrick DesRochers, Jean-Luc Grand-Pierre; and every sharp-cornered eastern European one: Valery Zelepukin, Roman Hamrlik, Igor Kravchuk. I live to hear *NHL 2Night* host John Buccigross say "Sven Butenschon." And vice versa.

To be sure, a few of hockey's traditions are idiotic and indefensible, foremost among them the sanctioned cross-checking of a player to the ice in the second or so after he has scored. It's as if Pudge Rodriguez had license to sucker punch a base runner who has just crossed home plate, though, I happily concede, that practice would enliven many a baseball game.

Mostly, though, I am captivated by hockey's manifold pleasures, even the simplest ones. There remains something deeply hypnotic about watching a Zamboni make its rounds, the oval of uncleaned ice getting ever smaller and smaller, a tableau too few Americans will ever appreciate.

Don't tell me it's not a television sport or that it's too Canadian. While recently screening, for the tenth time, footage of the 1980 U.S. Olympic team, my scalp was tingling. (I felt like a subject in a Selsun Blue commercial.) I still get chills when Mike Eruzione scores the game-winner against the Soviets, even though I know precisely when, and how, it's going to happen. By the time the U.S. team celebrates its gold-medal win over Finland and Jim Craig is wrapped in the flag like a marathoner in a foil blanket, I have full-body goose bumps.

Even now, just recalling the moment, my skin is pebbled like a plucked chicken's. Hockey can make me shiver, and I am here to tell you: it has nothing to do with the ice.

(April 30, 2001)

MR. STIV'S EXCELLENT ADVENTURE

B efore screaming monkeys fell from the sky to rob me and beat me and leave me for dead, before I sliced a three-iron into the crater of a volcano (and hit a perfect lava wedge out to save par), before a James Bond villain named Mr. Cedok served me up as a cocktail wiener for the water life of the Indian Ocean, I was told to idly bicycle around Bali.

Before I fluffed my hotel pillow and found a live lizard where the mint was supposed to be, before I set out to see this island in Indonesia with nothing but a German guidebook for company, I planned to pedal peacefully around Bali's 2,147 square miles of unreal estate.

That was the assignment: Ride a bike. Clear my head and fill my notebook, take in the sun and bang out the story. One of those life-in-the-slow-lane swimsuit-issue stories. The kind they would no doubt headline BALI HIGH! Or better yet . . .

GOLLY, IT'S BALI!

The island excursion was not what my editors had imagined it to be, though Bali was just as I had pictured it. Alas, my only picture of the island was the 1952 film *Road to Bali,* in which George (Bing Crosby) and Harold (Bob Hope) were stalked by the evil Mr. Arok, spurned by the lovely Princess Lalah and assaulted by Bogatan the Giant Squid.

These were precisely the sorts of things that would happen to me in my seven-day Balinese sojourn.

This was entirely my fault. My previous international travels had consisted of forty-five minutes in Tijuana (I know what you're thinking, but I was eleven years old and it was a family vacation) and a tour of Canada's Smythe Division cities. So once off the North American continent I went nuts, seeking out the exotic wherever I could.

Greenout greets all visitors to the Emerald Island. George and Harold arrived on Bali by boat, parting the lime Kool-Aid waters off the southern coast. I came by plane, flying in over the green rice terraces that descend from Bali's tree-studded central mountains, themselves more fertile than Jane Pauley.

The greens on the golf course at the Bali Handara Country Club in the mountain village of Pancasari, the first stop on my tour, were said to be the greenest swatches of the greenest mountains on the greenest island on God's green earth. Pancasari is a short van ride from the airport in Denpasar, a sprawling, noxious village of 200,000 that only twenty years ago was quaint and fairly untouched by tourism. Which raises an interesting question: Van ride?

I confess. My butt cheeks didn't touch a bike seat all week. For while driving in and around Denpasar in search of a bicycle rental shop, I saw:

- A giant stone pedestal displaying the twisted wreckage of an automobile whose driver, a disfigured crash dummy doused in red paint, hung from a window. HATI-HATI was the pedestal's inscription: "Be careful."
- A sign reading, in English, BETTER LATE THEN [sic] END UP IN THE HOSPITAL.
- Two fruit-marketing mopeders broadsided by a truck, sending melons heavenward and the two bikers flying into traffic.

- Countless pieces of spirit-appeasing roadside statuary skirted in black-white-and-gray-checkered cloth. ("Black for evil spirits," said Mr. Ade, whom we will meet later, "white for nice spirits." And gray? "For in-between spirits.")

I also saw zero bicycle rental shops.

On the island's roadways, life in the slow lane moves at breakneck speed. So I forgot about seeing Bali by Schwinn, and instead purchased a shrink-wrapped guidebook called *Bali,* rented a Mitsubishi Super Kijang van, and resolved to drive the seventy miles to Pancasari and the legendary golf course there.

As Denpasar receded and Bali's more breathtaking, break-down-and-weep-beautiful precincts passed the windows, I stripped the shrink-wrap from the guidebook and riffled through it for rudimentary directions to our destination. The introduction to the book began: "Als die Erstauflage dieses Bali-Fuhrers. . . ."

BALI ON ZERO RUPIAH A DAY

A bit of background would be helpful before we get to the excellent-adventure portion of our story.

Where Bali is. If the world were a cherry tomato, and you were to stick a toothpick through New York City, which isn't a bad idea when you think about it, the toothpick would come out the opposite side near Bali, virtually 180 degrees from Gotham.

Climate. It's not the heat, it's the humidity. The sheets on the bed that you *don't* sleep in are soaking wet when you wake up in the morning. The fattest James Michener paperback curls into a soggy cylinder on the nightstand. Even in an air-conditioned room, your pillowcase can be mistaken for the natural habitat of the Balinese gecko, as I discovered after turning in my first night on the island. Come daytime, it really gets humid.

Speaking of Michener. This island is not the fictional Bali H'ai of which he wrote in *Tales of the South Pacific,* which became the musical *South Pacific,* which spawned the song "Bali H'ai."

History. Java is less than two miles to the west across the Bali Strait, so Bali's history is as old as Java man's. But space limitations dictate that we jump ahead to 1596, when Dutch sailors first set foot on Balinese soil, and then to 1906, when some four thousand Balinese died in the suicidal *puputan,* a hopeless fight against the Dutch forces that had ruled Bali off and on for three hundred years. The Japanese occupied Bali in World War II, sometime after which the island became part of the newly independent country of Indonesia.

Religion. Bali is 95 percent Hindu and seems to have a temple for each of its two and a half million people. Thus Mick Jagger didn't wait in line when he got married and converted to Hinduism here last November.

Temple etiquette. Women bring elaborate offerings of fruit, carried Carmen Miranda–like on the tops of their heads. As for the non-Hindu: "It is better that you go to temple without Balinese people," said Mr. Ade, whom, I promise, we will meet later. "Because if you do wrong, you just say, 'Big sorry. I did not know.'"

What to eat. "Jackfruit may cause nausea," read a warning in the Bali Hyatt. "You should have a glass of boiled water before eating it, and avoid alcohol for three hours after." Otherwise, a treat.

Durian, which looks like a pale yellow softball, cannot be carried onto airplanes or into most hotels. It is said to "smell like hell and taste like heaven." I tried it. It smelled like a Greyhound restroom and tasted like a pale yellow softball.

Where to stay. The Oberoi hotel in Legian Beach has roofless bathrooms, which are nice until you discover that on Legian Beach you can rent motorized hang gliders. The Oberoi may be the only luxury hotel in the world whose bathroom sinks are equipped with spray cans of Bay-Gon, which combats, according to the label, nyamuk, kacoa, laba-laba, and kutubusuk. That's "mosquito," "cockroach," "spider," and "bug" if you're scoring at home.

On the downscale are the Bali Intan Cottages in Kuta Beach, a sort of Fort Lauderdale for vacationing Australian students. (AVOID HANGOVERS advises a sign at the Cock 'n' Bull Pub. STAY DRUNK.)

"We take any kind of card," said the man behind the desk at the Intan Cottages. I charged my room to a long-expired Minneapolis Public Library card but was busted at checkout.

"Big sorry," I said. "I did not know."

JOE VERSUS THE VOLCANO

English-language guidebooks to Bali do exist. "It's often said the Balinese look away from the sea and toward the mountains," reads one book. "The mountains are the abode of gods and the sea is the home of demons and monsters."

The sea, as I would discover when I became human crankbait, was indeed the home of demons and monsters. But the mountains, as I discovered at the Bali Handara golf course, were not all bougainvillea, either.

Lake Buyan and 7,467–foot Mount Batukau overlook Bali Handara. Two years ago, the Indonesian government banned hiking on Batukau, anticipating a volcanic eruption that has yet to come. Nevertheless, "I think Batukau will smoke soon," a Balinese man told me. "On top of Batukau, trees are growing up. I think they are very hot, yes?" But the most unsettling thought as I made my backswing on Handara's first tee was the knowledge that the golf course on which I stood was, literally, eighteen holes in one.

The Bali Handara course was laid out seventeen years ago in the crater of an unnamed volcano. Sure, the volcano is "long inactive," but so are Tony Orlando and Dawn. Should I not fear a return to activity?

Directly behind me on the first tee box, Mount Catur watched my follow-through like a three-thousand-foot instructor. And though my all-time lowest golf score would be a record-high temperature on Guam, I unaccountably spanked that first ball 275 yards down the center of the fairway. My caddy, a sixteen-year-old Pancasari village girl named Kadek Suartini, admired the flight of the Titleist. Then Kadek the Magnificent, more lovely than Princess Lalah herself, turned to me and gushed, "Luck-eee! Luck-eee, Mister!"

Somehow, she knew that when it comes to driving, I'm no Pope John Paul II who, of course, is notoriously long off the tee. In the Handara clubhouse hangs a photograph of the pontiff wearing red-white-and-blue Foot-Joys beneath his white vestments. Two Balinese are posed to the right of the Holy Father. All three stand behind Handara's eighteenth green. The caption below the photo reads: "1984 Bali Bash. L to R: Low Gross, Low Net and Long Drive Winners. (Golf Clothes Supplied by KB Petroleum Golf Fashion Wear.)"

That's right. Apparently, His Holiness not only won a long-drive contest on Bali when he visited the island, he also inked an endorsement deal.

Kadek spent the rest of my round exhausting her English vocabulary. When I told her I was from the United States, she began calling me Joe. When I blew putts, she screamed, "Aaargh!" When I sliced a three-iron into the flinty bottom of a small canyon and asked for a lava wedge to chip out with, she said, "Drop it."

Drop what? A new ball? My pathetic attempt at an icebreaker? Such language difficulties required that I hire an interpreter. And so, immediately after carding a one-twenty-something, I hired one.

Meet twenty-seven-year-old I Made Ade. His long left thumbnail was meant to show that he did no hard manual labor. He was to serve as guide and van driver. I called him Mr. Ade—it rhymes with "body"—and he called me Mr. Stiv. With the characteristic warmth of the (noncaddying) Balinese, Mr. Ade was soon describing to me his village, his wife, his wedding. "I am married one year," he said. "And I have six-month-old child. So I have very quick service, yes?"

We hit it off, Mr. Ade and Mr. Stiv. So why didn't I listen when he told me . . .

"IN SANGEH, THE MONKEYS ARE STUPID"

"Yes," he said, a nervous smile splitting his face. "I take you to Tabanan."

But I want to go to Sangeh, I repeated. I want to see Bukit Sari, the sacred Monkey Forest there. I want to see Pura Bukit Sari, the sacred Monkey Temple in the sacred Monkey Forest.

"But friendly monkeys in Tabanan," Mr. Ade replied. "In Sangeh, the monkeys are stupid."

Stupid?

"They go in your hair," he said. "They jump on your shoulders. They scratch you. They take your glasses, take your money, take your camera. They want many fruits to give them back. If they take expensive camera, they want many more fruits. Friendly monkeys in Tabanan."

Take me to Sangeh, I said. I want to see the stupid monkeys.

The Ramayana is one of the great Hindu epics. It holds that Hanuman, the monkey god and a flying white monkey himself, was toting a mountain across the sky when he dropped a chunk, studded with trees and teeming with monkeys, on the spot that is now Bukit Sari.

Bukit Sari is still teeming with monkeys. Teeming with thieving, murderous, corrupted monkeys. Monkeys who would mug me for my Minolta and hold it for a ransom of bananas. Monkeys who would gouge a fistful of flesh from my shoulder just to watch me bleed. More intriguing was the fact that in the deepest part of the forest stood Pura Bukit Sari, an ornate temple to all things monkey: a baroque, Hearstian, palatial San Simian.

Mr. Ade parked the van when we pulled within sight of the forest, a thicket of straight and leafy nutmeg trees. We could already hear the whine of what sounded like cannonballs ripping through the treetops as we read the sign posted at the side of the road: ATTENTION: BE CAREFUL WITH YOUR BELONGINGS (AC-CESSORIES) DURING VISIT TO THIS HOLLY MONKEY FOREST. TO AVOID UNDESIRABLE CASES CAUSED BY SOME AGGRESSIVE MONKEYS.

The sign was a model of understatement, if not of spelling and punctuation. The sign maker didn't mention that the human earlobe is an "accessory." For of all the "cases" Mr. Ade has had occasion to witness in the Monkey Forest, perhaps the most "undesirable" have occurred when "some aggressive monkeys" have snatched the pierced earrings—and accompanying pieces of lobes—from the heads of unsuspecting visitors.

On the threshold of the fenced-in forest, a toothless old woman bade me to take the stick she offered, and I did. She also urged me to remove my Coke-bottle-thick glasses, lest the monkeys rob me of my very vision. Impossible, I told her. As I pinned the glasses to the bridge of my nose with my index finger, Mr. Ade broke his nervous silence.

"Mr. Stiv," he said quietly. "Please do not taunt the monkeys."

I assured him that I had no intention of taunting the monkeys.

"Please," he repeated more quietly. "Do not taunt the monkeys."

In the forest, the sunlight disappeared. And so did all sound, save for the screeching of monkeys and Mr. Ade's constantly whispered admonitions against taunting them. As we walked down the single dirt path, I felt the eyes of a million monkeys on me—the new inmate on parade down Cell Block A at Monkeytraz.

Suddenly, a thirty-pound animal came cannonballing out of the trees. We half-circled each other as two wrestlers will at the start of a match. He lunged and I jabbed with the old lady's stick. The simpering simian hobbled away.

Another monkey picked the pocket of a tourist walking ahead of us, then bolted into the woods. The tourist sought out a forest ranger, who sought out the monkey, who was found waving a driver's license and motioning for peanuts.

There weren't more than twenty human targets in the forest, but soon all was a black marketplace of gray monkeys—here bartering for bananas, there making off with a baseball cap, everywhere pawning people's goods for a palmful of peanuts.

And just as I glimpsed the magnificent Monkey Temple, one of its tenants hijacked, humbled, and dehumanized the Aussie.

An Australian high school kid began bawling and flailing after a monkey had leaped onto his shoulder. A ranger ordered the boy to stand still. Thirty seconds passed, and the kid looked cautiously at the monkey. After a minute or so, the boy was beaming while his two friends snapped their Instamatics.

It wasn't until the boy began to—yes—taunt the monkey that the animal drew itself to its full three feet in stature and cackled maniacally. The monkey may also have beaten his chest with both fists, though I didn't pause to take notes. For at that very moment, as all activity froze around them, the monkey, standing like a hirsute hood ornament on the Australian's shoulder, loosed a hideous scream.

The monkey then took a long leak on the chump's bare neck, rappelled to the ground, and disappeared into the forest, howling and giving monkey high fives to his howling monkey friends.

Mr. Ade and I made tracks for the van.

LOOKING FOR MR. CEDOK

The last thing I remember thinking before I lost consciousness was: How exactly did I let this happen?

How does anyone let himself be ferried miles out into the Indian Ocean in a canoe, knocked unconscious, turned into chum, and dangled in the sea spray for the better part of four hours?

Well, he begins not by planning a fishing trip to end his life but by planning one to end his visit to Bali. Hire a boat. Cast a net. Crack a Bintang, the beer of Indonesia. Maybe tune in a prodigal ball game bounced off an errant satellite.

Which is how I innocently came to hire my own hit man.

I found Mr. Cedok (CHED-ock) in the fishing village of Jimbaran. He is, by his own estimate, "about twenty-four." (The Balinese year is two hundred and ten days long.) He is from infinite generations of fishermen. As Mr. Ade pointed out, *cedok* is an Indonesian word for "something like a spoon, used to scoop the water from the boat."

Of course, Mr. Ade begged off the excursion immediately after telling me that Cedok's very surname implies a boatful of water. I would meet Cedok alone the next morning at six.

"Tomorrow," Cedok said, "be lucky." I didn't know if it was a forecast or a command, but he said it in Indonesian. Cedok doesn't speak a word of English.

His twelve-foot boat, the *Lumayan,* was the same sort of outrigger canoe you see on the opening credits of *Hawaii Five-O.* Alas, the waves in the Indian Ocean the next morning were also the same sort as on the opening credits of *Hawaii Five-O*. I swallowed several Dramamine as Cedok zipped us out to sea on the power of the village's lone outboard motor.

I was handed a large plastic spool of fishing line labeled UN-BREAKABLE. An enormous multihooked lure dangled at the end of the line. I blindly followed Cedok's pantomimed instructions and realized too late what I had done. Miles from shore and a hemisphere from home, I had tightly wrapped unbreakable line twice around my waist and tied a knot from which there could be no escape.

I was bound to one end of the unbreakable line, which extended a hundred yards into the Indian Ocean. A sumptuous lure at the other end beckoned anything to bite. Nearby, commercial fishing boats were using industrial-strength cranes to haul in yellowfin tuna the size of Pontiacs. If I snagged one of those, I knew, I would be waterskiing barefoot behind it.

I sat down on the floor of the canoe and held, viselike, with both hands, onto my wooden-plank seat. Cedok did not seem to think that this was a bad idea. I prepared to die. And then everything faded to black. . . .

I had fallen sound asleep (too much Dramamine).

But in my sleep I had hooked an eight-pound tuna, and I fought it until the fish had no more energy. When I awoke, Cedok was laughing hysterically and pulling in the tuna hand over hand.

I fell asleep again for two more hours but failed to catch anything else. When we returned to Jimbaran Beach, Cedok, who hadn't said two words in the boat, began chattering excitedly to other fishermen. Mr. Ade arrived in the van, and I described to him an epic Melvillean struggle lost by the fish I was holding aloft.

All the Balinese on the beach tossed back their heads and laughed a good long time. "Mr. Cedok says you are very funny," said Mr. Ade, himself convulsed. "Mr. Cedok says you don't know you catch a fish even when it is flopping on the line."

"Tell Mr. Cedok this is the first fish I ever caught," I told Mr. Ade. "Tell Mr. Cedok that I think he is a very wise fisherman. Tell Mr. Cedok to keep the fish."

While Mr. Cedok *cedoked* the *Lumayan,* Mr. Ade relayed the message. I dropped the solitary tuna in the boat.

"Mr. Stiv," said Mr. Ade. "Mr. Cedok says, *Lumayan.* It means, 'Better than nothing.' It means, 'Just happy to be here.'"

(February 11, 1991)

NO HANDICAPPING
THIS FIELD

S ome years ago, while waiting on the first tee of a Minneapolis
golf course, my threesome was joined by a man with one arm,
which he used as the front arm of his practice swing, sweeping
the club forward in a graceful parabola, in the manner of Steffi
Graf hitting a backhand or a matador throwing open his cape.
When the amputee spanked his first drive 225 yards down the fairway, my brother turned to me and whispered, with a deep sense
of foreboding, "We're about to get our asses kicked by a guy with
one arm." And so we did.

I thought of that man last week, at the National Amputee Golf
Championship, at which I met the one-armed, one-legged, four-
fingered Bob MacDermott, who was shocked by high-tension
wires on his Edmonton farm sixteen years ago. "The worst part
wasn't taking fifteen thousand volts," he said. "On the way to the
hospital the ambulance blew two tires and threw me out the back.
That's when I thought, Game over. I'm playing that big golf course
in the sky."

Yet there he was last week—drinking a Harp, not playing one—
at Hazeltine National Golf Club near Minneapolis. A seven-
handicapper before his accident, MacDermott, who plays with a
prosthetic arm and leg, is now a one. This summer, he shot a six-
under 65 to win the championship at his club, Belvedere. He even

qualified for the Alberta Open. The forty-seven-year-old really has become a one-legged man in an ass-kicking contest.

"Hands," he told me, after a windswept round of 74, "get in the way of a golf swing." "I used to spray the ball all over the place," said forty-nine-year-old Dan Caputo, a railroad switchman, of the years before he lost his right arm between two boxcars in 1984. "Now I'm right down the middle." Indeed, in the first round last week Caputo, playing with a prosthesis, aced the par 3 seventeenth at Hazeltine and hightailed it off the course immediately after putting out on eighteen. "We were worried we'd have to buy a round for everyone," said his wife, Kim. "Have you seen the price of drinks at this place?"

All manner of athletic marvels were gathered at Hazeltine. "What this thing does to a football is awesome," said spectator Dave Reinhart, thumping his prosthetic leg on a folding chair. "I get hang time in the three digits."

To Reinhart, I was a TAB, a Temporarily Able-Bodied person. To Patrice Cooper, the left-arm amputee and seven-time Hazeltine club champion (six with one arm) who lured the tournament to her home club, I was a "normie," ironic shorthand for normal person. And single-leg amputees, who generally shoot the lowest scores at this tournament? "We call them normies-with-a-limp," said Cooper. "They don't get any sympathy on the golf course."

The fifty-fifth National Amputee Golf Championship was contested among one hundred sixty-five men and women from every limp of life. "This tournament is usually played in a warm-weather spot," said Cooper, fifty, who lost her arm to cancer sixteen years ago. "And at the hotel, around the pool, all you see are these prosthetic legs, leaning against deck chairs."

Though the golfers came from thirty-two states and nine nations, they shared a sense of humor that was—there is no other word for it—disarming. The one-legged Reinhart said he literally has one foot in the grave. But he's also missing two fingers, and so, when I asked him his age, he paused for a very long time before saying fifty-three. "I'm not good at counting," he explained. "I can only count to thirteen. [Smile.] Fourteen on a good day."

Moe Clayton of Richmond lost his golf scholarship at Vanderbilt ("bad grades") and then both legs in Vietnam (in 1970) and now buys a new pair of prosthetic gams every year. "And every year," said his buddy George Willoughby, a leg amputee from North Carolina, "Moe gets an inch taller. He was five-foot-eight when the military took him. Now he's six-four."

When the PGA Championship was played at Hazeltine last year, Tour players were tended to by on-site equipment-repair specialists. So too, last week, were the amputees, who availed themselves of a prosthesis-repair tent at the turn. "People are coming in for lube jobs," said Cara Koski, tournament publicist, escorting me into the tent. "They'll ask, 'Can you duct tape this for me?'"

The men's and women's winners of the three-day, fifty-four-hole tournament were two normies-with-a-limp. Twenty-one-year-old Kenny Green of Clarksville, Tennessee. (73–76–74), had his left foot amputated below the ankle at birth and said of the field, "I am just in shock at the skills of some of these players." Twenty-two-year-old Kim Moore of Fort Wayne, Indiana, (76–89–77), who lost her right foot at birth, said, "Doctors thought I wouldn't walk, until I started walking on my stump, pushing a Fisher-Price shopping cart." She was two at the time. Last month the aspiring pro missed the cut at Q school by five strokes.

"All golfers are after the same thing," said the unsinkable MacDermott, who finished third (74–75–77) among the men. And we all find that Eden equally—eternally—elusive. "People ask me if I throw my clubs," said Patrice Cooper, after removing her golf-specific prosthetic arm, which locks onto her club shaft. "I always tell them no. By the time I get it out of the clamp, I've calmed down."

(September 22, 2003)

BEERS & SHOTS

Ted Hankey sits at the bar. His left palm is slapped up against his brow so that a cigarette plugged between his fingers seems to grow from his forehead. It looks like a unicorn horn. Hankey's right palm rests on a cardboard coaster, as if he's taking an alcoholic's oath.

The barman sets a pint in front of him, and Hankey, with both hands, moves it a millimeter closer. Bald and badly tattooed, with skin the color of wallpaper paste, Hankey will look tonight, under the unforgiving lights of television, as if he were two decades older than his thirty-two years. Now, though, bent over his beer, he looks beautiful—born to the bar, one hand on his head and one on his Harp, lost in concentration, a Rodin sculpture: *The Drinker*.

Dublin once had its legendary pintmen, supernatural imbibers who could achieve a state of grace by consuming, in a single sitting, as many as thirty jars of Guinness. "The man behind the bar knows the pintman when he sees one," John Sheridan wrote forty years ago in a trade publication called *Irish Licensing World*. "It is not a matter of dress, or age, or social status; it is a sort of spiritual look. The pintman takes up the tumbler with ritualistic care. Nothing can touch him then. The clock ticks for you and me, but the pintman is on an island in time."

True, this is not Dublin, it's suburban London. And Hankey's no pintman; he's an arrowman. But the arrowman, or professional darts player, is a descendant of the mystical pintman. And for the moment Hankey is on an island in time.

In thirty minutes Ted (the Count) Hankey must burst through the doors of this backstage bar, stride up to a klieg-lit oche (the line behind which the arrowman must stand), and defend his title in the richest tournament in professional darts: the impossibly pressurized, internationally televised, £189,000 (about $279,000) Embassy World Darts Championship, held every January at the Lakeside supper club in Frimley Green, England. Beyond those doors lies madness. "A lotta blokes throw good darts in the pub," says arrowman Andy Fordham, "but out there under the lights"—he points to the doors and the stage beyond them—"they melt."

Thus the arrowman drinks before (and during and after) his matches. "Loosens the darting arm," Martin Amis noted in *London Fields,* his epic darts novel. Never ask the arrowman to abstain. That, as the great English dartsman Cliff Lazarenko said in the seventies, would be "like asking Mark Spitz to set world records in two feet of water." It simply isn't done.

Hankey's opponent will be formidable, for he is none other than Fordham, a three-hundred-pound publican from the southeast London borough of Woolwich. Fordham, thirty-nine, the third seed in the tournament, prepared for this semifinal match by rising early, finding a pub ten minutes from the tournament site, and persuading the barman to open up for him. Which is how he came to be drinking pilsner at half past nine in the morning, bottles passing before him as if on a conveyor belt in a bottling plant. He threw, in preparation for the match—the winner of which is guaranteed £23,000 and a place in the £46,000 final—precisely six darts.

Fordham is Popeye-forearmed, with a magnificent mullet that falls, like a brown Niagara, nearly to his waist. When I ask him how often he practices, he says, "I don't." When I ask him how he spends his time, he says, "I drink." When I ask him what that tattoo on his left forearm is, he says, "The Grim Reaper." So it is.

Onstage, master of ceremonies Martin Fitzmaurice is imploring the restless sellout crowd of twelve hundred—seated bingo-parlor-style at a hundred long tables—to behave. "Ladies and gentlemen," says the tuxedoed emcee, "please do not stand on the chairs or the tables. And please do not steal the chairs or the tables. We lost three chairs last night, and we do ask your cooperation."

At one of three bars at the Lakeside, another Martin—Martin the Barman—performs a marvelous inventory of intemperance. "We'll sell four hundred kegs this week," he says. "There are eleven gallons in each keg . . . that's forty-four hundred gallons, right . . . there are eight pints in a gallon, so . . . let's see . . . right . . . we'll do thirty-five thousand, two hundred pints this week." He whistles in exhalation and then double-checks the figures with a pencil. "That doesn't include bottles," he mumbles. "We do lots of bottles."

If you figure that one bottle of beer is sold for every two pints of draught, that works out to 52,800 beers consumed during the nine-night tournament—which is to say, five beers a night for every man, woman, and child in attendance at the Embassy. What's more, tournament sponsor Embassy is a brand of fags, or cigarettes, and thus everyone at the Lakeside is encouraged to smoke like an oil fire. Everyone complies, too. So a blue Los Angeles haze hangs over the proceedings. English photographer Julian Herbert, alarmed by my ambition to spend the week in these quarters, coined a vivid anachronism. "You will have a dry-cleaning bill," he said, "of biblical proportions." So I would.

Here's the rub, though. Sometimes the healthiest thing a body can do is get out of the sunshine off the green grass, out of the fresh air, and breathe in the opposite—air that is equal parts smoke, tension, and BO. Only then will you rediscover what first drew you, as a child, to games. "A sense of 'umor is what's missing from sports, don't you think?" says Bobby George, the King of Darts, aspirating his *h*'s in the Cockney accent of London's East End. "The footballers over 'ere 'ave all become prima donnas. Same in America. You don't get the 'umor in sports. Americans 'ave to win everything. Darts aren't about that. Darts are about 'avin' fun. Darts are about the *craic* [the good time you have] with your mates down at the pub."

So they are. So come with me. It's a beautiful day—much too lovely to spend outdoors.

"You can walk into most any pub, get a free set of darts from behind the bar, and make friends for life," says Irish publican Gabriel (Gabby) Nolan, who left Galway for England when he turned twenty-one, in 1968, to pursue his dream of driving a red London double-decker bus. He did so for four years, and it was a great gas. But then Gabby aspired to manage a pub, and he took classes and wound up pulling pints at the King George in Essex. Which is where he became mates with Bobby George, who sat at the bar for much of the mid-seventies, occasionally answering the telephone just to make it stop ringing.

"King George?" the callers would say.

"Speaking!" George liked to reply.

"And that's how I got my nickname," George says. "The King. King of Darts."

Indeed, George was, for some time, the King of Darts, a two-time winner of the News of the World world championship, a tournament—now defunct—that once drew seventeen thousand spectators to the Agricultural Hall in north London. By the late 1970s the News of the World had moved to a raucous London dance hall, the rough-and-tumble Alexandra Palace. Soon the News was usurped, in prestige and prize money, by the Embassy worlds, where players and spectators alike can (and do) bet at the on-site bookmakers.

"Dennis were an eighty-to-one shot when he won the Embassy in 1991," says Alan Critchlow, manager of the great arrowman Dennis Priestly. "He got twenty-four thousand pounds for winning. And I won twenty-eight thousand pounds betting on him. The next day the bookie sent a big Rolls-Royce 'round, and the driver took us to Ascot. They were trying to get their money back. They took a right canin' on that one."

Every face and every place in darts appears lifted from a Guy Ritchie film. George, fifty-five, never threw a dart until he was twenty-nine. "I dug tunnels and laid granite floors," he says. That explains his square physique, which supports three pounds of gold jewelry, including a ring on each finger of his left (or nondarting) hand. The chain around his neck would be more suitable on the tires of a snowplow. Not surprisingly, George is up for a role on the soap opera *EastEnders*. "They want him to play a character," says Gabby Nolan, "who is like himself." Which is to say, a working-class hero, for George is universally considered—in the vernacular of the East End—"a good guv'nor."

That's how he fell into darts. "One night a guy in a pub was bein' a bit of a bully," says George. "He was bullyin' people who couldn't play darts, and I said to 'im, 'You're a bit of a bully. You're out of order.' He said, 'Oh, yeah, can you play?' I said, 'I never played the game in me life. I'll play you for fifty pounds.' The guy was the best player in Barkingside. I beat him. Within a year I was the local masters champion. I had a gift."

To understand the gift you must know that tournament darts is 501, a game in which both players start with 501 points and try to "check out," or reduce their scores to zero, three darts at a time. The final dart must be either a bull's-eye (which is worth 50 points) or a double. Thus, 180 (three treble 20s) is the most an arrowman can score on three darts, a feat that always elicits an orgasmic cry from the referee: "One 'undred and aye-teeeee!" It requires extraordinary physical reserve to repeatedly hit, from an oche seven feet, nine and a quarter inches away, the double and treble beds, each of which has a surface area smaller than a fortune-cookie slip. That is why there is a £50,000 bonus offer at the Embassy to any arrowman who makes a "nine-darter": seven treble 20s, a treble 15, and a double 18 for 501—the lowest possible checkout. "A nine-darter is like making nine holes-in-one," says George. "You need a lot of skill, and a bit o' luck."

At its highest level, professional darts is almost entirely a mental game, and not merely because the arrowmen, nearly all of them school dropouts, are arithmetic savants. Give them any number below 170, the highest score from which a player can check out on three darts—treble top (top is 20, at the top of the board), treble top, bull's-eye—and they will instantly convert it into the currency of darts. One hundred nineteen? Treble top, 19, double top. One hundred twenty-six? Treble 19, 19, bull's-eye. All arrowmen can do this all night, and it is arresting to hear them do so.

"But the game itself is simple," says George. "We could all be world-class. If you can see and got nothing wrong with your arms, there is no reason you can't be the best in the world. One six-teenth of an inch on this side of the wire, you're good. One six-teenth of an inch on that side, you're world champion. The difference in the end is nerves, what we call bottle. You gotta have the bottle."

Ted Hankey was all bottle in winning the Embassy a year ago (with a final three darts of 170), for which he earned £44,000. The final is always best of eleven sets, with each set a best of five games. Hankey won last year's match 6–0, in an astonishing forty-six minutes. How had he made his living before winning the Embassy—and, with it, a year's worth of exhibition bookings? "I were on the dole," says Hankey, who lives in North Wales. And before that? "You name it, I done it."

"We're just working-class people," says his manager, a retired lorry driver named Dave Lovatt, and in that one word—*just*—is an aching multitude: of class repression, of quashed ambition, of knowing one's place.

The antihero of *London Fields* is a petty criminal, Keith Talent.

A casual darter or arrowman all his life, right back to the bald board on the kitchen door, Keith had recently got serious," Amis writes. "He'd always thrown for his pub, of course, and followed the sport: You could almost hear angels singing when, on those special nights (three or four times a week), Keith laid out the cigarettes on the arm of the couch and prepared to watch darts on television. But now he had designs on the other side of the screen . . .

And television was all about everything he did not have and was full of all the people he did not know and could never be. Television was the great shop front, lightly electrified, up against which Keith crushed his nose. And now among the squirming motes, the impos-sible prizes, he saw a doorway, or an arrow, or a beckoning hand (with a dart in it), and everything said—Darts. Pro Darts. World Darts.

Embassy Darts. A dart is not merely rocket-shaped. It can *be* a rocket and generate escape velocity to break free from the gravi-tational pull of poverty. An easy alternative is to accept your lot, to convince yourself that money and success are fraught with prob-lems, and that you're better off without them. Gabby Nolan illustrates that with a story one night in his current darts pub, Nolan's Freehouse, Vauxhall, South London.

"You know George Best?" says Gabby, referring to the Belfast-born bon vivant soccer star of the 1960s. "One of the great footballers of all time, liked to knock about with women and all that? Well, one night here in London, he won forty thousand pounds at the Hilton casino on Park Lane. Ended up in bed with Miss World. They order champagne, and an Irish porter brings it up. He walks into the room and sees George Best in bed with forty thousand pounds scattered about and Miss World in her knickers. And the porter just shakes his head and says, 'George, where did it all go wrong?'"

Bobby George, blessedly, has no such aversion to pleasure. He lives in a forty-room, eighteen bedroom estate that he built in Colchester. Darts has been good to George. He has flogged boards on QVC in the United States and thrown darts on the very stage trod by Elvis at the Las Vegas Hilton. ("They had a board backstage," says George. "Apparently, Elvis and them liked to throw darts before they'd go on.")

"When Bobby started winning," says Gabby, "he'd play a lot of exhibitions in pubs. He had to go up to Scotland on the train once, and he complained that he was gonna be bored. I told him to get a book, and he said, 'I can't read.' He couldn't read or write. People would ask him to sign an autograph 'To Mandy' or 'To Patricia,' and he'd ask me how to spell 'Mandy' or 'Patricia.' He educated himself."

Today George writes a monthly column in *Darts World,* does color commentary for BBC2 at the Embassy, and enjoys—in his spare time—what he calls the "booze, fags, and cars" lifestyle that darts has afforded him. He has, in other words, no complaints.

Then again, what is there to complain about? All the arrowmen are staying in a hotel adjacent to the Lakeside supper club. The hotel lobby has two bars. One is called the Lounge Bar. A sign on its door says, THIS BAR IS FOR HOTEL BUSINESS GUESTS ONLY. DARTS PERSONS USE PENINSULAR BAR. THANK YOU. Across the lobby the Peninsular Bar—whose sign has been modified, by Darts Persons, to read PENIS BAR—is full at eleven o'clock in the morning.

When I ask Hankey how he will prepare for his semifinal, he says, "I'm gonna lie in bed with a sandwich and watch the darts on the telly, and if anyone phones up for an interview, I'm gonna tell 'em to fuck off." Fair enough.

Still, the Count graciously agrees to remove his darts shirt—like a bowling shirt, or the shirts once favored by Ferdinand Marcos— and do a brief roll call of his manifold Dracula tattoos. "That's a Drac, that's a Drac, that's a Drac, that's a demon, and that's for me," he says of the tattoo on his right arm that reads DONNA. The full-length Dracula on his back, alas, is but one third complete. (Fordham, in addition to his Reaper tattoo, has, on his right forearm, a skull and the name BOB. I don't ask.)

Fordham versus Hankey is the second semifinal on a Saturday afternoon. The first semi is won by John Walton, whose nom de darts is John Boy Walton. "Fordham wants him banned from darts," emcee Fitzmaurice tells the crowd, "and the reason is— get this!—he doesn't drink." Lusty boos lap up at the stage.

Moments later Walton is serially drinking pints backstage. "I don't drink," he explains, "before matches." Which nevertheless makes him, in darts, a teetotaler. Walton is the rare arrowman who can abstain before a match and win. "Any one of those guys goes out there without a drink, and he'll do nothing," says Mary Nolan, Gabby's wife. Yet the arrowman must also know when to say when.

"I played Colin Monk here once," notes Fordham, "and I got him drunk beforehand." Fordham won that night.

Such "windups"—the head games played before matches—are often more memorable than the matches. "One that sticks in me mind," says Mike Gregory, who lost the most dramatic Embassy final ever, in 1992, "happened at the Old Nun's Head pub in London." Gregory played all comers in exhibition matches, occasionally for a few quid. "There was this bloke named Jake," he says. "Jake the Snake. He said, 'Before we play, we're gonna have you on a bit.' I thought, okay, the usual, here come the strippers. But the bloke brings out an albino python and hangs it around me. I'm deathly afraid of snakes. He says, 'You've had the baby, now meet the da,' and he brings out a thirteen-foot boa. These are the things people do for an advantage."

As for Hankey, he now rises from the bar and dons a black cape. Upon hearing his name introduced outside, he bursts through the doors of the bar and strides toward the stage. His fanfare is chilling vampire-movie music. Several women in the audience have battery-operated bats on their hats that flap their wings.

Fordham, whose face is three quarters covered by beard—which explains his nickname, the Viking—enters the arena to "I'm Too Sexy," by Right Said Fred. Alas, to the disappointment of the hundreds who have come wearing plastic Viking helmets, Fordham doesn't have it tonight. Hankey's darts are tungsten-tipped missiles, guided by laser. Fordham needs a mere 33 on his final three darts to keep the match alive, but he can manage only a 5, a bounce-out, and a 1, for 6. Hankey then checks out from 134 for a spot in the final. Even so, the crowd sings (to the tune of "Guantanamera"), "One Andy Fordham! There's only one Andy Fordham! One Andy Forrrrr-dham! There's only one Andy Forrrrr-dham!"

"Ladies and gentlemen," announces Fitzmaurice, eager to clear the club after five minutes of this ovation, "Andy Fordham has left the building!"

If Fordham is the most popular player in world darts, it's because he is—as anyone will tell you at the pub he manages, the Queen's Arms in Woolwich—"a lovely bloke." Pulling a perfect pint of Guinness there one night, Fordham says, "I'm just a normal laid-back geezer." Within minutes he is pulling out photographs of himself as a rail-thin twenty-one-year-old aspiring soccer player. "Lookit," he says, an eternity of longing in his voice. "Lookit what eighteen years'll do to you." He takes comfort in a giant novelty birthday card on the wall behind him, hanging above the cash register. IT'S NOT A BEER BELLY, reads the card, IT'S A FUEL TANK FOR A SEX MACHINE.

Three years ago his wife, Jenny, contracted a cancer she seems to have thrashed. She shows me an old photograph of herself, bald from chemotherapy but smiling broadly. She keeps another photo, of Andy, in her locket, for the arrowman travels often. The next day he is off to the Netherlands, where darts is second in popularity only to soccer among televised sports, and where Fordham—a fixture in the English press only during Embassy week—is like a rock star. "In 'olland," says Fordham, trying to phrase this diplomatically in front of his wife, "the birds get their tits out for you to sign." Jenny rolls her eyes, but he goes on. "I signed a bird's bum once. She pulled up 'er dress, and she 'ad a G-string on underneath. She bent over, and I went like that with a marker." He makes a Zorro slash. "You couldn't read it," he says, taking a pull of his pilsner, "but she couldn't see it anyway."

In England darts reached a peak of popularity in the 1980s. "Holland is now where England was then," says Gregory, speaking only of the public's appetite for the game. "They took over darts. That's the way it goes here: football, cricket—we used to be on top in them, too."

Holland's top two arrowmen are both at the Embassy. Ray Barneveld is a two-time winner of the tournament. (He's a former postman turned darts millionaire.) Co Stompe is an Amsterdam tram driver, matchstick-thin, who speaks impeccable English in a Cockney accent. ("Because we spend so much time 'ere," says Stompe, whom I later overhear saying, "Fuckin' 'ell.") The Embassy is televised live on the Dutch network SBS6. "There are seven million people in Holland," says English pro Kevin Painter, "and five million of 'em are watching us on TV." (In fact there are about sixteen million people in Holland, three and a half million of whom watched Barneveld win the highest-rated final.) In the United Kingdom, the Embassy has been exiled to a nightly tape delay on BBC2, though it is rerun endlessly throughout the next afternoon.

In the eighties, eight tournaments were televised annually in England (now only two are), and there was a popular darts game show (called *Bullseye*). Thus arrowmen like Jocky Wilson were famous beyond all reason. Wilson was a toothless Scotsman. Gabby Nolan's children bought him a set of false teeth, but they weren't made to measure, so he wore them on a chain around his neck. It didn't hurt that oche rhymes with Jocky and that Wilson always entered to an emcee calling, "Jocky to the oche," a phrase that still resonates in England. His appeal transcended darts. When Dexy's Midnight Runners appeared on *Top of the Pops* in 1982 to perform their hit "Jackie Wilson Said"—a cover of the Van Morrison classic—an engineer at the BBC keyed in, as a back-drop, footage not of Jackie Wilson (soul man) but of Jocky Wilson (arrowman), naturally assuming the song was about him.

When I ask Tony Green—the eminent darts play-by-play man for the BBC and a witness to all twenty-four Embassy tournaments—why darts declined in popularity in England, he pauses for a very long time and says, "I'm going to be perfectly honest with you. I think it was the introduction of the Breathalyzer. Pub leagues dwindled, and the game dried up a bit at the grassroots level. But you'll never take darts out of the pub. You wouldn't want to."

"A lot of youngsters go to university now and make money and don't have time to go to pubs," says Gabby Nolan, "but you'll still find good publicans who put their hearts into darts." So Nolan's pub has two boards and six league nights a week, and thirteen thriving teams whose kindly (if profane) members contributed £1,300 to charity last year. "All from one swear box," says Mary Nolan. "And we only enforce the swear box on Saturday nights. Even then, only during the karaoke."

Though professional darts is still great craic, the game I am witnessing at the Embassy is, incredibly, a sanitized version of its incarnation of the eighties, when players could drink and smoke on television. Now they're not allowed to drink alcohol on cam-era, and—absurdly—Evian bottles chill in a champagne bucket at the oche. "It was a mistake to take the drinkin' and smokin' off the stage," says Gregory. "Two thousand people in the audience are drinkin' and smokin', and the guy throwin' darts has a bottle of water? The reason people like watchin' darts is that they know the people onstage are like them."

Jocky Wilson, alas, is retired to Kirkcaldy, disillusioned with darts and the media machine that ate him. (At least the *Sun,* the lurid London tabloid, bought him a proper set of teeth in thanks for his years of providing fodder.) The best player in the world now—the best ever, by most estimates—is Phil (the Power) Taylor, who has won nine world championships: two Embassies and seven of the eight Professional Darts Corporation titles. The PDC is a rival tour, started in 1994, with Taylor and other players who don't play the Embassy, which is run by the venerable British Darts Organization. Darts, like boxing, has no unified title. The field at the PDC championship, televised on Sky, is said to be more talented at the top. The thirty-two-man Embassy has a deeper field and more prize money.

I arrange to meet Taylor at the players' hotel, and he brings a buddy: a big bloke, with half an ear, whom Taylor introduces as Holyfield. Last year the queen declared Taylor a member of the Order of the British Empire—one step short of a knighthood— an astonishing feat for an arrowman. Tonight he will be honored at the Embassy, in a rare rapprochement between the tours.

Astoundingly, Taylor didn't play darts until he was twenty-six. (He is forty now.) He threw every Tuesday night at his Stoke-on-Trent local, the Saggermaker's Bottom-Knocker. (Saggermaker was a job in pottery, and Stoke was once a pottery center. Whatever, pray tell, is a bottom-knocker is a question perhaps better left unanswered.)

"I was," Taylor says of those first league nights, "a natural." Within a year he was picked to play for his county, and within another year he quit his engineering job. He resolved to crawl through his television and into pro darts. The man had three children—he has four now—and his dole check afforded him, after household expenses, only £6 a week in pocket money. "That's what made me a winner," he says. "That pressure." At his first Embassy, in 1990, he went off at 250-to-1 with the bookies. Everybody in Stoke bet on him. "Everybody," he says. "An old lady told me she had seven pounds left from her pension check and put it on me." And everybody won.

Parked outside in the hotel drive is Taylor's blue Peugeot 406— a complimentary dealer's car, painted with his name and nickname and the outdated boast 8 TIMES WORLD CHAMPION. He has made roughly £2 million in tournament winnings, exhibition fees, and endorsements. "People have called me Tiger Taylor, but I don't think of myself on that level with Woods or Michael Jordan," says the Power, a short, potbellied, extremely polite man with the arrowman's requisite tattoo on each forearm. "I do get congratulated a lot. People are very proud of me here because England don't win at too many things anymore."

As we speak, Taylor's buddy, Holyfield, is at a grease board in this hotel conference room, silently drawing a detailed lion's head in orange marker. (It is majestic—moving, even.) "The biggest thing that will ever happen to me," says Taylor as we prepare to make our good-byes, "will be meeting the queen of England. No, I never, ever would have dreamed it."

It may never happen. Eight weeks after our conversation, Taylor will be convicted of indecent assault for having groped two twenty-three-year-old women with whom he had engaged in an epic drinking contest after a 1999 exhibition in Scotland. (His sentencing was scheduled for March 27.) Tabloid headlines will call Taylor a DARTY OLD MAN and his victims, DARTS TARTS. They will quote him as longing for his days on the dole queue and telling the judge, "This case may well split up my family." Even the quality broadsheets will report that the queen may strip Taylor of his MBE.

All this from a man considered to be, by professional darts standards, too boring. "I suppose Taylor is the best ever," Gabby Nolan says one night at the Freehouse, "but until fairly recently he could go into Sainsbury's supermarket and not be recognized." How different from a decade ago, when elegant Eric Bristow—the Crafty Cockney—was a charismatic rival of Jocky Wilson's. Bristow found himself in New York City, walking down the street, when a fan's disembodied voice came from across Fifth Avenue. It screamed, simply, "One 'undred and aye-teeeee!"

The bad news is, no one can turn back the clock. The good news: There's no need to at the Lakeside—*Club Mirror* magazine's Club of the Year from 1976 to '80—where a bygone age is preserved in amber. The walls are filled with signed publicity stills of long-forgotten or never-recalled acts: Grumbleweeds, Keith O'Keefe, the Fantasticks. Machines on bathroom walls dispense packets of cologne called Zazz and Obsess. The entire place exudes a touching (if maudlin) showbiz sincerity, with an 8-by-10 glossy of the Candy Man taking pride of place on one wall. "For as long as Lakeside has existed," reads the caption, "we dreamed of the day that Sammy Davis Jr. might appear. He was booked to appear on October 13, 1990. Unfortunately, he had a prior engagement—in heaven."

In Sammy's stead, this has become the Lakeside's biggest night, the Sunday evening of the Embassy final, Hankey versus Walton, televised live throughout the United Kingdom. At the backstage bar John Boy calmly throws darts, nurses a few fags, sips at his coffee. The Count, conversely, is sinking pints, smoking like Vesuvius, and making frequent trips to the loo.

Nerves don't serve an arrowman well. Sweating palms are the enemy. "I couldn't win in America," says Gregory, "because of two things: Budweiser and air-conditioning. The condensation from the longneck bottles got on my fingers and affected my release."

The enormity of tonight's match is inescapable. Kate Hoey, member of Parliament and Britain's minister of sport, has arrived. Backstage, Hankey sneers and snaps on his cape. Walton blinks madly through thick glasses. Standing with both players is a BBC announcer who opens the live broadcast by saying, "Beyond these doors is the most unique atmosphere in sports!"

With that, the doors are thrown open, and the players crash through—first Walton, to "Cotton-Eyed Joe," and then Hankey, to his vampire aria. The place goes absolutely batty. Perhaps literally so, in the case of the young female Count enthusiasts, who are back, wearing their hats with mechanical bats.

The match starts badly for Hankey. He makes a sickly 22 on his first three darts, while Walton makes "one 'undred and aye-teeeee!" From there, things quickly get worse for the Count, and he goes into his trademark stall, taking an eternity to walk to the board and remove his arrows. This actually helps a little, and he's only down three sets to two at intermission, when he steams into the bar backstage and shakes several empty cigarette boxes on as many unbussed tables, desperate for a fag. At last he finds one—and smokes and sips from a pint glass while his manager, Lovatt, slaps him softly on the face, whisper-shouting, "Stop fuckin' about!"

Walton sips coffee and coolly throws darts. The abstainer has stolen the pintman's tranquillity. "I was so relaxed," he'll say later,

"I felt like I was playin' in the pub." After the break Walton takes the sixth set, and the seventh, and in the eighth he needs only 25 on his final three darts to kiss the trophy. He throws only the first two. "Nine, double-eight, thankyouverymuch," the new champion says an hour later, recounting the highlight of his life in two digits. "I wanted to fly."

A thirty-nine-year-old former laborer from industrial Doncaster, Walton began playing darts at age nine, in the back room of a bingo parlor, while his parents, in the front room, looked for a B-8 or an I-17. He began playing professionally, he says, after wrecking his back on the job. "A laborer with no back," he says, "is no use to anyone."

No use to anyone? Tonight, with his weeping fiancée at his side, Walton leaves the Lakeside in the Mercedes 450 SEL with the JONBOY license plate and the oversized novelty champagne bottle in the backseat. The sterling Embassy trophy is in the front seat. In the mail is a check for £46,000. His life is changed forever. Yet it isn't changed even for a day. Tomorrow night he'll be back at his local, in his regular weekly league match. "At the Alma in Doncaster," he says. "I don't miss Monday night."

Because that's what darts is all about: the craic with your mates down at the pub. So the mixed league is playing Monday night at Nolan's Freehouse, where Gabby tells me one last story. Years ago he and Bobby George would drive around London in the latter's used Rolls. In those days, at the wheel, Bobby always played a tape of his favorite song, "American Pie," and he'd sing along in his Cockney accent: "Drove me Chevy to the levee . . ." So one night the pair washes up at Bill Bartlett's pub in Brentwood, and one thing leads to another, and three bookies at the bar bet Bobby five to one that he can't put three straight darts in the double-1 bed. Gabby slaps a hundred pounds on the bar, and Bobby sticks the first dart. Then, just next to it, the second. The King of Darts returns to the bar, and sips his pint, slowlike. The blokes are a bit wound up now, so they double the stakes for the last arrow, and Gabby slaps another hundred pounds on the bar. Bobby walks to the oche as if he were John bloody Wayne—and finds, with the final dart, the last square micron of space still available: double-1.

Gabby is giddy all over again at the memory—of himself and Bobby legging it out of there with what was, in their youth, a small fortune. "Some lovely stories," says the Irishman, wistfully recalling the people and places and predicaments one finds in thirty years as a London publican. "I've sometimes thought of writing a book."

When I tell him he ought to, lest the stories disappear, Gabby reassures me. The oral history of darts and pints and London pubs will survive unto eternity. "The cows come and go," says the wise publican, pulling another pint of Caffrey's and placing it, unbidden, before me. "But bullshit lasts forever."

We raise our glasses.

(April 2, 2001)

'TOGA PARTY

"This is my favorite place in the world," says David Cassidy, wreathed in a costly cologne, outside the paddocks at Saratoga Race Course. "I mean, on a day like today, where on earth would you rather be?" Then Cassidy, who has owned racehorses since the 1970s—when he made his fortune playing Keith Partridge on *The Partridge Family*—gestures sweepingly with his right hand, as if throwing open a cape. "Look around," he says. "What's not to love?"

I love everything about Saratoga, the 139-year-old track in upstate New York. It is the Wrigley of raceways, or would be if it weren't a half century older than the ballpark.

I love that every two patrons entering its grounds carry a heavy cooler between them, so that they look like pallbearers at a midget's funeral. I love the press box, which installed a men's room in 1978 and a ladies' room in 1998, a twenty-year interval in which women were asked, if you don't mind, to hold it a little longer. And I love that the only acknowledgment of a larger world beyond the track are the four sentences—out of 116 pages—that the *Daily Racing Form* devotes to nonequine news. On this day, opposite a long story on the forthcoming Best Pal Stakes, is a minuscule item headlined RUSSIAN COPTER CRASH KILLS 80.

Mayflies live for a single day, cherry blossoms bloom for but seventy-two hours, and Saratoga is open for racing only six weeks every summer, until Labor Day. Which is why, every August, the population of Saratoga Springs triples to seventy-five thousand and local channel 12 is devoted entirely to horse racing—reverential, low-budget, oddly hypnotic coverage playing without end. "It's like Bulgarian cable television," says *New York Times* racing writer Joe Drape, seated at the bar of the Spring Water Bet and Breakfast, a horseplayer's hostel a block from the track. After a full day of racing in the East the TV above the bar is tuned to action from Del Mar near San Diego. (Hours after those races end, live racing from Australia is carried in some of New York City's Off-Track Betting parlors, whose clientele is every bit as male as the priesthood, and more celibate.)

In the thirty-minute eternity between races at Saratoga, every walk of chain-smoking humanity watches televised simulcasts from Monmouth Park and Delaware Park while seated in row upon row of red, molded-plastic chairs bolted to the concrete behind the grandstand. It resembles the departure lounge at Indira Gandhi International Airport. Seating is almost impossible to come by, and when someone steals your chair here, he does so literally; a track employee, at an information kiosk, has her stool bicycle-chained to the table at which she sits. As for the unreserved seating along the rails, a courtly sign says: PLEASE DO NOT REMOVE BENCHES. It was necessitated, I like to think, by an unlucky bettor who figured that if he had to sleep on a park bench for the rest of his days, he might as well take one with him.

Make no mistake, races are especially hard to handicap at Saratoga, the Graveyard of Favorites. Man o' War suffered the only loss of his career here in 1919, beaten by Upset, who gave the upset its name. Hence the local lust for knowledge remains astonishing. "You're from *Sports Illustrated*?" says the high school kid slinging wieners at the Nathan's Famous stand, eyeing the credential around a writer's neck. "Then maybe you know: Whatever became of Lemon Drop Kid?" ("He's a horse," you want to reply. "What could he possibly be doing now—selling real estate?" But you don't, because his enthusiasm is infectious.)

And so we stand in line at the ticket windows, the idle rich and the idle poor, poring over tout sheets and the DRF, intoxicated by tips like "intriguing" and "dangerous" and "has a shot"—the same vague, could-mean-anything adjectives found in horoscopes and weather forecasts and Magic 8 Balls. But I don't realize that until after the race, when my losing ticket has been torn into ticker tape and tossed to the wind. Oh, well. The track can take your money, but it cannot take your dignity.

Or can it? Moments later, realizing the ticket is a business expense, I am on all fours, gathering the pieces, a confetti that now fills my pockets. I feel like Rip Taylor. The pieces will be assembled, mosaic-style, and filed with my next expense report.

But profit is hardly the point of Saratoga. Take a walk around the grounds, past the paddocks, to the famous Big Red Spring, where water pours perpetually from three spigots in a fountain that resembles Caligula's birdbath. Though the water tastes heavily of minerals—imbibing it is like sucking on a rock—retirees in cataract-surgery sunglasses drink it down lustily from paper shot glasses of the kind you get at the dentist. To judge by their expressions, they are happy citizens of Horse-opolis, and the spring is a fountain of youth.

A gentle breeze sends pari-mutuel tickets lazily cartwheeling across the concourse and tickles the toupee of the railbird next to me. For the moment—with a Furlong Frank in one fist, an oil can of Foster's in the other, and a "promising" horse in the seventh race—there really is no place on earth I'd rather be.

(September 2, 2002)

TOUR DE FRANCE

Sunday, June 28, 1998: New York to Paris

There are but two psychological states available to the transatlantic air traveler—torpor and terror—and the same might be said of spectators at the World Cup, that quadrennial showcase of scoreless soccer enlivened only by the clear-air turbulence of hooliganism. So why combine these activities? Why fly to France for a week's worth of "football," when the only touchdown on offer is an uneven landing in Paris?

Because something Wilbur Wright said of flight seems also to apply to soccer: "If you are looking for perfect safety, you will do well to sit on a fence and watch the birds. But if you really wish to learn, you must mount a machine and become acquainted with its tricks by actual trial."

What do I hope to learn in the next six days? Nothing less than the secrets of Kanu and Cafu and Camus. Nwankwo Kanu—not so much a name as an unplayable Scrabble rack—had a hole in his aorta nineteen months ago but recovered to compete for Nigeria in the World Cup. The mononymous Cafu is a defender for Brazil, the world's most stylish and self-absorbed collection of athletes, a team aptly described by one Brazilian newspaper as a "cauldron of vanities." And Albert Camus was a French philosopher who once said, "All that I know most surely about morality and obligations, I owe to football."

In these men you have the World Cup, to say nothing of the world itself. It is all there: elan, ego, and French pretentiousness. Morality, obligations, and a stout heart. As a sportswriter, I know little of morality and even less of obligations. So there is this, too: One week at the World Cup might—just might—make me a better human being.

Monday, June 29: Paris

Eleven P.M. on the Champs-Elysées and Yugoslav players are getting hammered. On television, that is, during a 2–1 second-round loss to the Netherlands, but is it really any wonder? "The Yugoslavian players are out until two or three every morning," U.S. coach Steve Sampson had said earlier in the World Cup. "The security officers [for the U.S. team] talk to the security officers for other teams. We have been informed that the Yugoslavian security officers are exhausted from staying up until two or three every morning watching Yugoslavian players."

"Excessive nightclubbing"—the offense for which South Africa reportedly dismissed a midfielder from its squad—is the game within the game at the World Cup. And so officially licensed World Cup condoms sell in Champs-Elysées souvenir shops, and Bulgarian superstar Hristo Stoichkov had nightclubbed so excessively that he couldn't get out of bed for one team meeting, and most English supporters would benefit from receiving Mickey Mantle's original liver. If the World Cup were an actual cup, it would be made of half a coconut and would come with an umbrella. At a sidewalk newsstand on the Champs-Elysées, I purchase a British newspaper, the *Independent,* and read the bold, above-the-fold headline: ENGLISH FANS WILL BE ABLE TO DRINK ALL DAY. Tomorrow bars will remain open from 8:30 A.M. until 11 P.M. in St. Etienne, where England is to play Argentina at nine o'clock in the evening.

Drunken English fans, of course, rioted on match days in Marseilles and Lens. And given the history of England and Argentina—Maradona's notorious "hand of God" goal beat England in the '86 World Cup, four years after the Falklands War—the failure of French officials to ban alcohol in St. Etienne is seen as curious at best, particularly when most English fans in the town of two hundred thousand will be without match tickets. "There will be a high level of frustration which will [leave] people looking for drink to find some other outlet for their energies," Tom Pendry, a member of the British Parliament, warns in the *Indepedent*. "This is a cocktail for disaster."

Yet reading this last line at midnight in Harry's Bar, at large in the land of the World Cup, I have but one thought, and it is a Homer Simpsonian one at that: mmmmmm . . . cocktail.

Tuesday, June 30: St. Etienne

"May I take your picture?" photographer Al Tielemans asks an English gentleman whose head is shaved—save for a four-foot ponytail—and whose body is tattooed with the illustrated history of Britain. It is an hour before England-Argentina, a mile from Geoffroy Guichard Stadium, and the man is drinking from a frothing forty-ounce bottle of Kronenbourg. "No, you cannot fucking take my picture," our friend enunciates with remarkable clarity. "Piss off."

Off we piss, ducking into a bar so grimly utilitarian that it has only the words SNACK BAR stenciled on the windows. The peeling wallpaper inside is supposed to look like wood paneling. This may well be a first in interior decor: simulated simulated wood paneling. To liven up the place, Big Al Moonie of Biggleswade, England, has hung an English flag—his name and hometown sewn to the cross of St. George—over most of one wall. Another hundred or so English, including as many as three women, have crammed themselves into Snack Bar, packing it from front door to fetid toilet.

"Are you a journalist?" asks a skinny, pop-eyed, prominently Adam's-appled eighteen-year-old with a close-cropped head.

"Yes."

"Then you should leave," he says. "You shouldn't be here."

"Is that advice or a threat?"

"Decide that for yourself," he replies.

"What's the problem?"

"What's the problem?" he says. "After what the journalists have done to us this week?"

A 250-pound bloke with hair spiked like pineapple skin cannot help overhearing. "You'll be all right here," he assures us, shooing away Adam's apple. The man is Butch from Bristol, and he says he has followed England—literally followed the team—for ten years. He and friends Marco and Joe are commuting to this World Cup from the west coast of England. This is their fourth trip to France in three weeks. "We're just here for the football," he says. "They were asking six hundred quid for tickets outside the stadium. That's what, a thousand dollars? So we're watching it here."

The entire bar sings "God Save the Queen" before kickoff, and the rest of the evening unfolds in song. Argentina scores first on a penalty kick and—to the tune of "If You're Happy and You Know It Clap Your Hands"—the whole of Snack Bar belts out a chorus of: "If it wasn't for the English you'd be Krauts."

When Alan Shearer gets the equalizer for England, a man to my right turns and hugs me, his train-wreck smile reminding me of Austin Powers. "Keep St. George in my heart, keep me English," the crowd sings. "Keep St. George in my heart, I pray. Keep St. George in my heart, keep me English. Keep me English till my dying day." Which segues, oddly and immediately, into "No sur-render, no sur-render, no sur-render to the IRA!"

Moments later eighteen-year-old English phenomenon Michael Owen scores a spectacular go-ahead goal, the best of the World Cup, and the crowd goes Snack Barmy. Snack Bar is a mosh pit. I am knocked to the ground but recover to sing—to the tune of "Michael Rowed the Boat Ashore"—"Michael Owen scores the goals, Al-le-loo-oo-ia!"

But just before half Argentina makes it 2–2, and English anger turns toward the retired Maradona. To Handel's "Hallelujah Chorus," everyone sings, "Mar-a-dona! Mar-a-dona! Isawanker! Isawanker! Isaway-ay-anker!"

So it goes, through David Beckham's being sent off for England in the forty-seventh minute for kicking an Argentinian player, through the entire scoreless second half, through thirty scoreless minutes of extra time. Before the grim vigil of the penalty kicks, a hundred English in Snack Bar sway as one, singing—to "Auld Lang Syne"—"We're proud of you, we're proud of you, we're proud of you, we're proud . . ."

But many in the crowd have turned their backs to the TV, unable to look, for penalties always go wrong for England, which lost on them to Germany in the semifinals of the '90 World Cup and to Germany again in the semis of the '96 European championships. As if prepared for the inevitable, three guys behind me sing—to the tune of "She'll Be Comin' Round the Mountain When She Comes"—"We'll be right nasty bastards if we lose!" They sound serious.

On the final penalty kick David Batty places the ball on the spot, measures off his steps, and bangs his shot off the goalkeeper's hands. England loses and Snack Bar goes batty. Several fans slump onto tables, but many more pour into the streets. Bottles are thrown, V signs are flashed, epic profanity rains on all unlucky pedestrians. Hundreds of police in riot gear rumble up the pavement of the narrow streets. Three men in handcuffs are shoveled into paddy wagons. Four paper-hatted teenagers stand inside a locked and unlit McDonald's, waiting until it is safe to leave.

We make for the car and head out of town after midnight, and from every precinct come three sounds: the barking of dogs, the breaking of glass, and the donkey bray of French police sirens going *ee-yore ee-yore ee-yore.*

Wednesday, July 1: Ozoir-Brazil

In the morning, over breakfast in a château in the vineyard village of Villie-Morgon, I meet a regal Argentine named Horacio Bernardo Scliar, who manages a factory in Buenos Aires. Attending the World Cup with his three adult sons, Fernando, Martin, and Esteban, Horacio is happy, but he cannot mask his concern for the Argentines. "That was not a good match stylistically," he frets. "Argentina did not play with flair." Playing with flair is of paramount importance to South America's teams, a fact that will hit home this afternoon when Al and I drive four hours north to Ozoir-La-Ferriere, which has officially changed its name for the duration of the World Cup to Ozoir-Brazil.

Ozoir-Brazil, the training headquarters of the Brazilian national team, is only seven miles from Disneyland Paris, which is appropriate as the Brazilians have attracted a Goofy, Dopey, Happy horde of hangers-on and hangers-out. Practices are open to the public— free tickets are required—and the stadium's four thousand capacity is filled every day. "You should come," the team's PR contact, a woman named Ana, had told me. "Everyone has fun. It is very relaxed."

So it is. From the stands the Brazil bus is cheered raucously as it rolls into the parking lot outside. Ten minutes later the players emerge from a tunnel to meet the Brazilian press corps, many of whose members extend balls and T-shirts to be autographed, hands to be clasped, cheeks to be kissed. Several carry disposable cameras and ask the players to pose. I am not making this up. The team's calisthenics get a standing ovation. I take a seat in the stands between a man wearing a hat decorated with the miniature heads of Brazilian national team members—they stick out from the crown of his cap like cherry tomatoes skewered on toothpicks—and a four-hundred-pound Brazilian man in a platinum blond wig who keeps standing up to samba. Did I mention that a band is playing throughout the practice? Of course it is.

Now picture the Chicago Bulls allowing this—inviting this— as they prepare for the NBA finals, or the Green Bay Packers practicing in such a way for the Super Bowl. You can't? Then you have just discovered, at 5:17 on a Wednesday afternoon, what makes the World Cup what it is—whatever it is.

As we bid adieu to Ozoir-Brazil, Ronaldo, the team's twenty-one-year-old superstar, is blithely chipping a ball into the goal from midfield and grinning that grin that looks like the grille of a badly used Mercedes.

Thursday, July 2: Lyons and Nice

Parked in downtown Lyons is a badly used Mercedes with German license plates. The owner has ripped off the hood ornament—which is the main reason most people buy a Benz in the first place—and replaced it with a miniature soccer ball. Having driven a thousand miles in three days in pursuit of football, Al and I somehow understand.

No World Cup games are scheduled today, so we drive to Nice, the town so nice they named it . . . Nice. The German team trains here, and though we don't see any players the trip is worth every four-dollar gallon of gas. For the sea is the color of antifreeze, and the sky is like stone-washed denim, and the only work people are doing is on their tans. Nobody cares about anything on the French Riviera. These people have more phrases for *apathy* than Eskimos have for *snow*. In addition to ennui and malaise and blasé, there are que sera sera and c'est la vie and—well, you get the picture. Nice is less than an hour's drive from the France-Italy border, and France plays Italy in a quarterfinal match tomorrow, but you would never know it to gaze at the thonged throngs on the beach.

Not that I do, mind you.

Friday, July 3: Menton, France, and Ventimiglia, Italy

In Menton, a seaside town one thousand meters from the Italian border, this afternoon's match is a civic obsession. On the beach, cones are set up, a ball is rolled out, and children gather to play . . . baseball. To be fair, one old guy at a produce stand has painted his handlebar mustache in the tricolors of France, and his buddy is reading the *Nice Matin* newspaper, whose front-page headline states bluntly, FRANCE–ITALIE—LE DERBY DES FAUS AMIS ("the match between phony friends"). So perhaps things will pick up.

We will watch the first half of Le Derby des Faux Amis in the Italian town of Ventimiglia, twenty minutes to the east of Menton. "My name is Tony," says a man who approaches in the Ventimiglia vegetable market, where flags reading FORZA ITALIA!

are planted in piles of garlic. "You speak French? My English is not so good. I work on a cruise ship. We get watches in Switzerland, you understand? Breitling, Rolex, Tag Heuer . . ."

We don't want to buy a watch, we tell Tony. We want to watch the football match.

"Go into any bar," he says. "No, go to the Festival Café. On the beach. A grand panorama. Talk to Rudy. He's a friend of mine. You drink a caffè, drink a beer, drink a caffè, drink a beer—like that. Pretty soon, people go crazy."

"Grazie, Tony," I tell him.

Tony looks crestfallen: "You mean you no want to buy a watch?"

A TV has been set up outside the festival, with its grand panorama of sea, and at the 4:30 P.M. kickoff, a very serious Italian kid of sixteen yells, "Silenzio!" This omertà is honored for most of the desultory, scoreless first half, in which Italy adopts a dreary defensive posture. But so what: Italian sports television is a revelation, with its gratuitous supermodel studio hostesses and split-second commercials wedged into dead-ball sequences, so that a shot of a toothpaste tube will suddenly flash onto the screen in mid-match. And the match itself has its moments. When French midfielder Zinedine Zidane falls to the pitch clutching his crotch, the café crowd erupts into song, joyously hand-gesturing various suggestions at the screen.

At the halftime intermission, we hightail it back to Menton, whose streets are eerily silent. In an outdoor café at the Hotel les Arcades, forty people variously sit and stand around a television, smoking and sipping and shrugging through a scoreless second half and extra time.

Then the funniest thing happens. The match goes to penalty kicks. France wins 4–3. And suddenly, instantly, a thousand tiny Renaults are racing around the town square, their little horns parping. Menton sounds like a thousand Felix Ungers clearing their sinuses.

Flags flutter from the French doors of apartments. Firecrackers begin to pop. On the beachfront avenue, the Promenade du Soleil, cars race up and down all night, flying blue-white-and-red scarves and parping endlessly. Strangers embrace, old men beam, waiters are fractionally less rude. France is a nation transformed.

The French get happy every twenty years, whether they need to or not, just to exercise their smile muscles. Tonight is that night. For one evening they pretend to like even tourists. Tonight, we are all their faux amis.

Saturday, July 4: Menton to Paris

The seven-hour drive back to Paris affords ample time to absorb lessons from this trip. There were many novel experiences: I got to write the phrase "Bulgarian superstar" for the first time. I know where to buy a Swiss watch in Ventimiglia, Italy. I will never hear "She'll Be Comin' Round the Mountain" in quite the same way.

I think I did discover the secrets of Kanu and Cafu and Camus— seeing stout hearts (England-Argentina) and Brazilian brilliance (in the person of Ronaldo) and learning something of morality and obligations (namely, that there is none of either at La Coupe du Monde).

Four years ago to this day, the United States was playing Brazil in the second round of the World Cup; in this Cup's thirty-two-team field the United States finished last. But if America has regressed in soccer I, as an American soccer fan, have come a long way. Quite literally, in fact. Al and I drove more than two thousand miles in the last six days, and our rented Renault Safrane now resembles a fuel-injected Dumpster. By climbing off the fence, mounting the machine of La Coupe du Monde, and experiencing its tricks by actual trial, I have become a more catholic sports fan. So perhaps the World Cup has made me a better human being after all. It has certainly made me a more smelly one.

We stop at a gas station near Auxerre. I buy a Coke to mark Independence Day, on which Americans celebrate shedding the shackles of a soccer-crazed nation, freeing us to form our own constitution, our own government, our own curious brand of football. Back in the car, as Holland-Argentina kicks off on the radio, I cannot help but think, if only for a moment: What ever were the Founding Fathers thinking?

(July 13, 1998)

RESIDENT ALIEN IN RED SOX NATION

North of New Haven but south of Hartford, running the breadth of central Connecticut, is the border that separates Yankees and Red Sox fans. It's a baseball Mason-Dixon Line—a kind of Munson-Nixon Line, below which you love Thurman, above which you love Trot. Just last week I moved north of that line, from Manhattan to New England, which share a currency but not a clam chowder. Nor much of anything else.

And so, like all relocated sports fans, I'm now forced to learn a new set of secret handshakes: the in-jokes, the back stories, the cultural touchstones my new neighbors have been accruing since birth. Like the subtle difference between NESN and Nissen. The former, I know now, is a cable carrier for the Red Sox, while the latter is a brand of bread endorsed for countless years by Ted Williams. In manifold local TV commercials, Williams could be seen fishing with Maine sportswriter Bud Leavitt, when talk would turn, as it naturally does between two grizzled men in a boat, to the orgiastic pleasures of J.J. Nissen's Buttertop Wheat.

This is not to be confused with Big Yaz Special Fitness White Bread, whose Carl Yastrzemski-adorned wrapper enlivened supermarket shelves in the 1960s. If Ted Williams was the best thing since sliced bread, this was the best sliced bread since Ted Williams.

Or so I'm now learning. But absorbing all of this is rather like learning a foreign language. Indeed, it is a foreign language when you consider that *tuna* in Boston is a stereo component, while *tuner* in Boston is former Pats coach Bill Parcells. And thus I'm literally illiterate in parts of New England. An enormous billboard that hangs in left center field at Fenway communicates entirely in Morse code. But any Fenway fan can tell you what it says: Red Sox Nation.

A resident alien in Red Sox Nation, I have much remedial research remaining. It isn't easy to commit to memory every beer-sponsor jingle in the history of New England sports. But I must try, if I'm to hold my own at parties. The Sox have pushed both Carling ("Hey Mabel, Black Label!") and Narragansett ("Hi, Neighbor! Have a Gansett!"), and the Pats once plied fans with Schaefer, whose slogan—"The One Beer to Have When You're Having More Than One"—was a bold invitation to binge drinking.

Indeed, I was having more than one last Friday night, inside the venerable Cask 'n' Flagon, the bar behind the Green Monster at Fenway, imbibing beers near a man whose T-shirt bore the phrase, libelously inaccurate, JETER'S GAY.

"There's a whole range of hatred T-shirts for sale out there," Sox season-ticket holder Kathy Gilmour, thirty-one, explained to me at the Cask. "That one makes YANKEES SUCK look classy." She appeared mournful for a moment and then added, apologetically, "Yay, Boston!"

John Burkett moved to Boston two seasons ago. That's when the thirty-eight-year-old Red Sox right-hander—who has bowled ten perfect games in his lifetime—learned that the lanes in New England are largely devoted to candlepin bowling. "Smaller ball, smaller pins, they leave the deadwood on the lanes," sighs Burkett. "I tried it once, two years ago, and haven't done it since. But I'd like to go again this summer."

Give him Tommy Points for perseverance. Tommy Points, awarded to hustling Celtics players by color analyst Tommy Heinsohn, are now bestowed, throughout New England, by ordinary citizens—as, say, when a friend agrees to take your shift at the Steak Loft.

The Steak Loft, in Mystic, Connecticut, is distinct from *The Movie Loft,* the late late show airing after Red Sox games on Channel 38 in Boston. If you've never heard of that, you're doubtless ignorant of "Brass Bonanza," the fight song of the Hartford Whalers, whose presence is still felt, like the phantom leg of an amputee, six years after the franchise fled for North Carolina. You can still consult devotional Whalers Web sites with names like The Blowhole. And you can still hear radio reports, like this one from Hartford last week, which identified white-hot Anaheim goaltender Jean-Sebastien Giguere as "Whalers draft pick J. S. Giguere."

But then this is New England, where Whalers are heroes and heros are grinders, which it helps to know when buying a sandwich. Indeed, all of this is vital information for anyone hoping to hold even the simplest conversation. So if you're asked to meet at the Red Seat, beyond the Pesky Pole, beneath the Jimmy Fund sign, will you know that it's in right field at Fenway, in the bleacher seat, painted scarlet in a sea of green, where Williams deposited the longest homer in park history, beneath a sign for the ubiquitous New England charity that honors a twelve-year-old cancer patient from 1948 whose name was not Jimmy but . . . Einar?

It's all very confusing, and I often mistake the Chowder Pot (a seafood joint on I-91) with the Beanpot (a college hockey tournament in Boston). But there's so much more that confounds me. The Big Dig. Wicked pissah. Make Mine Moxie. And the grin some grown-ups get when they think of George Scott, late of the Red Sox, examining his bats to see which ones had taters in 'em.

(May 26, 2003)

'RING TOSSED

The most unsettling thing about driving 142 miles per hour on the German autobahn in James Bond's convertible with the top dropped is not the sudden realization that your head juts above the windshield, so that any airborne object—a pebble, a lug nut, the shedding payload of a flatbed truck—will forever be embedded in your coconut, like the coins and keys you sometimes see in the hot asphalt of city streets.

Nor is it the banana-yellow Porsche GT3 that draws even with you in the passing lane, lingering off your left flank for thirty seconds, as if attempting the in-flight refueling of a Stealth bomber, while its leering driver hand-gestures you to drag-race him. (That terror passes quickly enough when the pilot of the Porsche loses patience and leaves you in his vapor trail at one fifth of Mach 1.)

No. What makes a man vow to change his life, to say nothing of his underpants, should he survive such a journey is this: The journey hasn't even begun.

For you have come to test your driving skills not on the speedlimit-less autobahn but on the Nurburgring, the ribbon of road that Germans drive when they find the autobahn too tame; the ribbon of road that racing legend Jackie Stewart called, without hyperbole, "the Green Hell"; the ribbon of road that a twenty-four-year-old German named Mika Hahn told me, with furrowed brow, "is very, very dangerous"—far too dangerous for him to drive on, and he's a likely future world champion of speedway motorcycle racing.

The Nurburgring has long been too harrowing for Formula One racing. Since 1927 the picturesque Grand Prix track has lain, like a gold necklace on a rumpled bedspread, in the Eifel Mountains of western Germany. But over the decades, as cars became faster, the fourteen-mile, 170-turn course became deadlier. It closed forever to F/1 racing in 1976, after Austrian star Niki Lauda was famously set alight there when he crashed on the approach to a turn known as Bergwerk. By 1983 the 'Ring prudently had been closed to nearly every form of professional racing. Yet—and here's the rub—the Nurburgring remains open, as it ever has been, for the general public to drive on as fast as it pleases for as long as it pleases in whatever it pleases: race cars, jalopies, or crotch-rocket motorcycles, many of which have become sarcophagi for their drivers.

Why on earth would anybody want to race there? "If you studied piano all your life and had a chance to play Carnegie Hall on a Steinway, you would want to do that," says Dan Tackett, forty-two, a financial services manager from San Diego who has made eleven trips to the Nurburgring in the past sixteen years. "This is the most difficult, challenging, and rewarding racetrack in the world. For serious drivers, it remains the Holy Grail."

It is Everest in asphalt—"the single greatest piece of motor racing architecture in the world," says *Motor Sport* magazine of England—and it demands equipment that is up to the task. Which is how it is that I'm heading for the Nurburgring in a cherry-red BMW Z8, the model driven by 007 in *The World Is Not Enough* but piloted at this moment by English photographer Bob Martin, who is not licensed to kill and is, truth be told, barely licensed to drive.

We retrieved this astonishing feat of automotive engineering at the world headquarters of the Bayerische Motoren Werke in Munich. The company's skyscraper is a kind of architectural pun, constructed of four cylinders. Directly across the street is the 1972 Olympic athletes' village. The site where eleven Israelis were taken hostage at the Summer Games is now the world's most poignant apartment complex. Mesmerized by the view, I absentmindedly signed a three-page document in German that rendered me legally responsible for returning, scratch-free, the $125,000, 400-horsepower, eight-cylinder, zero-to-sixty-in-4.5-seconds dream car that Bob was soon driving off the lot in the giddily overmatched manner of someone who has been given the keys to the space shuttle.

Or rather Bob, a giant of a man, was not so much driving the two-seater as he was wearing it. He looked like a man in a kayak, a very happy man. As we negotiated the streets of Munich, Bob began speaking in tongues about the "Zed 8" and its "bloody brute" of an engine, its "stop-on-a-sixpence" brakes, and, "oooh!—all the beautiful bulgy bits" on its chassis. By the time we entered the autobahn and were swept away like a raft on rapids, all of Bob's bulgy bits were aflame with excitement. He was fearless in his phallic chariot. "BMW!" Bob cackled, merging into traffic, throwing down the hammer, the wind whining in our ears. "Bob Martin's Wheels!"

"BMW," I muttered darkly, not liking the looks of this at all. "Bob Martin's Willy." He didn't respond. So, with an ever-deepening sense of disquiet, I shut up and rode shotgun toward a 'Ring of Hell unlike any imagined by Dante.

We overnight in the Alps and discover, in the morning, that our five-hour route to the 'Ring will take us roughly from Ulm to Bonn—from the birthplace of Einstein to the birthplace of Beethoven—in a vehicle that weds science and art. Construction of Ulm's Munster cathedral began in 1377. Its 536–foot steeple remains the tallest in the world. Mankind, alas, no longer builds such wonders. Or do we? "I think that cars today are almost the exact equivalent of the great Gothic cathedrals," French social critic Roland Barthes wrote of postwar Western civilization. "I mean the supreme creation of an era, conceived with passion by unknown artists, and consumed in image if not in usage by a whole population which appropriates them as a purely magical object."

Nowhere is the automobile more talismanic than in Germany, the country that gave us the concept of wanderlust, the word *fahrvergnugen* ("joy of driving"), the world's top driver (F/1 king Michael Schumacher), and high-performance automakers Mercedes-Benz,

BMW, Porsche, and Audi (as well as mid-performance auto-makers Opel and Volkswagen, and nonperformance automaker Trabant). Americans think of themselves as car crazy, but they don't know the half of it. "Germany is a car culture," says Tackett, the American 'Ring veteran. "America is a drive-through culture of convenience."

"In America cars are appliances," adds U.S. Air Force captain Todd Fry, twenty-six, a motorcycle-riding F-16 pilot based at Spangdahlem Air Force base, an hour's ride from the Nurburgring. "Here, cars are the objects of passion."

So Bob and I continue hammering toward the village of Nurburg. Two hours south of the Green Hell, when we cross the Rhine at Karlsruhe, a black Mercedes SL 500 convertible with full body kit and mag tires appears suddenly in our rearview. Bob takes little notice, for he is dozing, an alarming prospect given that he is—at the same time—driving on hundred miles per hour with the top down.

In our cramped cockpit (we will later discover) Bob's right leg is mashed against a button that activates his electronic seat warmer. It is ninety-five degrees on this afternoon, and Bob is being bum-toasted by red-hot coils hidden beneath the black leather uphol-stery of his seat. He is being lulled into a coma by heatstroke and highway hypnosis when the Benz—headlights strobing madly—gets on our back bumper like one of those KEEP HONKING I'M RE-LOADING stickers so popular in the United States.

We are both nodding like junkies when the horn sounds be-hind us. Bob snaps to attention. In a panic, he reflexively jerks the wheel. We career into the right lane, and the Benz passes. But as soon as it does, the middle-aged maniac in the driver's seat (Bob is now calling him a "plonker") maneuvers the Merc into the right lane, decelerates, and begins to ride our front bumper. After two hundred yards of this mouse-and-cat game, he exits the autobahn slowly, so that we can see him pointing at the exit sign as we pass. The man is laughing through his elaborate mustache. (The men—and not a few women—of this German region all have mustaches like the CBS golf announcer Gary McCord.) The plonker keeps pointing at the exit sign—a sign, we now see, for the Daimler-

Benz complex in Worth. The man in the Merc, evidently in the employ of that automaker, grins as if he's just won something. Perhaps he has.

Still we're one hundred fifty miles from the Green Hell. If drivers on the autobahn are hypercompetitive and brand-loyal, what kind of psychotics await us at the Nurburgring? "They are people who enjoy the sheer pleasure of driving," says BMW event manager Werner Briel when we pitch up at the 'Ring's parking lot. "They are concerned not only with velocity but with . . . style." Then, holding on to his homburg, he leans over and strokes his sweatered pet dachshund, Katya.

The Nurburgring drivers, in turn, attract an audience of rubber-neckers almost as interesting as the motorists themselves. "They come to see the cars, they come to see the crashes," says Reinhard H. Queckenberg, whose name sounds like that of a Groucho Marx character but in fact belongs to the owner of a small racetrack not far from the Nurburgring. "It is living theater."

The elevation changes a thousand feet along the track's fourteen miles. The road rolls out, like a rucked red carpet, over hill and dale and through primeval forest. Three towns and a twelfth-century castle are contained within the Nurburgring's infield. But then you have already, no doubt, seen the circuit. Countless car commercials are filmed on it, the kind that carry the disclaimer, PROFESSIONAL DRIVER ON A CLOSED TRACK. DO NOT TRY THIS YOURSELF.

Yet, every year, thousands of drivers do try it. Each of them pays 21 deutsche marks—about $9.50—per lap and joins the hundred-plus vehicles that are allowed on the loop at any one time. For most of its length the road is little more than two lanes wide. Unlike modern F/1 circuits, the Nurburgring doesn't have a thousand yards of run-off area beyond its shoulders. Rather, it has no run-off area. If you leave the road, you collide with a tree or a cyclone fence or steel guardrails. Crash through the guardrails, and you, or your estate, must pay to have it replaced.

One ambulance and one flatbed wrecker truck are forever on standby at the 'Ring's starting line. Drivers sign no waiver and are given no warnings. "This could never happen in the States," says Roger Scilley of Laguna Beach, California, whom we meet ten minutes after arriving. "Lawyers wouldn't allow it. But over here, you're responsible for your own actions."

Which isn't to say that there are no warnings whatsoever at the Nurburgring. No, all along the perimeter of the track are signs that shriek LEBENSGEFAHR! (Mortal Danger!), but those are for the spectators—and the ones behind the fencing, at that. There are no words for those race fans, like the four teenagers we'll encounter on our second day at the track, who watch the festivities, with a cooler full of beverages, from inside the guardrails. Imagine enjoying the Indy 500 while standing against the wall of Turn 2. Now imagine doing so when all the drivers are amateurs.

Germans are, generally speaking, better drivers than Americans. "In Germany," says Louis Goldsman, a fifty-seven-year-old retiree from Mission Viejo, California, on pilgrimage at the 'Ring, "you're required to attend a driving academy for four months before you can get a license. It costs the equivalent of twenty-five hundred dollars to obtain a license, and you can't get one until you're eighteen. Insurance is more expensive. All this makes for more serious drivers. The average eighteen-year-old German girl can outdrive the typical testosterone-polluted American male any day."

Goldsman has come to the Nurburgring with a group from the BMW Club of America. At 10 A.M. Eastern time on Monday, March 6, many of the club's fifty-five thousand members called a toll-free number in hopes of getting one of the seventy-two available spots on the trip. Richard George speed-dialed the number 240 times from Dallas before securing one of the berths, which sold out in three hours. The trip cost each driver $2,500, plus airfare, and required him (or her) to have attended at least three high-performance driving schools. "We're freaks," says a woman who underscores the point by giving her name as Robyn McNutt. "Freaks."

The club has rented the track for three days. The first two days were devoted to learning the line of the course, mile by mile. Bob and I stumble upon these people on the final day, as they are grimly preparing to put the pedal to the metal and make their "graded lap" of the Nurburgring, at full speed, as expert judges stationed about the circuit make notations on their clipboards.

"We will be graded on a scale of one to ten, one being good and ten being what the Germans call *totalkaos*," says Tackett, the club's best driver and de facto leader, in a pre-lap speech to his fellow motorists. "Now, you've all had some hot laps in practice, maybe even incurred the need for some laundry attention. You might want to slow it down a little this time. I have pictures of a car that rolled here to show you that this is serious business."

"Two years ago," whispers Dan Chrisman, a fifty-three-year-old from Austin, "one driver on this trip took out thirty feet of fencing and wound up on his top in a BMW 328." The driver of that car suffered nothing more than a cut, and his passenger walked away uninjured, but not all cars are that safe. Thirteen kilometers into the clockwise course is an infamous hairpin turn called the Karussell. It is a concrete former drainage ditch that drivers plunge into, leaving the track looming above them, like a paved wave threatening to break through the right-hand windows. "I have seen families in camper vans out on the course," says Chrisman, a three-time veteran of the circuit. "I've gone into the Karussell and looked above me to see a double-decker tour bus with little old ladies on the upper level looking down at me through their cameras."

There will be two hours of public racing after the BMW club completes its graded laps on this Friday evening, and already some heavy artillery is massing in the parking lot: Lancias, Porsches, Mercs, Ferraris, Vipers, a Lamborghini Diablo, a rare Dutch Donkervoort, a Fiat Uno with valve springs popping through the bonnet. Many cars have but a single seat, with a racing harness. There are racing motorcycles of every description, their leathered riders doing push-ups in the parking lot. "Those bikes," points out Mike Valente, a veteran English motor-sports photographer, "will be going a hundred and eighty miles an hour on the final straightaway. On two wheels. Each wheel has a footprint the size of your shoe."

I am told to expect madness when the track opens to the public. "The Germans who live locally," says Tom Doherty, forty-one, an Indianapolis native who has attended every Indy 500 since 1966, "are all driving souped-up BMW M3s"—modified racing cars—"and they drive blindingly fast out here."

But before the public can have a go, Tackett has agreed to take me as a passenger on his graded lap. Everyone tells me that I'm lucky, that Tackett is the best American driver on site. But bad juju is confronting us everywhere as I hop into Tackett's BMW 523i sedan and we make our way to the starting chute.

Before Tackett and I set out, BMW of America Club member McNutt points to a spot on her map of the Nurburgring. "That's where Niki Lauda," she volunteers brightly, "had his barbecue."

Fritz-Jurgen Hahn, a fifty-nine-year-old member of an auto club in Düsseldorf, fondly recalls for me the first time he raced on the Nurburgring. "It was in 1963, in a Porsche Spyder," he says. That is the car James Dean died in.

"The track was built in 1927 as the German equivalent of a WPA project," Tackett says, attempting to soothe my nerves with conversation as we wait for a starting flag. "There are a hundred and seventy turns, and I'm going to alert you to every one of them in advance, not to bore you, but to protect the interior of my car." With that, a flag drops and Tackett accelerates and the world goes by in a blur. I find myself riding a rail-free roller coaster at 125 miles per hour, and I won't have a single coherent recollection— apart from removing my bucket hat and holding it over my mouth—of that first circuit.

"It's just a red fookin' mist out there, innit?" says Tom Thompson, an English motorcyclist we shall meet in a moment. "It is brain out, brick in."

Tackett takes me for two more laps when the course opens to the public. Though he follows the line expertly, the ride is sickening. For most of it I stick my head out the window like a black Lab. Ahead of us Bob Martin rides in the backseat of a convertible, facing backward through 170 turns at up to 140 miles per hour, gamely taking pictures of the cars behind him. His shirt is pulled up over his mouth: At these speeds—and I am as serious as a heart attack here—a shower of vomit on a car windshield may prove fatal to the showeree. Bob had the Wiener schnitzel for lunch.

Bikes and cars flash past on either flank. The Nurburgring is exactly like a Grand Prix video game sprung to life, only instead of getting a GAME OVER message after crashing, you die.

Drivers must exit the circuit after each lap. Following my second shotgun lap with Tackett, one hour into public racing, cars are suddenly forbidden to go out again. The PA announcement in German states that the track is being cleared. The ambulance and the flatbed wrecker are dispatched, sirens wailing. Vague reports come back from the last drivers to cross the finish line that a yellow car spun out somewhere in the red fookin' mist. The wrecker truck will take fifteen minutes to reach the far side of the track, seven miles away. After ten minutes, a second ambulance sets out from the starter's chute, followed by a police car. The silence is hideous.

Twenty minutes later, a black Opel GTE crosses the finish line, its driver ashen-faced, evidently having lingered at the site of the accident. He drives through the parking lot and off into the dusk without telling any of us what he witnessed.

Many drivers at the Nurburgring mount video cameras in their cars. A young German who has just recorded his ride cues up the video for a crowd in the parking lot. About halfway through the circuit, as a diabolical turn comes into view, a spot of yellow begins to take shape on the shoulder. We view the tape in superslow motion until three Zapruder-like frames reveal everything: a yellow Lancia marooned askew on the outside shoulder, its rear left wheel jammed all the way up into its well, the car's driver and passenger standing next to it, miraculously unharmed. The flatbed does not take the wreckage through the main gate, where all the drivers are parked waiting for the track to reopen. The driver of the Lancia is also spirited out some side gate. An announcement is made that the Nurburgring is closed for the night, but it will reopen on Sunday for ten hours of public racing.

Tonight's public racing lasted sixty-two minutes before a near-catastrophe occurred. But we will be back on Sunday. We want to see the cars. We want to see the crashes.

Reinhard H. Queckenberg was right. It is living theater.

A modern F/1 track has been constructed next door to the Nurburgring, and on Saturday it hosts an extraordinarily dangerous event: vintage motorcycle-and-sidecar racing. The sidecars are really just square metal platforms bolted to the bikes. Sidecar passengers, called monkeys, ride a foot off the pavement at 135 miles per hour, sometimes prone, sometimes supine, their helmeted heads an inch off the track when leaning into turns. "Last year at this race, there was a bad accident," says Mika Hahn, a sometime monkey. "Four sidecars went into a turn together, two touched and overrolled. One person was totally killed and had to be—how you say?—reanimated. He survived."

"The perfect sidecar passenger should weigh six stone [eighty-four pounds] and have a pointed nose for aerodynamics," says a six-seven, forty-year-old biker whom I meet in the pits, "but I got this one: six-foot-seven and built like a brick shithouse." He hooks a thumb at his towering seventeen-year-old son, who wears a black leather jumpsuit with his nickname stitched to the back: TINY.

"At least," says Tiny, "I got the nose."

Tom and Tiny Thompson are from Bulkington, England. Cheryl Thompson—Tom's wife, Tiny's mother—is a petite woman with painted nails who also wears full leathers. She too is a monkey. When her husband was twenty-eight, she explains, he rode his 1938 Triumph 250 everywhere. "He's so tall, he looked ridiculous on it," says Cheryl, a former sales executive with Prudential in London. "Like an elephant on a matchstick." She told him he needed an "outfit"—a sidecar—for aesthetic balance.

"Get an outfit and I'll ride it," she promised, though she had no intention of doing any such thing. "Blimey if two weeks later he doesn't come home with a sidecar," says Cheryl. "I thought, Crikey." The couple painted THOMPSON TWINS on the Triumph. "The Thompson Twins," she says sheepishly of the new-romantic eighties band, "were popular at the time."

Cheryl sighs and says of Tiny, her only child, "He could ride a bike before he could walk." In 1983, Tom rigged a remote-control accelerator to his bike, tied a rope to its frame, and let Tiny ride in a circle around him. Says Tom, "He was nine months old at the time."

"The other mothers in the park went mad," says Cheryl. "They said, 'Look at him, with no helmet!' I said, 'You try finding a helmet for a nine-month-old!'"

Tiny was allowed to drop out of school at fourteen—"They didn't want me back," he explains—and now spends the summer traveling from race to race with his parents, living in the back of a rented van. He loves his parents, and they clearly love him. How many seventeen-year-olds would be willing to spend the summer with their parents, sharing a single mattress? Tiny may have quit school, but the Germans have a phrase that fits him well: *Reisen bildet.* "Travel educates."

The Thompsons are protective not only of each other but of their fellow amateur racers as well. "We take calculated risks," says Cheryl. "The last thing you need is some barmy git out there who's trying to kill people. But you do get them. At [England's] Mallory [Park speedway], on a hairpin, someone tried to push us out—to take a hole that wasn't there—and he smashed into my right hand. I could have killed him. Afterward, he looked at my hand and said to me, 'At least you can still peel the potatoes, luv.' I wanted to punch him out.

"We took a nasty bump at the gooseneck bend on [England's] Cadwell Circuit," Cheryl says with classic British understatement. "This chap was going full out, and his stupid idiot passenger rolled onto the track, and it was either hit the passenger and kill him or go into the wall. So we hit the tire wall at ninety miles an hour." Cheryl says she was "black from top to toe" for two months. Tom was catapulted over the tire wall and lay motionless for thirty seconds with a ruptured kidney and three broken ribs. He slowly returned to consciousness and shouted, "I'm alive!" He wiggled his toes: "My legs work!" He wiggled his fingers: "My arms work!" Then, after a pause, he wailed to his wife, "Oh, my God, I'm blind!"

"There was mud in his helmet," says Cheryl, rolling her eyes.

The point is, they risked their lives to save a monkey, and that says something hopeful about human nature. "We are all ever so close," Cheryl says of the amateur vintage sidecar community, "no matter what nationality. At the start of every race, we all look at each other and cross our fingers—we get sorta jinxy-like. Solo riders aren't like that. But sidecar racers have camaraderie."

The Thompsons' enthusiasm for amateur racing renews my desire to get behind the wheel on the 'Ring of Hell the next day.

I am—how you say?—reanimated. Before leaving the vintage bike rally, I buy a Red Baron helmet and goggles from a Swiss trafficker in old-time driving gear. (His business card reads, somewhat salaciously, that he also purveys "accessories in leather.") Cheryl kindly cuts a piece of fabric from the Triumph's tarpaulin, creating a white scarf that will billow behind me as I whip the Zed 8 'round the Nurburgring on a public-racing Sunday.

"I would never ride over there," Tiny says as Bob and I prepare to take our leave. "They say one a week goes over there." By "goes" he means dies. Then Tiny bids us a cheery farewell.

On Sunday I see it all: a man doing 110 with his dry-cleaning hanging in a back window; an Opel Kadett hammering into an S-turn while its gas cap flaps against the rear quarter panel; a guy getting airborne at Kilometer 4, his children's dolls looking impassively out the rear windshield; three teenage girls smoking in an Opel Swing hatchback, the driver applying lipstick in the rearview while idling in the starting chute; and a man in a drop-top whose hat flies off at the Flugplatz. Happily, the hat doesn't suction itself to the face of a biker behind him. Heaven knows it could.

Todd Fry, the young air force captain, likes to race his Honda CBR 900 RR Fireblade around the Nurburgring. "I'm not one of these guys who's an adrenaline junkie," says Fry, of Pompton Plains, New Jersey, roasting in his red-white-and-blue leather jumpsuit. "I've scared myself more often on the motorcycle than in an F-16. But fear is a good thing to have. Fear is life insurance out here."

If so, I am well insured. As Fry and I speak, an Opel Esona race-prepared road car blazes by on the track. A dozen Lotus Elises go into the starting chute together. A pink-and-white tour bus full of seniors from Kaiserslautern enters the raceway, hazard lights blinking absurdly. A ding-a-ling in a camper van survives two passes around the 'Ring, both times plunging into the Karussell turn. "Just pass him," advises Fry. "Everyone has a right to be out there. For the most part, you're just racing the road anyway."

Tell that to the driver of the Porsche GT2, an earlier, more aggressive version of the car whose driver wanted to drag-race Bob and me on our first day in the Alps. Tell that to the pilot of the Nissan Skyline GT-R, a Japanese-only supercar that was probably towed over here from England, street-illegal as it is. Tell that to the nutter in the purple Lamborghini Diablo. Tell that to all the mustachioed Germans doing 160 on their Italian-made Aprilia racing bikes.

"The biggest rush is when you're fully leaned over into a turn and you're scraping your knees on the track," says Mike Leong, twenty-four, an air force lieutenant from Cincinnati who rides a Yamaha YZF-R1 racing bike. "When you take a turn right, you have four hundred forty pounds and one hundred fifty horsepower and all those G's acting on you." He shows me the deep scuffing in the plastic guards sewn over the knees of his leathers. "That," he says, "is how you know you've made a good turn."

"The military isn't crazy about us doing this," says Fry, unnecessarily.

"My parents don't know I ride," says Leong, "but my brother gets *Sports Illustrated,* so I guess they'll find out. Oh, well."

The Zed 8 beckons from the parking lot. I have been reluctant to drive it even on the rural highways around the Nurburgring, which attract almost as many racing bikers as the raceway. Everywhere on those roads are signs that say RACEN IST OUT! (Racing Is Out!) above a silhouette of a biker sliding off his cycle into oblivion. "You know it's a good road," says Leong, without a trace of false machismo, "when you see those signs."

Leong and Fry have the Right Stuff for the Nurburgring. Michael Schumacher, who was winning the Canadian Grand Prix in Montreal on this Sunday afternoon, has the Right Stuff. Eighteen-year-old girls in Opel Swing hatchbacks have the Right Stuff. James Bond has the Right Stuff, and I have his car. But the question remains: Do I have the Right Stuff?

I came to the Nurburgring to test my driving skills—which is to say *nerve*—on the most difficult roadway in the world, the San Diego Freeway on acid. Of course, I really came to learn deeper truths about my courage under extreme duress. From afar, it seemed as if it would be good for a laugh. This is what I've learned: I will not drive 125 miles per hour on an automotive minefield in a borrowed car costing more than I'm worth, solely for the momentary diversion of a magazine editor back in New York City. Now I know. *Reisen bildet.* Travel educates.

I call that courage. You call me a wuss. Fine. But you'll have to say the same to Tiny, and trust me, you don't want to do that.

(January 15, 2001)

NAME PLAYERS

If you're like me—one of twelve Steves at your workplace—you envy pro football players not for their money or their fame but for their breathtaking names. Zeron Flemister, Cletidus Hunt, Emarlos Leroy, Armegis Spearman, Sulecio Sanford, Flozell Adams, Shockmain Davis, Antico Dalton, Tebucky Jones, Peppi Zellner, Cheston Blackshear, Wasswa Serwanga, Laveranues Coles, Na'il Diggs, and Mondriel Fulcher are all employed in the NFL, as is the insuperable Hannibal Navies, whose name always conjures in my head a fleet of amphibious elephants—in bathing caps and nose plugs—swimming ashore at Normandy en route to the Alps.

Whatever its pretensions as the new national pastime, pro football has surely displaced baseball as the best sport to announce. Any knucklehead in a network blazer can paint one thousand-word pictures on Sunday simply by reciting the starting lineups. Receiver Chafie Fields, late of the 49ers? A verdant but rash-bearing pasture, downstream from Flushing Meadow. Raiders running back Napoleon Kaufman? A short accountant in a tricorn, riding a white steed to Price-Waterloo. Giants receiver Amani Toomer? Two words: designer disease.

For some years now I have been unable to hear the name of Steelers center Dermontti Dawson without seeing, instantly and all too vividly, the label for Del Monte Creamy Style Yellow Corn. (I wish it weren't so.) More often the images that illustrate my

Sundays are lyrical—almost poetic—and is it any wonder why? The name of former Dolphins guard O'Lester Pope, when intoned by Pat Summerall, sounds like the opening of a poem or song. (Behind him on the depth chart: O'Holy Knight and O'Cursed Fate.)

If names are destiny, and your son's destiny is to be a pro football player—and to marry a woman named Destiny, as so many do—then give his name a stylish spelling. Marty Jenkins will one day manage a Pizza Hut, which is perfectly fine. But MarTay Jenkins will play wide receiver for the Cardinals. (Indeed, he already does.) The difference between a Marty and a MarTay, it goes without saying, is the difference between a party and a par*tay*.

Of course, parents can't always encode a child's fate in his or her name. As it turns out, the mother of Priest Holmes could not preordain her child's occupation; he became a Ravens running back. The power of suggestion likewise failed the parents of Patriots defensive back Lawyer Milloy. The Burress family of Virginia Beach was no doubt displeased that young Plaxico became a receiver for the Steelers rather than the multinational plastics conglomerate they had hoped he would be. Such failure to fulfill one's fate can be a source of bitter disappointment—Ravens linebacker Cornell Brown attended neither Ivy League school—or of great relief: Browns defensive end Stalin Colinet hasn't executed thirty million of his countrymen.

NFL games are three hours of tedium occasionally interrupted by action. So in the course of a telecast one's mind will wander to Yalta and beyond. Every down poses a diverting question: Was the mother of rookie defensive back (cut last Sunday by the Buccaneers) Earthwind Moreland an Earth Wind & Fire fan? What do Rams linebacker London Fletcher, Giants offensive tackle Rome Douglas, and former Cardinals defensive back Paris Johnson make of the stagnating euro?

The perception of gladiatorial grandeur that surrounds pro football, I am convinced, has everything to do with the Greco-Roman grandiloquence of its players' names. Aeneas Williams, Octavious Bishop, Adalius Thomas, Roman Fortin—no wonder the Super Bowl is Roman numeraled. Thank heaven that another season has arrived, with all its lovely neologisms. Jammi German, Stockar McDougle, Errict Rhett, Lemanski Hall, Olandis Gary, La'Roi Glover, Alshermond Singleton: they are priceless peers of Peerless Price.

I salute you, Orlando Bobo.

(September 4, 2000)

BAD BEYOND BELIEF

Q: What is there to say about a man who couldn't make the worst
   baseball team of this century?
A: That he didn't want to play badly enough.

Evans Killeen was cut from the 1962 New York Mets. The pitcher
sliced open his thumb while shaving on the morning of a scheduled spring training start. The Mets cut the right-hander when he
couldn't satisfactorily explain why, exactly, he was shaving his thumb.

Steve Dillon did not make the 1962 Mets. But manager Casey
Stengel saw something in the left-hander that nobody else did, and
he promoted him the following season. "Dillon probably shouldn't
have been up there," recalls Craig Anderson, who pitched for the
Mets from 1962 to 1964. "But Stengel was real big on him. Dillon
was Stengel's middle name, you know."

Craig Anderson, of course, did make the 1962 Mets. Pitching
in relief, Anderson won both halves of a doubleheader against the
Milwaukee Braves on May 12 of that season to run his record to
3–1. Anderson never won another game in his career, which ended
with *nineteen consecutive losses* spread over parts of three seasons.
Pardon my italics, but such factoids as these fairly demand the
Ripley's Believe It or Not treatment.

Three decades have done nothing to diminish how bad the Mets
were in 1962, the franchise's first season. Those Mets were bad

like God is good: their badness will endure forever. "I get three to five letters every day," says Marvin Eugene Throneberry, the Mets first baseman whose monogram and misadventures afield made him a mascot for the '62 season. "I throw 'em all in a box. When it rains, I answer 'em. No, I never thought it would carry on this long."

To understand why a fifty-eight-year-old salesman for the Active Bolt and Screw Company is up to his knees in S.A.S.E.'s at his home in Collierville, Tennessee, one must understand those expansion Mets embodied by Marvelous Marv. And frankly, that summer of '62 is as difficult to fathom as a Stengel soliloquy. So if this backward glance at that season jumps ahead of itself occasionally or doubles back in spots or tends to ramble here and there, well, it could be no other way.

Stengel-like, the story often makes no sense whatsoever. Nine games into the 1962 season, for instance, the Mets were nine-and-a-half games out of first. Is that possible? In fifteen tries, the Mets never once won on a Thursday. Bad? The team was mathematically eliminated from the pennant race on August 7.

This is true—cross my heart, hope to die, stick a needle in my eye: The '62 Mets continued to lose ground in the National League standings after the season had ended. Is that possible? As we shall discover, it was possible for the Mets, whose record of 40–120 left them sixty and a half games behind the first-place San Francisco Giants.

Thus, being cut from the '62 Mets was to low self-esteem what the Buick Roadmaster was to low gas mileage. A snub from that club was like having a Hare Krishna on your threshold say that no, really, he couldn't possibly come in for coffee.

Or was it? In hindsight, who would you rather be, the standby passenger who was bumped from the *Hindenburg* or one of the chaps who went down with the zeppelin? "Oh, I'm glad that season was a part of my career," says the genial Anderson, now an associate athletic director and assistant baseball coach at Lehigh University. "I got to play with Gil Hodges. I got to meet Stan Musial. I got to play for Casey Stengel. I still get letters. How many people can say they were in a ticker-tape parade through New York City?"

Oh, the humanity. The Mets' home opener that April was scheduled for—and these stories have been fact-checked for accuracy; we do not make them up—Friday the thirteenth, at the Polo Grounds, the Mets' unlucky horseshoe in Harlem. On April 12 the Mets were given a ticker-tape parade up lower Broadway, culminating with ceremonies at City Hall. Among the dignitaries on the rostrum was William Shea. A local attorney and civic leader, Shea was the man most responsible for bringing National League baseball back to New York following the westward flight of the Dodgers and Giants four years earlier.

"At City Hall, Bill Shea—who was lionized in New York—made a speech in which he apologized for the players," recalls Richie Ashburn, the center fielder who would be dubiously distinguished at season's end, named Most Valuable Player on the worst team of this century. "It still sticks in my craw. Before we had played a single home game, Shea told the fans, 'Be patient with us until we can bring some real ballplayers in here.' And the players—we were standing right there! I mean, he was probably right, but he didn't have to say it."

Ticker tape. Nineteen sixty-two was the dusk of that innocent postwar age when America's leading industrial product was . . . the hyphen. Remember? The United States was a veritable Hyphen-Nation of Ban-Lon and Sen-Sen and La-Z-Boys and Speedy Alka-Seltzer and un-American activities and movies like *Ben-Hur*.

And so the expansion Mets would stay at the Hi-Way House in Houston when they played the league's other expansion team, the Colt .45s. Little news nuggets about the team were tacked onto the end of longer stories in New York City newspapers, beneath bizarre column subheads like "Met-Ro-Nomes," "Met-a-Morphoses," "Met-Cellaneous," metc.

And from the very start, the New York pitching staff would induce runs like Met-a-Mucil. Opening Day starter Roger Craig and more than a dozen other Mets were stranded in an elevator for thirty minutes at the Chase Hotel in St. Louis, where the Mets were to begin the season against the Cardinals. Going down? Indeed. Rained out on Tuesday, the New York Mets debuted on Wednesday, April 11: Craig lasted three innings and balked in one run. His teammates committed three errors. The Cards won 11–4.

It was the first of Craig's twenty-four losses in 1962. Now the manager of the Giants, Craig recalls with humility pitching against the pennant-winning Giants of Willie Mays and Willie McCovey thirty seasons ago. "We would have pitchers' meetings before every series, and we would go over the scouting report," Craig remembers. "One time when the Giants came to town, Stengel asked me, 'Mr. Craig, where would you like us to defense McCovey: upper deck or lower deck?'"

They say the best things in life are free, but the worst things, it turns out, also come pretty cheap. Mets owner Joan Payson had spent a trifling $50,000 as a fee for the franchise, a mere $1.8 million in payments to other clubs for players in the expansion draft, and all of $600,000 in salaries to field her team. Of course, general manager George Weiss was tighter than a Speedo two sizes too small. In making a salary offer that spring, he is said to have egregiously lowballed traveling secretary Lou Niss, then conspiratorially whispered these words of encouragement: "You know, traveling secretaries are usually voted a full World Series share."

So Mets management got what it didn't pay for. On opening night, Hobie Landrith was Craig's batterymate, and what an apt term that was. Gil Hodges, the erstwhile Brooklyn Dodger star who had just turned thirty-eight, was at first base. Charley Neal was the second baseman. Felix Mantilla was at short. Don Zimmer played third base. The left fielder was Frank Thomas. Ashburn, thirty-five, was the center fielder. And the right fielder was . . . the rightfielder was . . .

Understand that Stengel had trouble with names the way Ronald Reagan has trouble with dates. When Stengel was hired at the age of seventy-two to be the Mets' first manager, he told the press that he was delighted to be taking over "the Knickerbockers" and playing in "the Polar Grounds."

And while Stengel had two pitchers named Bob Miller on his team—they were roommates on the road, in fact—he called one of them Nelson. Still, it is startling to see Stengel on a flickering black-and-white television screen during that first week of the '62 season trying to name his starting lineup for broadcaster Lindsey Nelson. Stengel makes it all the way to his right fielder before treading air.

"He's a splendid man and he knows how to do it," says Casey on camera. "He's been around and he swings the bat there in right field and he knows what to do. He's got a big family and he wants to provide for them, and he's a fine outstanding player, the fella in right field. You can be sure he'll be ready when the bell rings—and that's his name, Bell."

Having returned from the Wednesday game in Saint Louis to be disparaged at their own parade on Thursday, Gus Bell and the rest of the Mets then lost their first home game, amid snow flurries at the Polar Grounds on Friday the thirteenth. Still, advance sales were as brisk as the weather at the Mets' Manhattan ticket office, located seven blocks from the Metropolitan Opera in the Hotel Martinique. Legend has it that an opera buff mistook the Mets' ticket window for the Met's ticket window one spring day, requested "two for *Traviata,*" and was asked by an eager-to-please Mets employee: "First base or third base side?"

Apocryphal, you say? Hey, don't rain on our parade. Bill Shea did that once already.

Remember Miss Rheingold? Remember King Korn trading stamps? Remember when Ford Frick was baseball commissioner? Remember when people had names like Ford Frick? Remember cruising with the top down in your Ford Frick?

If so, you may also remember that the Mets began the '62 season 0–9. And because the Pirates got out of the gate 10–0, New York was indeed nine and a half games back after playing only nine. In fact, the Mets beat those Bucs on April 23 for their first win, 9–1 on Ladies' Night at Forbes Field. The following day Frick fined Stengel $500 for appearing in uniform with the voluptuous Miss Rheingold in a Rheingold Extra Dry Lager ad. Why ask why?

Two days later the Cleveland Indians announced that they had traded catcher Harry Chiti to the Mets for a player to be named later. The deal would not be completed until June 15, when Chiti was returned to the Tribe as the player named in compensation for himself. That's when the New York media—tough crowd, the New York media—suggested that the Mets had been fleeced in the Chiti-for-Chiti swap. And thus began a Mets tradition that continues to this day, in which fans in the street endlessly second-guess the team's front office. *Yo, I can't believe Weiss couldn't get more for Harry Chiti than, you know . . . Harry Chiti.*

Chiti, by the way, was one of seven catchers who would do time with the Mets in 1962. Hobie Landrith, another, had been the Mets' very first selection in the expansion draft. "You gotta start with a catcher or you'll have all passed balls," explained Stengel, who then, just a few weeks into the season, had Landrith traded to Baltimore for Throneberry.

Stengel tried Clarence (Choo-Choo) Coleman behind the plate, and the former Phillie showed early promise. "He was one of the best low-ball catchers I've ever seen," says Craig. "But if it was high stuff, you could forget it. Choo-Choo would also give you the sign and then look down to see what it was."

Coleman was also fidgety in the crouch, so animated that when journeyman pitcher Chuck Churn was once asked to name the toughest man he ever pitched to, he answered, "Coleman." Coleman was equally elusive in interviews. Mets broadcaster Ralph Kiner recalls, in his seminal prose opus *Kiner's Korner,* asking Coleman on the air how he got his nickname. Coleman responded that he didn't know. Flustered, Kiner then recovered by blurting, "Well, what's your wife's name, and what's she like?"

"Her name's Mrs. Coleman," replied Coleman. "And she likes me."

What does David Letterman say? Do we have time for one more? Here goes. On May 12, Stengel inscrutably sent the left-handed Landrith to pinch-hit against Hall of Fame lefty Warren Spahn of the Braves. As soon as Hobie reached the batter's box, Stengel called time, hobbled out there himself, whispered in Landrith's ear, and then returned to the dugout with a smirk on his mug. Hobie hit Spahn's first pitch for a game-winning home run. What had Stengel told him? "I told him," Stengel said afterward, "to hit a home run."

What does David Letterman say? These are actual letters from actual viewers. Well, these are actual stories from actual players. "Some of the stuff is myth," says Hot Rod Kanehl, the utility infielder who spent the eight seasons before 1962 kicking around the minor leagues. "Some of it sounds better than it actually was." But Kanehl not only fails to refute a single story, he also enthusiastically antes up with others and then embroiders those with delightful detail.

So on July 6, Hot Rod didn't just hit the Mets' first grand slam, he won fifty thousand King Korn trading stamps for doing so. "King Korn had a store in Chicago, and I traded the stamps in there," says Kanehl, who now manages a Garcia's Mexican Restaurant in Rancho Mirage, California "I got a living room suite, a Deepfreeze, an end table—a lot of junk." Go deep, win a Deepfreeze. Mets home games were like Wheel of Misfortune that summer of '62.

The decrepit Polo Grounds, erstwhile home of the Giants, had undergone $350,000 in renovations for that season, which is to say the place was painted white. The Polo Grounds were, in fact, more like a state-fair grounds, full of ridiculous sideshows and carnival-midway games that diverted attention from the Mets games themselves.

"They had circles on the walls down the foul lines at the Polo Grounds," recalls Ashburn, who is now a broadcaster for the Phillies. "If you hit a ball in a circle during a game, you got so many points. Ball boys were stationed down the lines, and they decided whether a ball landed in the circle or not."

The player with the most points at season's end would win a boat. Keep in mind that Ashburn would eventually be named the team's MVP, and for that he would win a twenty-four-foot Owens powerboat that slept four. "Well, I hit one ball that I know was in the circle, but the ball boy didn't see it," Ashburn says. "And there was no appeals process. That ball would have given me enough points to win the boat. So I should have won two boats that season. But what the hell, I didn't even know what to do with one. I lived in Nebraska."

Remember, this nautical intrigue occurred during the games. Frank Thomas, in fact, tried to jerk so many balls boatward down the 279–foot left-field line that Stengel is said to have chastised him at one point, saying, "If you want to be a sailor, join the navy!"

In any event, Ashburn would dock his boat in Ocean City, New Jersey. "It sank," he says. "But it didn't just sink. The sucker took five or six days to go down. So they dragged it up, and I sold it. Oh, and the guy I sold it to—his check bounced."

No it didn't. "Yes," says Ashburn. "That really happened."

The Mets' official mascot was Homer the Beagle, and he lived at the Waldorf-Astoria on Park Avenue. Oh, what a wonderful time that was to be young and single and a beagle living in Gotham! And if you happened to be a big league mascot on top of that, well, then the world was indeed your Gaines-Burger.

Homer was trained by Rudd Weatherwax, the man who taught Lassie everything she knew. Alas, the Weatherwaxian magic didn't always work on Homer, and the beagle never quite got the hang of circling the bases at the Polo Grounds. Then again, neither did Throneberry.

Matriculating in the Yankees' farm system of the 1950s, Marv Throneberry was thought to be the next Mickey Mantle, not the first Mickey Klutts. But by 1962 he'd found happiness in simply having one of the five hundred big league jobs that then existed. As for his often erratic play? "A lot of it," Throneberry says now, "is nothin' but fiction."

Let us pull a nonfiction classic from the shelf. Throneberry lashed a triple off Chicago Cub starter Glen Hobbie in the first inning of a game at the Polo Grounds on June 17. But Chicago first baseman Ernie Banks motioned for the ball, stepped on first, and Throneberry was called out on appeal. Says Ashburn: "We could all see from the dugout that Marv really didn't even come close to touching first base."

All except Stengel, who shot from the dugout as if catapulted. Second base umpire Dusty Boggess intercepted the skipper and informed him that Throneberry hadn't touched second base, either. "Well, I know he touched third," went Stengel's timeless punch line, "because he's standing on it."

"I can kid about it now," says Throneberry, relaxing after dark at his fishing house near Collierville. "When people ask me about it, I ask them, 'Have you ever seen an umpire who could see?'"

He is good-natured enough to have done thirteen self-deprecating beer commercials for Miller Lite. His name resurfaced nationally in 1983 when the incriminating bat George Brett used in the Pine-Tar Incident was discovered to be a Marv Throneberry model. When a young New York writer named Jimmy Breslin wrote a book about the 1962 season called *Can't Anybody Here Play This Game?*, Throneberry was, naturally, the comic lead. "Jimmy Breslin went on the TV once and said that I made him famous," says Throneberry. "I think it was on Johnny Carson. He admitted it."

Having said all that, Throneberry is still fiercely proud of his seven seasons in the major leagues. "I still don't know why they asked me to do this commercial" was one of his signature lines in the Miller Lite ads. And in wrapping up your conversation with him about the '62 Mets, you get the feeling that he still doesn't know why you asked him to be in this story.

"People always ask me to tell them some of the funny stuff that happened that year," says Throneberry. "Really, I don't remember that much funny stuff happening."

Some people, of course, wouldn't know funny if it sprayed seltzer in their face. Marv Throneberry is not one of those people. He simply needs to have his memory refreshed.

You want funny? The New York Mets celebrated Old-Timers' Day before their game against the Dodgers on July 14, even though the franchise was four months old. Who were they supposed to bring back—Harry Chiti?

You want funny? After five and a half innings of the main event that day, the Mets trailed the Dodgers 17–0. "We were bad," says Galen Cisco, and he didn't even join the Mets until September. "If you could just win one game out of a series with the Dodgers or the Giants, you were good for the week. We weren't expected to win. We had a horseshit team. There were a lot of clubs we just couldn't beat. We were as bad as our record."

And so they were. Two weeks before their Old-Timers' Day loss to the Dodgers, the Mets were no-hit by Sandy Koufax in Los Angeles. Koufax struck out the first three Mets he faced that afternoon on nine pitches on his way to the first of his four no-nos.

The Mets didn't go bad, like lunchmeat. They were bad from the beginning. Wire-to-wire bad. Yet on the glorious first Saturday of August, they did sweep a doubleheader from the Reds at the Polo Grounds. This rendered Cincinnati manager Fred Hutchinson so distraught that he remained alone in the visitors' dugout for a full half hour after the second game had ended. "If you were playing the Mets you had to win four," explains Don Zimmer, who was traded from New York to Cincinnati in May. "Winning three of four wasn't good enough."

It was in another series against Cincinnati that summer that Ashburn pursued a fly ball to shallow left center field. Now, the Mets' Venezuelan shortstop, Elio Chacon, recklessly laid claim to every ball hit in the air. Before this game, Ashburn had asked bilingual teammate Joe Christopher how to say "I got it" in Spanish. "Yo la tengo," he was told.

So here comes the fly ball, and sure enough, here comes Chacon to invade Ashburn's airspace. "I see him whipping out from shortstop like a little kid on a scooter," says Ashburn. "So I yell, 'Yo la tengo! Yo la tengo!' And Elio puts on the brakes." It was at that precise moment that left fielder Frank Thomas, a native of Pittsburgh, ran headlong into Ashburn and knocked the ball loose.

There is no *i* in team, but there is an *e* or, in the case of the Mets, 210 of them. That's how many errors they committed in 1962. Their team ERA was 5.04. Their team batting average was .240. They crafted separate losing streaks of eleven, thirteen, and seventeen games and generally gave the Cleveland Spiders, who finished 20–134 in 1899, a run for their money.

The most remarkable statistic from that season is the 922,530 unshakable fans the Mets drew to the Polo Grounds even while, minutes away, the Yankees were fielding what would be their ninth world-champion team in fourteen years and drawing 1,493,574. So before their final home game, against the ninth-place Cubs on September 23, the Mets thanked their public. Each player was given a lettered placard to hold, and when the team assembled on the field they spelled out WE LOVE YOU METS FANS TOO. Stengel then moved to the end of the line as an exclamation point.

"We had a big meeting in the clubhouse before the game about whether we should do this," says Craig Anderson. "Most of the guys were saying it was bush league and we weren't going to do it. We were Major Leaguers. We weren't doing this. Then Stengel came in and made a fifteen-minute speech that began, 'You guys don't have to do this.' Fifteen minutes later we ran out there with our placards. I don't know what the hell Casey said, but we did it."

Because the Mets were to move into their new Queens ballpark, named for the parade-pooping Shea, at the start of the 1963 season, this was to be the last ball game at the historic park beneath Coogan's Bluff. At the end of the Mets' 2–1 win over the Cubs, the Polo Grounds' public-address system played "Till We Meet Again."

Stengel, seventy-three, was awarded home plate. As he made the long walk with the dish to the clubhouse, six hundred feet away behind the center-field fence, "Auld Lang Syne" wafted down from the speakers. The 10,304 spectators stood and wept openly. "And we all stood outside the clubhouse," recalls Hot Rod Kanehl, "and we cried."

Of course, "we did the same thing at the end of the next season," Kanehl notes. The Mets returned to the Polo Grounds in '63, you see: Shea Stadium would not be ready until 1964.

As befits a truly atrocious ensemble, the Mets closed on the road, far away from New York City. They lost their 117th game, in Milwaukee, to tie the 1916 Philadelphia Athletics as the most prolific losers of the twentieth century. They lost their 118th game the next day and their 119th two days later, before 595 fans at Wrigley Field.

Well, all good things must come to an end, and the bad things have to stop eventually too, and so the Mets' season finally concluded on a frigid September 30 in Chicago. New York trailed the Cubs 5–1 going into the eighth inning, but Sammy Drake led off with a single, and Ashburn advanced him to second base with a single of his own. With the tying run on deck, catcher Joe Pignatano strode to the plate and promptly hit a blooper toward right field.

Trouble is, Cub second baseman Kenny Hubbs caught the lazy liner, threw to Ernie Banks at first to double off Ashburn, and then watched as Banks threw to shortstop Andre Rodgers to catch Drake off second base. Triple play. It was Pignatano's final at bat in the big leagues.

It was also the final play of Ashburn's fifteen-year career. He hit .306 in 1962, made the All-Star team, was offered a $10,000 raise to return in '63, but walked away from it all. "I often wondered why a guy who hit .306 would retire," says Zimmer, who was Ashburn's roommate while with the Mets. "Three years later I asked him, 'How could you hit .306 and retire?' He said, 'I could see us losing a hundred games again. I couldn't lose again.'"

"This was a group effort," Stengel told the team assembled in the visitors' clubhouse that afternoon in Chicago as they surveyed the foul waste left in their wake. "No one player could've done all this." And yet hadn't the season been fun?

The question was put to Stengel by Louis Effrat of the *New York Times*. Responded Stengel: "I would have to say no to that one."

The Dodgers and the Giants—the two teams whose departures from New York necessitated the Mets and this first unfathomable season—finished September in a tie for first place. L.A. and San Francisco would meet in a three-game playoff, the results of which would count toward the regular-season standings. Thus the Mets did indeed drop half a game in the race after their season had ended.

Richie Ashburn, Most Valuable Player on the worst team of this century, has returned to Chicago to broadcast a Phillie game. He was one of the Whiz Kids, Philadelphia's National League champs in 1950. His lifetime batting average was .308. He is not in the Hall of Fame, but Red Smith once wrote that he should be, and that, says Ashburn, is good enough for him.

And yet as he tugs on a pipe in his room at the Hyatt Regency, what is it that he finds himself talking about? The triple play that ended it all in the ballpark ten minutes north of here. "That last season was a year I didn't want to go through twice," he says. "But I am glad I went through it once. I made great friends—I still talk to Marv a couple of times a year. I got to spend a year with Casey. You know, I get more mail for that one season than I get for all of my years before that."

Those Mets truly were bad like God is good. Their badness will endure forever. Three miles from Ashburn's downtown Chicago hotel, at a club called Lounge Ax, a professional rock 'n' roll band has been booked for the weekend. The band's lead singer was raised in Brooklyn in the 1960s. The band's name is Yo La Tengo.

(May 25, 1992)

MY BIG FAT
SPORTS WEDDING

We met, by chance, in a smoke-filled bar better suited for curing hams. She asked if I was the scribe who once mocked, in *Sports Illustrated,* women's professional basketball. Reluctantly, I said that I was. She asked how many games I'd actually attended. I hung my head and said, "None." And so Rebecca Lobo invited me to watch her team, the New York Liberty, play at Madison Square Garden. We both reeked of secondhand Camels. (And, quite possibly, of secondhand camels: it was that kind of a dive.) But my insult had been forgiven. It was—for me, anyway—love at first slight.

She had the longest legs, the whitest teeth, the best-sown cornrows I had ever seen, and I imagined us to have much in common. I ate Frosted Flakes right out of the box, and she was *on* boxes of Frosted Flakes. I am ludicrous, and she was name-dropped in a rap *by* Ludacris. We were, I thought, made for each other.

So I went to her game and then asked her to dinner, where I babbled earnestly about two memorable free throws I had hit in a high school game. Bear in mind, she is the all-time leading scorer in Massachusetts high school basketball history, girls' or boys'. Her high school—in Southwick—is on Rebecca Lobo Way. In 1995 her unbeaten team at the University of Connecticut won the national championship, and she was named the tournament's Most Outstanding Player and the consensus national player of the year. She dropped in on *Letterman,* was cut out of *Jerry Maguire,* won an Olympic gold medal, had her own Reebok sneaker, had her own Barbie doll, and had the president of the United States sing "Happy Birthday" to her in front of two thousand people—all by the age of twenty-three.

But she didn't say that. Instead, she looked at me with pity and nodded politely as I nattered on. I was mad about her. She guest-starred on *Mad About You.* Seemed like fate to me.

She showed me around Connecticut. It looked, in many ways, like a benevolent Baghdad. Her face was on checks at People's Bank, on a wall at her gym, adhered to the stucco interior of the Guadalajara Grill in Granby. We were crawling in traffic on I-84 when her head emerged, one story tall, on a billboard in downtown Hartford. (She actually blushed, and we rode for a moment in embarrassed silence.)

But then her forbearance is breathtaking. At St. Francis of Assisi Catholic Church, a block from Madison Square Garden, a congregant whispered to her at the handshake of peace, "I'd like to see you get more aggressive on the boards." She said she would do her best.

The world, I discovered, is her friend. Barry Bonds approached in an airport to say he was a fan. Michael Strahan said the same. And Charles Barkley. At the NBA All-Star Game a photographer took our picture with former president Bill Clinton, then asked me to step out of the frame. "Happens to me all the time," a Secret Service man whispered in consolation. "You'll get used to it." Another day, at O'Hare Airport, a man asked to take Rebecca's picture and then motioned me into the frame. He said, "Get in there, Andre Agassi."

Her middle name, Rose, is constantly made manifest. In downtown Boston a man popped from the back of an idling landscaper's van, jogged over to us, and handed Rebecca an enormous white rose. She thanked him, pointed to me, and said, "He's never given me flowers."

In her rookie season, outside the Garden, Rebecca was hugged by a ten-year-old girl from the Bronx. An hour later, when she emerged from a restaurant, the girl was still there, and this time she handed Rebecca a red rose. Children send the school reports they've written about her, hand her cards outside arenas, walk up to her in the grocery store, as one did the other day, and say, "I have your Barbie." And though it happens daily, it is never routine. We'll walk away in silence after one of these encounters, and then Rebecca will say—when we're on the subway or in a parking lot—"That just warmed my heart."

Mine too. Last September, on my birthday, she gave me a vintage 1984 Minnesota Twins jersey, with the two fat twins shaking hands on the sleeve and Kirby Puckett's number 34 on the back. That afternoon, glazed in flop sweat, I wore it to a meadow in Central Park. Rebecca lay sunbathing when I abruptly took a knee, so that I appeared to be—while kneeling over her—attempting to administer CPR. Instead, I proposed, in the V-neck jersey of a disgraced icon. She said yes. A homeless man, immediately, offered us malt liquor from his shopping cart.

Last Saturday we were married. Among our guests was a sixteen-year-old girl from the Bronx named Natalia Orta, who had handed Rebecca that red rose six years ago. The two have been friends ever since. Last December, in New York City, Rebecca attended one of Natalia's high school basketball games. Afterward, outside the gym, Rebecca waited for Natalia. I was there too, and all I could think, on our walk to the subway, was, That just warmed my heart.

(April 21, 2003)

HOW WE GOT HERE

CHAPTER ONE

History has thrown a thunderous combination. Blacks are voting in South Africa today; Richard Nixon awaits burial tonight. In the office of the president of ABC News, nine muted televisions, recessed in a mahogany wall, monitor global events. Nine TVs, arrayed in a grid, frame the faces of Clinton, de Klerk, Mandela. They look like the Hollywood Squares of high office.

"It is so striking," says Roone Arledge, the owner of this louvered window on the world. "You look at Nelson Mandela and you look at Muhammad Ali. I can't help but see one in the other. The indomitability of spirit that both men have. You know, with the exception of the pope, Mandela may be the most famous man in the world today. Ali was that for many years."

Nixon's face pops onto a screen, like fruit in a video slot machine. True story: When Arledge was the president of ABC Sports in 1971, he hired the anvil-headed Frank Gifford away from CBS. Gifford's first assignment at ABC was to announce the Hall of Fame exhibition football game in Canton, Ohio. But when Nixon decided to drop in on the game, suddenly—horrifically—Gifford's first assignment was to interview the president.

Minutes before the broadcast Nixon told Arledge what a fan he was of the New York Giants in those days when Gifford embodied that team. In fact, when Nixon practiced law in New York, he often attended postgame parties at Giff's place. And then the president of the United States said a most curious thing to the president of ABC Sports. RN told RA: "I'm sure Frank would remember me."

Sometime in the second half of this century, sports became an axis on which the world turns. The most famous man on earth was a heavyweight fighter; the leader of the free world boasted fretfully of his friendship with Frank Freaking Gifford. Earlier this day, in his ABC office, Arledge had mentioned the name Michael Jordan, an American export as ubiquitous and profitable as Coca-Cola, and was asked how in heaven's name this had all come to be. How and when, exactly, did the globe become an NBA-licensed, Charles Barkley–signature basketball spinning madly on God's index finger?

Resplendent in a navy-blue suit, Arledge considered the question as an aide brought coffee, which was placed on a coffee table, next to a stack of coffee-table books: one on the Dalai Lama, one on Abraham Lincoln, one on Muhammad Ali.

"There have been comparable times in history when sports have been at the center of a culture and seemed to dominate the landscape," Arledge began. "Whether in Greek society or in what used to be called the golden age of sports. But everything . . . " Pause. Sip.

" . . . everything is magnified by television."

Roone Arledge returned to his coffee. And nine muted televisions fairly lit the room.

American scientists solved the conundrum in 1954. How might mankind minister to its own sustenance—without missing a minute of *Mr. Peepers*? An Omaha company developed technology by which a meal of turkey, corn-bread dressing, peas, and sweet potatoes could be frozen, boxed, sold, thawed, cooked, and safely eaten without an ounce of effort by the consumer. Swanson and Sons called this 98¢ mealsicle the "TV Dinner," to be eaten on a "TV tray," in front of, of course, the "TV." Godless Soviet scientists, meanwhile, frittered away their time developing the earth-orbiting satellite.

Nineteen fifty-four was a dizzying breakout year for television. Steve Allen starred in the network debut of *The Tonight Show* on NBC. Johnny Carson starred in the network debut of *Earn Your Vacation* on CBS. The U.S. Army and Joe McCarthy starred in the Army-McCarthy hearings on all four networks—NBC, CBS, ABC, and Dumont—as Senator Joe rooted out Reds through the riveting summer of 1954.

In that same summer Roone Pinckney Arledge Jr. was a twenty-three-year-old corporal waiting at Aberdeen (Maryland) Proving Grounds for his imminent discharge from the army, at which time he could begin to transform television, and television could transform sport into something truly stupendous. Upon graduation from Columbia University in 1952, Arledge worked briefly at Dumont, and ever since, though his duties in that job had been menial, TV had coursed through his veins.

In 1954 a New York attorney named Howard Cosell left the practice of law (and his $30,000 salary) to embark on a career in sports broadcasting (for $250 a week), despite the fact that he had turned thirty-six years old that March, his receding hairline in need of reseeding.

In 1954 a twelve-year-old child in Louisville had his red Schwinn bicycle stolen. "I'd walk out of my house at two in the morning, and look up at the sky for an angel or a revelation or God telling me what to do," the boy turned man would later tell biographer Thomas Hauser. Cassius Clay learned boxing to avenge the theft of his bike.

Soon all of these celestial events would be confluent, meeting before the world on television, which stood poised to dwarf every other communication medium by 1954. That year Jack Warner forbade the appearance of a television set in the home scenes of any Warner Bros. movie, the film industry futilely attempting to wish TV away. It was too late.

"By 1954," wrote David Halberstam in *The Powers that Be,*

there were 32 million television sets throughout the country, CBS television's gross billings doubled in that single year, and CBS became the single biggest advertising medium in the world. The real money, money and revenues beyond anyone's wildest dreams, was in television and above all in entertainment. The possibilities of nationwide advertising were beyond comprehension; afternoon newspapers quickly began to atrophy; mass-circulation magazines, which up until the early fifties had been the conduit of national mass advertising—razor blades, beer, tires, cars, household goods—were suddenly in serious trouble; within little more than a decade they would be dead or dying—*Collier's, The Saturday Evening Post, Look, Life.* Television was about to alter the nature and balance of American merchandising and journalism.

Amid all the withering print, 1954 also saw the birth of a mass-circulation magazine. The launch of *Sports Illustrated* on August 16 was especially propitious, for television, beginning almost that very year, was going to infuse sports with fabulous wealth, beam iconic images of athletes through space and around a wired world, push the Major Leagues to realize their manifest destiny in the American West, elevate interest in games to unprecedented heights, and attract the professional interest of some vastly talented men and women, not to mention Rudy Martzke.

As Corporal Arledge riffled through those first issues of SI, the magazine seemed to encompass all that interested him about sports. "It incorporated art and journalism in a way that was totally compelling," he says now, and he wondered then why TV couldn't do the same. He and friends lived a Sunday-to-Sunday existence as followers of the National Football League. Looking at photographs of these warriors, their hands gauze-wrapped like burn patients', steam clouds bursting from their mouths, he wondered why you never saw that on a telecast?

A magazine could offer a tight, clear photograph of Y. A. Tittle at the instant he stepped out of bounds. Why couldn't television? A scribe could write what he saw happening on the field, no matter how unflattering. So why couldn't a television announcer . . . tell it like it is?

Despite the wild success of its all-octogenarian talk show, *Life Begins at 80,* the Dumont network went telly-up in 1955. When the newly discharged Arledge found a job that year, it was as a stage manager at NBC, where he would soon become a producer for a Saturday-morning children's show. The program, hosted by Shari Lewis, was prophetically titled *Hi Mom,* a phrase that would resonate in NFL end zones some ten years later when Arledge took the NFL to prime time.

Hi Mom brought Arledge his first Emmy, in 1959, and within two years he was producing sports at ABC, where everything he touched turned to gold statuettes. There was really little hope of competing with him when you think back on it; after all, the man had won an Emmy producing a puppet show. What would he do with the Olympic Games?

Before he made the Olympics Olympian, fathered *Wide World of Sports, The American Sportsman, Monday Night Football, The Superstars, Nightline, 20/20, This Week with David Brinkley, Prime Time Live,* and Howard Cosell; before he pioneered and/or perfected the use of instant replay and handheld cameras and isolation cameras and sophisticated graphics and underwater video and split screens and field microphones; before he miked a dead zebra so that *Sportsman* viewers could better hear it being devoured by lions; before this ruddy-faced man named Roone fashioned a grand, safari-going, desk-dodging, expense-vouchered, limo-driven life for himself, he wrote a famous memo to his superiors at ABC telling them he was going to do all of that. The year was 1961.

Nineteen sixty-one happened also to be the year that FCC chairman Newton Minow famously called television "a vast wasteland." Television's presentation of sports, specifically, was something worse altogether.

"The prevailing attitude was summed up by baseball commissioner Ford Frick," wrote Marc Gunther and Bill Carter in their book *Monday Night Mayhem.* " 'The view a fan gets at home,' Frick once said, 'should not be any better than that of the fan in the worst seat of the ball park.'"

Turnstile-obsessed baseball owners agreed, and the networks fulfilled their wishes with primitive coverage. It would be uncharitable to say what your typical baseball owner was at the time, but it rhymed with Frick. If you wanted to see a ball game, went their shortsighted thinking, you would simply have to buy a ticket to the ballpark.

None of this mattered to ABC, which had no pro football and only a piece of baseball when Arledge arrived. But the development of videotape and the DC-8—cassettes and jets—allowed him to go "spanning the globe to bring you the constant variety of sport," which was really a fancy, Roone-ified name for auto racing.

To be fair, *Wide World of Sports* also brought heavy coverage of figure skating and gymnastics, sports that would stir a quadrennial appetite for ABC's coverage of the Olympics and vault a few female athletes into the ether of superstardom: Olga Korbut and Peggy Fleming, Nadia Comaneci and Dorothy Hamill, Mary Lou Retton and Katarina Witt, Tonya and Nancy. Nevertheless, it was a measure of television's meager interest in the Games that ABC paid $50,000 for the 1960 Winter Olympics in Squaw Valley and then skittishly reneged on the deal. But the space race was on, the cold war was at its hair-trigger, missiles-in-Cuba, shoe-pounding peak, and, says Arledge, "it became apparent with the Olympics in those days that if you had an American against a Russian, it didn't matter what they were doing, they could have been kayaking and people would watch it."

Soviet cosmonaut Yury Gagarin had been shot into space, and U.S. pilot Francis Gary Powers and his U-2 spy plane had been shot out of it. So eager were Americans to see vanquished Russkies of any athletic stripe that even twenty years later, when the host nation would finally beat the Soviets in ice hockey at Lake Placid, the United States would go bananas over a sport about which it knew precious little. The victory would be consecrated by many as the greatest sporting achievement of the second half of this century, and the moment of triumph would be punctuated by announcer Al Michaels's asking in all sincerity, "Do you believe in miracles?" The game was brought to Americans by Roone Arledge and the American Broadcasting Company, which had been serving the cold war hot for two decades.

In the mid-1960s the Olympics and a new college football package were ABC's only familiar showcases, which meant that *Wide World* lavished extraordinary attention on exotica, Arledge flying around all creation to buy the rights to anything that wasn't already owned: the 24 Hours of Le Mans, golf's British Open, the Japanese All-Star baseball game. While in Tokyo to negotiate the rights to that extravaganza, the peripatetic Arledge took in a Japanese film. The action often occurred at half speed, in the grand tradition of the bad martial-arts movie. Not for the first time Arledge wondered: Why couldn't this be done on television?

His return to New York included a layover in Los Angeles. In a bar called Julie's, Arledge asked ABC engineer Bob Trachinger how TV could become master over time itself. Trach sketched it all out on a sodden cocktail napkin—how an image could be taken off an Orthicon tube and replayed at half speed and . . .

ABC first used slow-motion instant replay on Thanksgiving Day of 1961. The most scintillating play in the game between Texas and Texas A&M was . . . a field goal. The network replayed the chip shot as if it were historic, just as they would replay the scene two Novembers later when Ruby shot Oswald. But on this November day, as Arledge recalls, "the earth did not shake."

The temblor came one weekend later. Syracuse was at Boston College, whose quarterback, Jack Concannon, scampered seventy yards for a first-half touchdown, a black-and-white streak across the television set. But when ABC replayed it, defenders could be seen clearly missing tackles, key blocks were suddenly thrown into sharp relief, and announcer Paul Christman was able to narrate every nuance of the run. The screen flickered like hell, but Concannon was balletic at half speed, and any Ban-Lon-wearing, Ballantine-swigging, Barcalounging viewer at home could see the whole field opening up before him. Look closely, and you could see much, much more. "You could see," says Arledge, "a whole new era opening up."

The National Football League was not always a vaguely sinister and monolithic American institution, something like General Motors, the single biggest advertiser on the league's Sunday-afternoon telecasts. But then came December 28, 1958, when CBS broadcast the enervating NFL championship game between the Baltimore Colts and the New York Giants, starring friend-to-Nixon Frank Gifford. From that day on NFL games would be presented as if they were somber pursuits of grave national importance.

"CBS was the paragon of professional football broadcasting," notes Arledge. "Ray Scott was its voice, and it treated every game as if it were played in a cathedral. The CBS style was very sedate, always has been: Pat Summerall followed in that tradition. But Ray Scott—Ray Scott was a voice from behind the altar."

ABC, meanwhile, began televising something called the American Football League. What was it about using the word American in its name that always seemed to render a corporation second-rate? The American Football League and the American Broadcasting Company were to the early 1960s what the American Basketball Association and the American Motors Corporation were to the 1970s, the latter two producing some ugly Pacers and seemingly little more.

Eventually, however, the underdog ABC and AFL would elevate each other. Because AFL players were largely unknown, Arledge ordered up omnipresent graphics. When Don Maynard of the New York Jets caught a pass, his name would immediately materialize on the screen. Three plays later, when he caught another pass, his name would appear again, with an interesting factoid to let you know that this was the same guy who had caught the last one and perhaps you should keep an eye on him.

"Before ESPN and CNN and talk radio, we only had the time of the game to tell all of these stories," explains Arledge as if talking about the Bronze Age. (In fact, at a production meeting on the day of Nixon's funeral in April, Arledge demanded that his staff acquire a list of everyone who would be in attendance at the ceremony in Yorba Linda. "If Alexander Haig shows up," he said, "I want to put on the screen ALEXANDER HAIG, NIXON'S CHIEF OF STAFF.") The technique of on-screen graphics began in earnest with those first ABC broadcasts of the AFL. Alas for Arledge and ABC, after four years the league sold its broadcast rights to richer NBC and then, four years later, merged with the NFL.

By 1969 the NFL had played five games on Monday nights, the first of them in 1966. All five were carried by CBS, to mediocre ratings. But with ABC the odd web out on pro football games, Arledge of necessity approached NFL commissioner Pete Rozelle about playing a game every Monday night beginning with the 1970 season. The idea had always appealed to Rozelle, who had loved the night exhibition games the Los Angeles Rams played when he was their publicist in the early fifties. "There was something special about the spotlight hitting the players when the starting lineups were announced," Rozelle has said. "It created a different aura than day football. It was decidedly more dramatic."

Once persuaded of the idea, though, Rozelle maddeningly offered the Monday-night games to his loyal networks, CBS and NBC. But CBS took a pass. They had a hit in *Mayberry RFD* on Monday nights, and besides, God intended for you to go to church on Sundays, not on Monday evenings. (And make no mistake, the NFL was church. To his lasting regret Rozelle ordered the league to play on the Sunday after the Kennedy assassination, in part because a landmark television contract was in the works and in part because the league was feeling a thou-shalt-keep-holy-the-Sabbath inviolability.)

In any event NBC, which had its popular Movie of the Week on Monday nights, also spurned the offer. So ABC had football for the fall of 1970 with one condition: Arledge insisted that he be able to choose his own announcers without interference from the NFL. Television contracts in that day called for approval of network announcers by the leagues; indeed, it had been only four years earlier that CBS broadcaster Jack Whitaker was thrown off the Masters' telecast by tournament officials for impudently calling the Augusta National gallery a "mob." But Rozelle agreed to give a free hand to Arledge, and the first person Arledge hired for his new *Monday Night Football* was Howard Cosell.

A few years earlier Arledge had signed Cosell to appear as a boxing analyst on *Wide World* and to cover the sport at the 1968 Olympics. Cosell instantly seized a high profile with his interviews of Muhammad Ali, whom Cosell insisted on calling . . . Muhammad Ali. This was deemed outrageous and deliberately provocative, even though Muhammad Ali was the man's legal name and had been for four years. "We've forgotten how weird some people's opinions were," says Arledge. Indeed, when ABC asked Ali—who had been stripped of his heavyweight title for resisting the Vietnam draft—to commentate on its boxing coverage, it did so despite warnings against the idea from the U.S. State Department.

In those first giddy days following those first Monday nights, Arledge had to dance a conga to his desk, sidestepping bushels of letters and telegrams tottering in piles throughout his office. He could peel one off a stack at random and invariably the missive would read, "Get him off the air!" Of course, "him" was Cosell, who later estimated that half of his mail began with the cheery salutation "You nigger-loving Jew bastard . . . "

The essence of the outcry was clear. "We were desecrating something," says Arledge. "CBS had Ray Scott, and now we had this loudmouthed Howard on TV questioning everything, yelling about what a dumb trade that was, and asking, 'Don't football players have rights?' And a lot of the owners just couldn't deal with it."

It was clear, too, that television could create a collective national experience, could unite a country in something, if only in its distaste for this toupeed boor spouting polysyllables in a broadcast booth. By the fall of 1971, thirty million viewers were tuning in to ABC on Monday nights.

With those kinds of numbers, it became a fait accompli. Within four years the World Series was made a primarily prime-time affair, and by 1978 the Super Bowl had also encroached on that rarefied space. Don't blame television or him, says Arledge; blame baseball and football owners: "Because they want to get more money, and the way to get more money is to play your games in prime time."

Sure, advertising dollars were wallpapering the networks' Sixth Avenue offices as well, but before long those dollars would return to the NFL as ten-dollar bills. CBS paid $14 million a year to televise the NFL in 1964 and '65. By 1982 the three networks paid a combined $2.1 billion to televise NFL games for five years. By 1990 five networks paid $3.6 billion for three years. And in 1993 Rupert Murdoch and the Fox network paid $1.58 billion for the rights to televise just the National Football Conference for four years.

Football would be played no more in the CBS cathedral but in a Fox-hole where coverage will likely owe more to ABC and

Arledge. In 1974, when he hired Fred (the Hammer) Williamson to briefly join the *Monday Night* lineup—a position that in 1983 would be filled by a more glamorous football entity, O. J. Simpson—Arledge noticed, on a chain around the Hammer's neck, a clenched black fist and a solid-gold penis, two items of jewelry seldom worn by Ray Scott of the CBS television network.

His ABC press-kit biography used to end with the unbecoming (and highly dubious) boast that Roone Arledge holds the records "for shooting the largest leopard and Cape buffalo—the latter considered the most dangerous animal in the world—on an African safari." How could anyone know that those two animals were the largest of their kind ever shot on an African safari? As for that clause between dashes—"the most dangerous animal in the world"—it seems a rather subjective and gratuitous flourish, does it not?

Arledge has occasionally been accused of creating yards of his legend from whole cloth. Tony Verna, a former director at CBS, will tell you that he and his network were first on the air with slow-motion instant replay, on an Army-Navy football telecast on New Year's Eve in 1964, though the historical record is obstinately unclear on the matter.

Certainly Arledge has known virtually every world leader and athletic giant of our time as head of the News and Sports divisions at ABC, and his is the world's grandest TV résumé. Even among his myriad achievements, one stands above all as the Cape buffalo of his accomplishments. It happened in Munich in 1972.

Arledge produced ten Olympics, and they are collectively the pride of his twenty-five years at ABC Sports. But the prices were dear, and he can tick off each of them to this day: Innsbruck in 1964 cost $250,000. Mexico City in 1968 cost $3 million, and that one really got to him. His colleagues thumped him on the back after he won the rights to those Games, but Arledge felt like vomiting. "Why are you congratulating me?" he asked. He was sick and remorseful, bedeviled by the buyer's guilt you and I might get after shelling out for a Chevette.

Munich ran $13.5 million, and four years later the '76 Games in Montreal cost $25 million, and suddenly it was all insane. "It used to be in those days," says Arledge, "that you'd rebuild an entire city if you had the Olympic Games." Montreal got new roads, a refurbished infrastructure, and a soon-to-be-domed stadium for its two weeks before the world.

Still, there were two sticking points with the Montreal Olympic Organizing Committee as Arledge was negotiating the rights to those Games in the middle of a Quebec night. The MOOC-a-mucks demanded 1) that Cosell not be assigned to the Olympics and 2) that no mention be made of the Munich Games in ABC's coverage of the opening ceremonies.

Arledge calmly responded with a question of his own, not out of anger but with a bemused, almost clinical detachment: "Are you out of your minds?"

The Montreal rights had drawn such a high price precisely because of what had happened in Munich. For starters, the 1972 Games had been the first to take over the whole of a network's prime-time schedule. (The Mexico City Games had been shunted to ABC's worst time-slot ghettos.) What's more, those Olympics had been a riveting athletic success. When they were over, Mark Spitz had more gold hanging from his neck than Fred (the Hammer) Williamson, and the U.S. men's basketball team had had its own gold stolen by those villainous, still-invincible emissaries from the Evil Empire in an epic final.

Yet the lower-case games themselves had become but a jot on history's seismograph after the events of September 5, when eleven Israeli athletes were taken hostage by Palestinian terrorists in the athletes' village at 4:30 that morning.

Jim McKay, ABC's Olympic studio host, was preparing to take a dip in the hotel pool on his only day off in the fortnight when he was summoned to duty. He would be on the air for the next eighteen hours, anchoring field coverage from Cosell and from Peter Jennings, the network's Beirut correspondent, who was in Munich for the Games.

Citizens of the world sat gathered around their televisions, the electronic hearth hissing and spitting bad news like sparks. In the end even some relatives of the hostages themselves received the sickening news from McKay, who, wearied and wan, could say little more than, "They're all gone."

Within a day Arledge and his staff had produced a forty-minute instant documentary on the murders, featuring reaction from Willy Brandt and the Munich chief of police and members of the Israeli Knesset and Golda Meir. He was puzzled when, Rozelle-like, Avery Brundage ordered the Games to go on that day; he was puzzled, likewise, when ABC News told him it did not want his documentary, that this was somehow still about sports. So Arledge moved all of his commercial spots in that day's Olympic programming to the beginning and middle of his show and ran the damn documentary in his own time, forty minutes uninterrupted at the end of the Olympic program. And don't think he forgot the slight when he took over last-place ABC News (in addition to Sports) in 1978 and made it the More-Americans-Get-Their-News-from-ABC-News-Than-from-Any-Other-Source king of Broadcast Row.

Arledge's coverage from Munich "changed television itself," wrote Gunther and Carter. "From then on, whenever a catastrophe struck, viewers no longer were content to wait for film at eleven; they expected television to afford them a chance to be eyewitnesses to history." In short, these "viewers" were about to become voyeurs, a phenomenon that would seem to reach its apocalyptic apotheosis on a Friday night in the summer of 1994 when ninety-five million Americans stayed tuned to several networks to see if O. J. Simpson would commit suicide on the San Diego Freeway.

ABC won twenty-nine Emmys for its Munich production. Even the president of archenemy CBS, ABC's own evil empire, approached Arledge at a post-Olympics luncheon in New York and congratulated him, something that just doesn't happen on the graceless weasel farm of network television. "It was," Bob Wood told Arledge, "like the nation was reading the same book together."

You can hear it. Power thrums through the corridors like traffic through the streets of Gotham, five stories below. Roone Arledge became president of ABC News exclusively in 1986, and from his elegant office here he can now look at sports as a father might look at somewhat disappointing children who have left the nest.

He sat by, gaping like the rest of us, as CBS overpaid for baseball by half a billion dollars in 1990. He calls the NFL's most recent television contract "a stroke of luck," after watching the league stuff Rupert Murdoch's money down its pants like a frenzied participant in a Dash for Dollars contest.

Arledge worries that these price tags may one day hang like toe tags on American sports. "The basic ill in sports today has got to be money," he says, "and it's ultimately going to corrupt everything. You have owners who can't control themselves giving all this money to players. You have twenty-five-year-old kids making several million dollars a year and thinking they're entitled to it. They argue that rock stars and movie stars make that kind of money, and they're performers just like athletes are. But I would like to think there's a difference between an athlete and a rock star. Unfortunately, it may well be that as new generations come along, they won't miss the virtues that used to be at the center of sport. They may see sports only as a means to a sneaker deal."

With all these chickens coming home to roost, doesn't this television executive feel a little like Harlan Sanders? Arledge acknowledges his and TV's place in "the feeding chain." But network execs—and team owners and athletes, for that matter—are entrepreneurs who can do as they please. Arledge makes $3 million annually, but he also made his sports division, traditionally a loss leader for a network, eminently profitable.

It is state-sponsored sports fanaticism that he finds particularly vexing, all of these modern-day ancient Romes across America, obsessed with gladiators and lavish Colosseums. Think of all that a new NFL team will do for Charlotte, Arledge says—wonderful, inestimable things—but think also of all that a new NFL team will not do for that city.

"I think a question that has to be asked is, In a time of poverty and homelessness and crime and all the other problems this society has, should we be building four-hundred-million-dollar stadiums with public funds?" he says. "In most cases these stadiums are publicly financed but privately profitable. And there are very few other places where that is true. It is not true of the Metropolitan Opera. We are notorious in this country for not subsidizing the arts and politics and things that we should. And yet, we do it in sports without even thinking about it. In fact, it's a hall-mark. If you don't do it, you're somehow second-rate."

In other words, you're not . . . major league. Up-and-coming cities need Major League franchises to be considered major league, and they need gleaming new stadiums to attract the franchises. It is the magical mantra of the film *Field of Dreams*: If you build it, they will come. One man understood this better than any other. Nobody built a bigger field from bigger dreams than Judge Roy Hofheinz, who was himself as big as all of Texas.

CHAPTER TWO

The Judge smoked twenty-five cigars a day, great tobacco-filled dirigibles that befit a man of his dimensions: the fifty-seven-inch waistline, the cuff links as big and loud as cymbals, the long Cadillac limousine in which he drove himself through Houston. It was said that Judge Roy Hofheinz could not find a chauffeur willing to work his hours, which were roughly the same as a 7-Eleven's.

Sleep, and you cannot graduate from high school at sixteen (as the Judge did), pass the Texas bar at nineteen, be elected to the state legislature at twenty-two and to the judgeship of Houston's Harris County at twenty-four. To the Judge life was a Whitman's Sampler of possibilities. He devoured the legal profession, poli-tics, the slag industry, real estate, radio, television, and professional sports—licking his fingers clean of each career before plucking out a new one.

The son of a laundry-truck driver, Hofheinz was also at vari-ous times Lyndon Johnson's campaign manager, the mayor of Houston, the builder of the Astrodome, and the owner of the Ringling Bros. and Barnum & Bailey Circus. The last two roles best suited the Judge's personality, though a Houston contempo-rary named Willard Walbridge once found it insufficient to equate Hofheinz with P. T. Barnum. Said Walbridge, "He made P. T. Barnum look like fourteen miles of bad road."

Thus in the early 1960s, when the Judge was planning sport's first domed stadium, he insisted that the dugouts be an extravagant

120 feet long. This was done not as a pioneering concession to player comfort but so that as many ticket buyers as possible could be obliged when they asked for seats behind the dugout.

When those seats, fully upholstered, theater-style, were installed, their various colors formed a garish palette that the Judge (whose garb ran to canary-yellow pants and test-pattern blazers) thought profoundly beautiful. "I'm inclined to think the Lord agrees with me a little bit," he explained, "'cause I've never seen the flowers of the fields all one color." It is instructive to note that the Lord agreed with the Judge, not the other way around.

After all, it was the Judge, not the Lord, who carved out the modern physical landscape of professional sports, a terrain blistered by domes and green with the fungus of artificial turf. Both were the brainchildren of Judge Roy Hofheinz.

Even as baseball emerges from the architectural dark ages of the 1960s and '70s, marked by the blight of the multipurpose stadium, and begins once again building traditional parks like Camden Yards and The Ballpark in Arlington, these—and all big-time sports stadiums and arenas constructed today—are designed around the luxury skybox and the elaborate electronic scoreboard. Both are the intellectual offspring of the Judge, who changed the very way Americans attend their games.

"We combined baseball with a cocktail party," says Fred Hofheinz, fifty-six, the Judge's younger son, himself a former mayor of Houston and his father's right-hand man in the first years of the Astrodome. "You can wander around your box with a drink in your hand and sell some guy some insurance. And I promise you, there are people all over sports now who never look at the sports event. The whole time, they're selling. I was at a Rockets game last Saturday, and I don't even remember who won."

On an April night in 1965, the Astros flew from their spring training home in Cocoa, Florida, to Houston, where they bused directly to the brand-new Astrodome to drop off equipment. Larry Dierker, an eighteen-year-old rookie pitcher on that club, bounded from the clubhouse into the concourse-level seats that night, taking in the multiple miracles before him: the air-conditioning, the grass growing indoors (artificial turf was not laid until the following year), the translucent roof (greenhouse by day, a planetarium by night)—the whole otherworldly quality of this $32 million marvel on the Texas prairie. To this day, Dierker recalls the moment exactly. "It was," he says, "like walking into the next century."

As the story of Los Angeles begins with irrigation, so the story of the Astrodome begins with air-conditioning. Willis H. Carrier was the Edison of the air conditioner, a mechanical engineer who predicted in 1939 that man would soon live beneath climate-controlled bubbles, with God powerless to impose weather on his creatures. To many of his contemporaries, Willis H. Carrier was, well, downright daft.

But was he? The globe is now goitered with domed stadiums, everywhere from Tokyo to Toronto. In Carrier's native upstate New York, Syracuse Orangemen play basketball and football in the Carrier Dome, an eponym that suggests Carrier was right after all. He was right. But it was the Judge who made good on the prophecy.

Roy Mark Hofheinz began relieving Texans from the sun—and of their money—as a nine-year-old during Prohibition, when he set up a refreshment stand in his front yard, displaying a hand-lettered sign that read NEAR BEER SOLD HERE, BUT NO BEER SOLD NEAR HERE. He was still cooling customers in the 1970s, when his AstroWorld amusement park hummed with the sound of that ultimate Texas extravagance: it had outdoor air-conditioning.

At home in the dead of a Houston summer, the Judge would often turn his own AC up high enough to frost the family room; when he had the house feeling like a refrigerated boxcar, he would build a fire in the fireplace and bask in its crackling warmth.

Yes, sir, air-conditioning could bring Christmas in July. So together with Houston oilman R. E. (Bob) Smith, who had a bigger pile than God, the visionary Judge decided to build the world's largest air-conditioned indoor shopping complex, just off Westheimer Road in Houston. That was the late fifties. The word today is *mall*.

About that time a group of local investors was trying to land a Major League Baseball team for Houston. Frustrated in its efforts, the group began planning a third big league, the Continental League. "This was the heyday in ownership profitability, in control of ballplayers," Fred Hofheinz points out. "The reserve clause was still in place. Most baseball clubs were privately held by rich individuals. Baseball was a club—an inside club. And the Continental League was designed to put pressure on everybody to expand the American and National leagues."

In little more than a decade, baseball's reserve clause would be challenged by Curt Flood of the St. Louis Cardinals, and the mahoganied country club of owners in the other three major professional sports would be gate-crashed by a couple of California hepcats named Gary Davidson and Dennis Murphy. But in 1960 the baseball establishment forestalled these events by simply allowing two more members beyond the red velvet ropes, granting National League franchises to New York and Houston. The latter team would be called the Colt .45s. And the Colts would be owned by Judge Roy Hofheinz, who abandoned his plans for a shopping mall when he alighted on a better, more colossal use for the cool, gentle breezes stirred by the man-made miracle of air-conditioning.

Understand that the Judge blew a lot of smoke, and not all of it came from a lighted corona. He always said that he was inspired to build the Astrodome after a visit to Rome with his wife, Dene. "Mama and I were standing there looking at the Colosseum," he would say of the ancient arena, which was at times roofed by a tarplike velarium in inclement weather. "It was a large, round facility, and most of the stadiums in the U.S. had been built to conform to the shape of the playing fields. Rectangular."

And, indeed, the Astrodome would be round, built to fit baseball and football and basketball and boxing and tractor pulls and concerts and what-have-you. So would the four undomed ballparks that would follow rapid-fire in the late 1960s and early 1970s: the abominations of Busch Stadium in St. Louis, Riverfront Stadium in Cincinnati, Veterans Stadium in Philadelphia, and Three Rivers Stadium in Pittsburgh. Those parks are called octorads, or rounded rectangles, and it was precisely that kind of esoterica—architectural and otherwise—that had a dead-bolt lock on the Judge's imagination.

For his intellect was as sharp as the crease in his trousers. The Judge wore a gold watch, but it concealed a tiny slide rule, which says a lot about the man. "I remember vividly a stack of books on the kitchen table," says Fred. "All of them about domes."

Convinced that man could raise a dome higher than man could hit a baseball, the Judge and Bob Smith purchased 494 acres of scrubland, empty save for a lone mesquite tree, from the Hilton Hotel Corporation. The city had already planned fourteen lanes of freeway to run past the site, and ground was broken for the Harris County Domed Stadium, to be opened in 1965. For three seasons the Colt .45s would play outdoors in a temporary, low-budget ballpark called Colt Stadium. By day fans would be hotter than bejesus and by night would be buzzed by Cessna-sized mosquitoes.

The name Colt .45s evoked the old Houston, whereas the Judge was looking to help shape the new, Space Age city, which was already home to NASA. So he telephoned a friend, astronaut Alan Shepard, one evening in the winter of 1964 and asked him if the Mercury Seven crew would like a ball club named for them. Of course, replied Shepard, who was such a sports fanatic that he would carry golf clubs to the moon on his trip there in 1971.

Thus the Colt .45s would become the Astronauts, a name the Judge preemptively clipped to Astros, knowing that newspaper-headline writers would do so anyway. (Defiantly, newspaper headline writers briefly referred to the Astros as the 'Tros, and to this day they are often the 'Stros.) The Harris County Domed Stadium would become the Astrodome, and the Judge would become master of what he called his Astrodomain: the Astrodome and the Astros, the Astrolite scoreboard and the Astrotots puppet theater, the Astro-Bowl bowling alley and the AstroWorld amusement park and the AstroHall exhibition arena. They were enough to make you AstroSick, but the names took root.

The Astrodome was paid for with municipal bonds, but the Judge built fifty-three luxury boxes with $2 million out of his own silken pocket. "It was done," says Fred, "to attract people who used baseball games as a backdrop to sell their products." And the Judge could sell nasal spray to the noseless. When players refused to appear on the Astros' pregame radio show because they weren't receiving watches or lube jobs or golf shirts or gift certificates in compensation, the Judge made an impassioned clubhouse speech to his charges: "Radio is the only link that a blind man has to his beloved Astros, for God's sake, and . . . "

"I don't even remember what-all he said," recalls Dierker, "but for weeks after, players were lining up to do that show."

So the Judge had no trouble renting his luxury boxes, which he said were inspired by, of course, a trip to the Colosseum. "I found out that the emperor and all the bigwigs sat at the top of the stadium," he used to say. The truth is, the bigwigs did not sit at the top of the Colosseum, and the Judge did not set foot in the old arena until 1967, when he flew to Rome to purchase the circus from John Ringling North.

For publicity purposes the papers were signed in the historic showplace. When the Judge's photo-opportunists tried to move a large stone into the picture, Colosseum guards went berserk. The stone had been in place for two thousand years, having been laid there by the emperor Vespasian.

When the Astrodome opened for its first exhibition baseball game, on April 9, 1965, it was proclaimed the world's single largest air-conditioned space. When the first home run was hit that day, by Mickey Mantle, of all people, the 474-foot-long scoreboard flashed TILT! If an Astro hit a homer, on the other hand, the scoreboard (with the world's largest screen) would produce a smoke-snorting bull, American and Texas flags flying from its horns like the flags on the fenders of a presidential limousine. (All of which would soon prompt Chicago Cub manager Leo Durocher to say, portentously, "Houston is bush.") On this day of the first exhibition, in fact, the president himself was in rapt attendance; the Judge's close friend Lyndon Johnson watched the 'Tros beat the Yanks 2–1.

"There was a mania to get inside the Dome that first year," says Astrodomophile Chuck Pool, a former Astro publicist who is now media-relations director for the Florida Marlins. "There was a Boy Scout Circus in the Dome in 1965. Ordinarily the Scouts would sell fifty thousand tickets for these things, but maybe three thousand people would attend. People bought tickets as a donation. But in 1965 they sold sixty thousand tickets, and everyone with a ticket showed up to watch the Boy Scouts, with thousands more outside screaming to get in."

Sixty thousand people paid to watch a Webelo tie a slipknot. Millions of tourists would pay a dollar apiece to enter the Dome and watch nothing at all. Fifty-three thousand would watch UCLA and Houston—Lew Alcindor versus Elvin Hayes—play on January 20, 1968, the night college basketball came of age. And nineteen million worldwide watched five years later as Billie Jean King and Bobby Riggs caricatured the battle of the sexes by playing a preposterous tennis match in the Astrodome.

While King's 6–4, 6–3, 6–3 victory that night was trumpeted as a sporting milestone, her triumph would prove fleeting, as two decades later only a handful of women in golf, tennis, and Olympic sports would be able to match the handsome incomes of their male counterparts. Yet on this night of spectacle in the Dome, King made her testosteroned tormentor look ridiculous.

Nothing was quite so ridiculous, though, as that week the Astrodome opened, when baseballs fell like baseball-sized hail on the Astros and the Yankees and the Baltimore Orioles and the Philadelphia Phillies. The Dome's translucent roof panels created such a glare during day games that Baltimore's Boog Powell took the field in a batting helmet. The league tried different-colored balls— red, yellow, cerise—to combat the problem, which was basically this: The Astros were in danger of becoming the first team to call a game on account of sunshine.

The club immediately painted over the roof panels, banishing sunlight. "And that was the death knell for grass," says Fred. The grass, Tifway 419 Bermuda, had been specially developed by scientists in Tifton, Georgia. But without sunlight the grass was going, going, gone. And yet the death knell for Tifway 419 Bermuda would be the life knell for another kind of turf being developed by scientists at Monsanto—as well as the life knell for knee surgeons for decades to come.

For the remainder of the 1965 season, the Judge simply painted over the dead grass and dirt in his outfield, mixed in some sawdust, and called it grass, though it was essentially a sandlot.

"I think he suspected all along that the grass wouldn't work," says Pool. "Artificial turf was developed in '64 through a Ford Foundation study that indicated city kids entering the army had lower coordination than suburban and rural kids. The study concluded that it was because city kids had no play areas. The first artificial turf was installed at Moses Brown Playground in Providence. And Hofheinz had installed a patch at spring training in '65."

Before sealing the deal to introduce artificial turf into the year-old Astrodome, the Judge procured a thirty-foot-long sample of the wonder-stuff from Monsanto, installed it at old Colt Stadium, and assaulted the surface in sundry Hofheinzian ways that would never have occurred to the manufacturer. Among the durability tests administered by Hofheinz: Rented elephants urinated on the nylon rug while trampling over it—approximating the kind of abuse a Lenny Dykstra might one day deliver to the surface.

In March 1966 carpet was laid in the Dome. In the first Major League Baseball game played on AstroTurf, a Los Angeles Dodger rookie named Don Sutton got his first Major League win. The Astro starter was Robin Roberts, who was headed for the Hall of Fame, and it appeared that AstroTurf was headed there as well. Busch Stadium in St. Louis, which opened later that year, would forsake grass in 1970 for low-maintenance AstroTurf. By 1973 five more stadiums would have synthetic surfaces, and AstroTurf welcome mats would join lawn jockeys and pink flamingos as staples of American exterior decorating.

As would be expected of a man who knows where to rent an incontinent elephant, the Judge traveled widely in life. The 1970 stroke that left him in a wheelchair (until his death, in 1982, at age seventy) did little to slow him. No, the Judge smoked life down to the butt end, as if it were one of his Sans Souci Perfectos, the cigars he snuffed out in gold ashtrays shaped like upturned fielder's gloves.

Aides would simply carry the Judge up to the Parthenon, like the potentate he was, on a visit to Athens. Like Lord Elgin, the Judge assembled all sorts of curiosa—unsightly statuary, antique furniture, garish baubles—to cart back to Texas. The crates piled up at his Houston homes, not unlike in the last scene of *Citizen Kane*.

"I'm surprised they haven't made a movie about this man," says Pool. "He was truly larger than life. At the end he had grown a beard and looked like Orson Welles. And his voice, it had this . . . riveting intensity."

What was the epigraph that began *Kane*?

"In Xanadu did Kubla Khan, a stately pleasure dome decree . . ." The Judge had moved into his Dome following the death of Dene in 1966, into his famously sybaritic apartment above the right center field–pavilion seats.

Behind the odd-shaped windows the Judge lived for eight years, surrounded by a billiard parlor, and a minigolf course, and a beauty salon, and a barber shop, and an interfaith chapel, and a children's library, and a presidential suite reserved for LBJ, and bathrooms with gilded toilet seats.

The Judge had another sometime residence, the Celestial Suites at the AstroWorld Hotel. A bathtub there was so large, it required an indoor-pool permit. In fact, the $3,000-a-night Celestial Suites penthouse was listed in *The Guinness Book of World Records* as the planet's most expensive hotel room. Elvis stayed there, though rumor has it that he found the place, decorated with the detritus of the Judge's European shopping sprees, too gaudy.

On weekends the Judge relaxed at his bayfront retreat, called Huckster House. The great man unwound there by clanging a locomotive bell he kept in the front yard, ringing the thing like Quasimodo at ungodly hours of the night "just to let the neighbors know we're around."

Alas, it is all lost now: Huckster House, the Celestial Suites, the apartment at the Astrodome. Pool took the media through the Judge's chambers for one last tour before the Astros gutted the residence in 1988. It had been fifteen years since the Judge lived in the Dome, but parts of his crib remained spookily intact. Pool, rummaging through the rooms alone, opened one door in the dark, flipped on a light, and was greeted by a disembodied head falling off a shelf. It was the overstuffed noggin of Chester Charge, the Astros' first mascot.

It is all lost now, but in its day the Judge's Astrodomain was a spectacle the likes of which the world had never seen, nor will likely ever want to see again. "I've stayed in some pretty good places," columnist Art Buchwald said after a night in the Celestial Suites, "but nothing quite so ridiculous as that joint."

There will never be another Judge. There will never be another Dome. French ambassador Herve Alphand visited Houston in 1965 and compared the steel-girdered roof of the Astrodome to the Eiffel Tower. "The Eiffel Tower is nice," agreed the Judge, "but you can't play ball there."

They all came: Bob Hope and Billy Graham. Buchwald and Buckminster Fuller. Lyndon and Lady Bird. Huntley and Brinkley. Princess Grace and Prince Rainier. When the (Astro)world was young, a Houston Astro might meet anyone upon arrival each day at the park.

On the eve of the 1967 Houston Champion International golf tournament, there was a pregame closest-to-the-pin contest. Various Astros drove golf balls from home plate to a flagstick in center field, competing against a team composed of PGA veterans and . . . Lawrence Welk. "I can still remember, [Astro infielder] Doug Rader kept calling Lawrence Welk Larry," recalls Dierker wistfully. "Hey, Larry . . . " The Astros were brash and young, and expected to remain so forever.

But time passes. Huntley and Brinkley split up, Princess Grace was killed in a car wreck, and sometime in there the Astrodome went flat, like a sunken soufflé. The Camelot optimism that ushered in the 1960s—that ushered in the Astrodome—had long before gone flat, like old champagne. Or the champagne music of Larry Welk.

The erstwhile Eighth Wonder of the World is now another dreary pitcher's park, albeit one that gave us fake grass and turf toe and rug burn and corporate boxes and those infernal cartoon clapping hands that tell us when to cheer. Happily, the legacy of the Astrodome is more than that, as the legacy of the 1960s is more than Vietnam and assassinations.

"I think what has happened to professional sports since 1960 is what I call the gentrification of it," says Fred Hofheinz, who chooses his words carefully, as if selecting tomatoes at the market, turning each possibility over in his head before speaking. "Up until then, there were sports fans and there were sports pages and a lot of people who followed sports. But beginning about the time that my dad and other promoters around the country became involved—with the advent of television—sports became something that everybody followed.

"Enormous new markets opened up, and the Dome was part of that. If you were to go to a Houston Buffs minor league game, you would have seen the die-hard fans, the people who kept scorecards and read the box scores every morning. That guy was in the minority at the Dome. At the Dome the wives came. The children came. Suddenly it was a whole new milieu of fans. The Dome greatly broadened sports' appeal for these people. In Houston it became a social event to go to the Astrodome. Women went to the Astrodome in heels!"

Indeed, the Judge created an entire press box for women society-page writers. The "hen coop" produced Astrodome stories that turned on such questions as "Is it proper for a man to wear his hat indoors?" Of course, the hats in question were cowboy hats, this being Texas; other American men had stopped wearing snap-brimmed fedoras to ball games (or anyplace else) after John Kennedy went bare-noggined on Inauguration Day in 1961.

Let the word go forth. The 1960s were to herald a new, hatless era. The Space Age. In Living Color. If the new decade wasn't exactly a new century, well, you could see a new century from there—from a concourse at the Astrodome in Houston, Texas. That city, it should not be forgotten, would fairly redeem the violent 1960s, just 165 days before the decade expired, by landing Americans on the moon with a bronze plaque. WE CAME IN PEACE FOR ALL MANKIND

As for the stadium named for the astronauts: When the Judge was still living in his famously sybaritic apartment above the right-field bleachers, an electrician named Don Collins had cause to work in the Astrodome at all hours. In the middle of some nights, in the vast, empty, dark arena, Collins could look up to a window of the

Hofheinz residence and see only the glowing ember of a cigar, floating there like a firefly, high above the synthetic playing field.

The Judge is gone from this life some twelve years now, but the ember still glows, a spectral stogie. Its blue smoke hangs like a spirit above every arena in the land.

CHAPTER THREE

Gary Davidson has a lot of balls: gold-and-orange-striped footballs that flew like kited checks in the World Football League, and red-white-and-blue basketballs whose pigmented leather was hard to grip in the American Basketball Association. He has dark-blue hockey pucks held over from the World Hockey Association, smart little slabs of rubber that look alarmingly like those urinal-disinfectant cakes.

To be fair, Davidson had originally lobbied for a less subtle fire-engine-red puck for his new WHA to use, but that notion was angrily shot down by the general manager of the Alberta (eventually Edmonton) Oilers, Wild Bill Hunter. "That is the most ridiculous thing I've ever seen," Hunter said when first affronted by the proposed scarlet puck. "Our players will never be able to see that puck."

Why not?

"Because," said Wild Bill, "they'll be looking for a black one."

The word *ridiculous* comes up often when speaking of the spawn of Gary Davidson, who made his way through only slightly fewer leagues than Jules Verne and turned out more acronyms than the New Deal of Franklin Roosevelt. This is the man who was the first president of the ABA, a cofounder of the WHA, and the founder of the WFL. In the 1970s Davidson's rebel leagues were designed to be the mod alternative to the square professional sports establishment, or at least the 1974 WFL media guide would have you believe that. "The Detroit Wheels are a 'now' team," grooved the guide. "The World Football League's 12 teams are 'where it's at.'" When the Wheels later went defunct, Detroit was somehow . . . de-funked.

It wasn't just the Wheels. Most of Davidson's teams and all of his leagues would eventually go south, metaphorically emulating the Toronto Northmen of the WFL, who became the Memphis Southmen before playing the first game in their unspeakable "Burnt Orange and Old Gold." But while the leagues lived fast, they also died young, leaving creditors and historians to sort through the bad checks and ridiculous nicknames left behind. (It is doubly instructive that one of the first checks ever written to the WHA was the initiation fee for the Miami Screaming Eagles. It bounced.)

The leagues were sublimely ridiculous from day one, literally from the moment that the formation of the ABA was announced in 1967. Davidson's autobiography is entitled *Breaking the Game Wide Open*. He calls it "a terrible book," and indeed it has more dead spots than the floor of the Boston Garden. But the book's account of the press conference held to launch the ABA, at New York's ultratony Hotel Carlyle, is enlightening.

"The buffet was loaded with delicacies of every description," Davidson wrote. "The whiskey flowed like water. A free ABA basketball was given to every writer and broadcaster in the place. Naked dancing girls circulated everywhere—well, they weren't really naked, and they weren't really dancing girls, but you get the idea. I don't know what they were or what they were doing there. . . . We spent $35,000 and we got a circus for our money. Everyone had fun, but no one took us seriously. It was a joke, and it made us look ridiculous."

It also made them look prophetic. You want to know what the most ridiculous thing was about Gary Davidson and his rebel leagues? It was this: In many ways, they weren't ridiculous at all.

"Gary Davidson," noted *Sports Illustrated* in 1975, "has been one of the most influential figures in the history of professional sport."

"What man, more than any other, has had the greatest impact on professional sports in America?" asked an editorial in *The Sporting News* in 1977. "You'd have to say Gary Davidson." In the months that passed between those two pronouncements, sports were undergoing a Davidsonic boom, and yet the name Gary Davidson, to hear it now, has little resonance for Joe Fan.

He was a Ted Turner who colorized the games even as he terrorized the existing salary structures. He and a team of fellow attorneys unshackled athletes from their restrictive contracts in the established National leagues: the NHL, the NFL, and the NBA, the last a league whose average player salary quadrupled, to $109,000, during the ABA's nine-year life span. In the Davidson lexicon, those leagues and the three TV networks made up the professional sports establishment. "Never met Roone," Davidson says, "because I was never part of the establishment."

Of course, Davidson also helped professional sport to establish itself, to realize its manifest destiny in North America. He spread franchises like fertilizer to all corners of the continent as he scattered his sales pitches (like fertilizer) to prospective owners in San Antonio and Winnipeg and Indianapolis, cities that became major league the instant a local millionaire industrialist said yes to Davidson's alluring offer of sporting eminence.

This is the primary legacy of Davidson's leagues. "A lot of new cities that had never had teams proved they could carry teams," says Tim Grandi, the former associate general counsel for the WFL. "And certainly, whether Gary intended it or not, players acquired new freedoms and prosperity that didn't previously exist. He wasn't Moses, but he did take control of professional sports away from a clique of owners and opened it up to more people and more cities."

"Walter O'Malley and Horace Stoneham are viewed as being extremely important in the evolution of modern pro sports," says Max Muhleman, a former vice president of the WFL. "What they did was induce other owners to view the sporting landscape in much larger terms. I can see a lot of that in what Gary Davidson did."

"I was probably responsible for more benefits to the players than Pete Rozelle or any other commissioner," Davidson says quietly today, "but I don't think that that will come up much anymore."

It won't come up because Davidson has been forgotten. His was a colorful streak across the 1970s sky, but one that ultimately fell short, like Evel Knievel at the Snake River Canyon. And yet his improbable story is worth reviving. Raised by a divorced mother, he worked his way through his first year of UCLA Law by picking up freshly murdered corpses at the coroner's office while on the night shift of an L.A. mortuary. Not many years after graduation, having established himself as a tax and finance attorney in Orange County, Davidson got in on the ground floor of something called the American Basketball Association. Once again, and for many years to come, Gary Davidson would be working with stiffs.

"In the 1950s," Davidson notes in his autobiography, "men who had been unable to obtain major league franchises formed the Continental League. It never got off the ground, but the threat of it forced expansion which brought some of the Continental League members into baseball's major leagues."

Spectator sports never much interested Davidson. Professional leagues captured his imagination only when he realized they could be used as a Hofheinzian financial lever. Only then did he find fifty ways to love his lever.

As the Continental League gave us the New York Mets and the Houston Astros, so are Davidson's rebel leagues responsible for the Edmonton Oilers and the Denver Nuggets and the Hartford Whalers and the Indiana Pacers and the Quebec Nordiques and the San Antonio Spurs and the Winnipeg Jets and the New Jersey Nets; for three-point shots and goalposts in the back of the end zone; for Julius Erving and Wayne Gretzky.

Wayne Gretzky. Davidson had never seen a hockey game until he cofounded the World Hockey Association in 1971. Before the league began play in '72, three potential franchise owners visited California from the hockey Holy Land, Canada. The idea was to get better acquainted with the thirty-seven-year-old Davidson and his forty-five-year-old colleague, Dennis Murphy—who had founded the ABA—by attending a Los Angeles Kings game with them.

"I'll never forget," says Murphy. "We're all sitting there in a row, the game is about to start, and the linesman goes to center ice and is about to drop the puck when Gary says, 'What are they doing?'"

Wild Bill Hunter, a profane, white-haired frontiersman who conjured images of Yosemite Sam, looked at Murphy and barked, "Who the hell is this guy?"

"Later," says Murphy, "Gary would fall asleep during the game. But in fairness to him, he never purported to know anything about hockey."

Well, he purported to know something. When the WHA named Camille Henry, a former star with the New York Rangers, to be coach of its New York Raiders, Davidson made the announcement at a press conference in Manhattan. He confidently began, "I'd like to welcome Henry Camille . . . "

As waves of laughter washed up to the podium, Davidson reddened like one of his prototype pucks. "No, no," he pleaded with the media hyenas, desperate to correct his mistake. "I mean . . . Hank. Hank Camille!"

The whole point was to make money, and to make money you had to make headlines, and for this pursuit Gary Davidson was perfectly appointed. He possessed what imaginative reporters called "Robert Redford good looks," and his habitual speech impediment magically evaporated when the camera lights came on. Davidson was a Skippy-smooth pitchman in a new era of sound bites, an era when there was no government undertaking, however massive, that could not be expressed in an insipid little slogan: Think metric. Whip inflation now. Fifty-five saves lives . . .

In both the WHA and the WFL, Davidson personally took a franchise as his own, for free, as if by birthright. He then sold them immediately. In the WFL he got $690,000 for his franchise, which became the Philadelphia Bell, whose offices routinely fielded complaints from citizens unhappy with their telephone service. Davidson would also draw a hefty salary to run the leagues from his law office—that is, once he had sold enough franchises to form a league.

Along the way Davidson was abetted by his old friend and law partner Don Regan, and by Murphy, a former marketing executive and former mayor of Buena Park, California, an Irishman from County Flimflammery with a winning smile and a world of energy. Together the trio played magnificently the egos of small-town, big-money megalomaniacs throughout the continent, men who simply couldn't resist owning their own pro team.

"Back then there were guys who had made millions making widgets in Omaha, but the only guys who knew them were maybe their bankers and the guys at the country club," says Grandi. "But with a sports franchise, they recognized an opportunity to be known in L.A. or Detroit. Maybe ninety percent of them were flakes, but . . . "

"Dennis Murphy would go into a town," says Davidson, "and call an accountant or call a lawyer, and ask if he had any clients who were interested in professional sports. He wasn't saying, 'Do you have any interest in a vinyl-dye factory?' Within two days he would have gotten enough leads for us to have someone to talk to. We would then come in, and the line would be, 'Would you rather be known as the owner of the Detroit Wheels or as a manufacturer of brassieres?'"

"Pick a city you had never been to before," says Regan. "Say Quebec City. We flew into Quebec City during the WHA days. We had the mayor, the governor, the biggest businessmen in town . . . We'd fly in, they'd run a bloody carpet out to us, they'd drive us away in Rolls-Royces, they'd treat us like we were the potentates of the world. And the whole reason was, the existing establishment then was so monopolistic and arrogant."

The monopolistic and arrogant establishment of the NHL and the NBA and the NFL drove the rebel leaguers, fueling them with a loony motivational paranoia. "We fought for everything we got," says Murphy, "to the point where we had bugs in our chandeliers. I'm not accusing the NHL or the NBA, but who the hell else would put them there? Before we'd go into our meetings, we'd have guys go in there with debugging devices. It was war."

Though it may sound like Murphy has bugs in his chandelier, Davidson corroborates these theories of industrial espionage. "We thought," he says ominously, "that Al Davis had our office bugged."

Installing a surreptitious listening device at any rebel-league meeting would have been a logistical challenge; the league drafts, for instance, always had a quintessentially 1970s mind-if-I-crash-here spontaneity to them. They were held in just about any joint that could provide an impressive dateline. Thus, World Team Tennis—which Murphy helped found in 1973 with the staunch support of Billie Jean King—conducted its first draft in New York in the auditorium of the Time and Life Building, home of *Sports Illustrated*. (To this day in our editorial meetings, we mind what we say about Al Davis.)

To be fair, there were grounds for genuine suspicion in the days of the WHA. Gordie Howe, a luminary with that league's Houston Aeros during the 1973–74 season, was a member of Team Canada '74, a squad composed entirely of WHA players. An eight-game series with the Soviet national team included four games in Moscow. "The Soviets put us all in this real ratty hotel," recalls Murphy, who adds that Howe was particularly appalled by two seedy chairs in a corner.

Howe strolled over to the chandelier in his room. "Colleen," he said loudly to his wife, "I wish these people in Russia would recognize what a great star I am and give us a couple of nice chairs." The Howes left to attend practice, and they returned two hours later to a new pair of beautiful chairs. "Thank you very much, my Russian hosts," Mr. Hockey told the light fixture.

"We were known," swears Murphy, "as the Bug League." You don't have the heart to tell him that everyone was bugged in the Soviet Union, that the KGB did not target the WHA specifically— but then you suspect that Murphy already knows this.

Such self-important self-delusion was vital to the rebel leagues. When Davidson was trying to sell a franchise in a strange city, he arrived with a manufactured air of centuries-old regality.

"You'd created this story, this image, this mirage, but all of a sudden you begin to have value," recalls Davidson. He gestures across his office; in a trophy cabinet sits a mounted replica of the check for $1,000,000 made out to Robert Marvin Hull from WHA Properties, Ltd., dated June 27, 1972. Winnipeg owner Ben Hatskin was given the WHA rights to Bobby Hull because he was willing to kick in an additional $1.75 million in salary to lure the NHL's premier scorer. This was an unheard-of sum in 1972; Hull's 1971 salary with the Chicago Blackhawks had been $150,000. "We weren't sure Bobby could even play," says Davidson. "But that check created so much publicity around the world that even though Winnipeg hadn't played a single game, that franchise had value."

Davidson wasn't sure the Golden Jet could play in Winnipeg because the NHL had filed suit to retain Hull and all the other players who had signed with the WHA. The WHA, in turn, filed an antitrust suit against the NHL and was granted an injunction to play its games while the court cases were pending. In the mid-seventies the NHL abandoned its reserve clause—the legal absurdity that bound players to a team perpetually after their contracts expired—and in 1979 agreed to absorb four teams from the WHA. The lawsuits were dropped, but the WHA was rendered extinct.

By this time Davidson had already resigned from the WHA and turned his attention to his dream of a world football league. He was going to do nothing less than conquer the globe. Says Regan, "We were young enough and naive enough that we didn't know there were limits, that the world has finite boundaries."

These men were feeling immortal, the success of the WHA standing as a monument to themselves. Of course, there were other, smaller monuments. In the WHA's first season of existence, Andre Lacroix won the W. D. (Wild Bill) Hunter award as scoring champion, J. C. Tremblay was honored with the Dennis A. Murphy award as best defenseman, and Bobby Hull was the Most Valuable Player and proud recipient of the Gary L. Davidson trophy.

As Davidson prepared to breathe life into the WFL beginning in 1974, athletes' eyes were on a bigger prize. The prize would be won in baseball, the one major sport that Davidson had not challenged. In '73 a former steel-union boss named Marvin Miller, the executive director of the Major League Baseball Players Association, had secured salary-arbitration rights for his constituents. Two years later an arbitrator's decision would grant "free agency" to pitchers Andy Messersmith and Dave McNally.

In the year between those two milestones, egregiously ill-timed plans were revealed for a new rebel baseball league, an opera buffa that would have nothing to do with the Davidson clique. Emboldened by the impact of the WHA and by the gaudy promises of the proposed new football league, a man named Sean Downey announced in April 1974 the imminent formation of the thirty-two-team World Baseball Association, to play in the United States, Latin America, and Asia. "Baseball as presently played and structured," said Downey, one of several original owners of the New Orleans franchise in the ABA, "is a bore." He would have known: Sean Downey was himself an insufferable gasbag with an ego like a detonated self-inflating raft. In the 1980s he would create his own abrasive, right-wing television talk show with himself, using his middle name, as the host. Morton Downey Jr. presumably figured that the show was the next best thing to owning a baseball team—and not all that different, as Marge Schott would one day demonstrate.

There is a remarkable photograph in the May 1, 1974, edition of the *San Francisco Chronicle*. Gary Davidson is shown "discussing matters," according to the caption, with tight end Ted Kwalick, formerly of the San Francisco 49ers but newly signed by the Honolulu Hawaiians of the World Football League. Kwalick is indoors, but he is wearing Foster Grant sunglasses. His spectacular dress shirt bears stripes so wide that there is room for only two of them. *Two stripes.* His shirt collar resembles a pair of pterodactyl wings. The knot in his tie is slightly larger than a baby's head. As for the tie itself, it is simply enormous, as if Kwalick were still wearing the napkin he had tucked into his collar at lunch.

The WFL's promotional literature boasted that this was a "now" league, which may explain why the league now looks so "then." Nineteen seventy-four turned out to be the WFL's only full season, but that season somehow began with bold promise in that summer of the Watergate denouement. Play began on Wednesday nights in July, as striking NFL players were printing T-shirts emblazoned with a fist and the slogan NO FREEDOM, NO FOOTBALL. The new league had the look of a high-salaried land of milk and money, flush with the wealth of men like Hawaii owner Sam Battistone, the czar of Sambo's Racially Insensitive Family Restaurants. The future was a grand boulevard, as wide as a Kwalickian lapel, and the King himself blessed the new endeavor: Elvis sat in a skybox on opening night in Memphis. The Philadelphia Bell drew a reported 120,000 fans to its first two home games.

Tax records, however, would show that only some twenty thousand tickets in Philly had been sold at full price. John F. Kennedy Stadium was a paper house, filled with fans in free seats. In fact, the entire league was a heavily mortgaged paper house, losing $20 million in its first twenty-week season. Members of the Florida Blazers were not paid for the final ten weeks of the season. Paper house? Coach Jack Pardee personally bought toilet paper for the Blazers' home locker room. "You've heard of hungry football teams?" his wife, Phyllis, once told a reporter. "The Blazers really *were* hungry."

Somehow the Blazers still managed to make it to the optimistically named World Bowl I, which historians have since renamed World Bowl I-and-Only. Their opponents in that game, on December 5, 1974, were the Birmingham Americans, whose uniforms were confiscated on behalf of a creditor by sheriff's deputies the day after their 22–21 triumph. As for the losers, well, at least they didn't go home empty-handed. Legend has it that following the opening coin flip, a Blazer captain put the silver dollar in his sock.

Gary Davidson exhumes his past from a sad little grocery sack. "I didn't want to lose all this," he says while dipping his hand into a paper bag full of brittle press clippings. "I don't think too much of this stuff is preserved in people's memories."

Seated in his Orange County real estate office, he lets his fingers alight on a yellowed piece of newsprint. "Here's an *L.A. Times* story about 1974, with pictures of Agnew, Nixon, and Davidson," he says with a sigh. "A bad year." He lifts his photo to the light, regarding himself as if in a mirror. "Good god," he mutters softly.

Good god. The Me Decade was supposed to have been his, and 1974 was to have been the most glorious year yet for him. He began writing his autobiography that February. He was photographed for the April 15 cover of SI, flanked by Kwalick and Calvin Hill of the Hawaiians. He confided to friends that he was thinking of running for the U.S. Senate in '76. He had everything, and *People* magazine came to photograph it: the millionaire at home in exclusive Emerald Bay, with four handsome children and a wife named Barbie, a former cheerleader at UCLA.

Trouble was, the man's life was a shimmering mirage. Where to begin? Hank Aaron hit his 715th home run on April 8, and Davidson was bumped from the front of SI; a copy of that unpublished cover hangs in his office, near the check to Robert Marvin Hull. (Says Davidson's secretary, beholding these mementos, "He had fifteen minutes to evacuate his home during the Laguna Beach fires last fall. What do you think he went back for?")

The glamorous Hawaiians turned out to be a hollow coconut, struggling to survive like every other team playing the hollow-sounding game of "WiFfLe ball," as sportswriters called it. "I remember when Dan Rogers was hired to be the first general manager of the Hawaiian franchise, and he was given a lifetime contract," says Grandi. "It wasn't too long after that, the owner called and said, 'I'm sorry, Danny, but I'm afraid you're dead.'

"So Dan came back and worked for the league, and during those final days he was talking on the phone at his desk. The desk and chair were rental furniture, and the league had fallen behind on its payments. Sure enough, the rental company comes by and takes away the desk and chair. But Dan kept right on talking on the phone."

By the end of 1974 there had been the indignity of World Bowl I-and-Only, Gary and Barbie had begun divorce proceedings, Davidson had wrecked his Jaguar, and he had been knifed in the parking lot of a Newport Beach restaurant, Woody's Wharf, while arguing with some drunk. Our Redford double got seventy stitches in his face from the last two incidents. Nineteen seventy-four literally scarred him for life.

"I turned forty," he says, continuing to recite this litany. "I ended up upside down about four million dollars, and that did not make for a good year." Nixon was exiled to San Clemente in August. And you begin thinking that maybe that old *L.A. Times* story got it right, that Davidson's photo belongs on the same page with Nixon and long lines at the gas station and those WHIP INFLATION NOW buttons, just another relic of an America gone bust in the mid-1970s.

If you think it is a stretch to connect Watergate and pro football, consider this: A sign in the war room of CREEP—the Committee to Re-elect the President—at the time of the Watergate break-in read WINNING IN POLITICS ISN'T EVERYTHING, IT'S THE ONLY THING. Nixon knew Frank Gifford. He surely knew Vince Lombardi.

Since 1974 Davidson has been as elusive as Bobby Fischer, the chess prodigy who went into his own self-imposed exile that summer. "I think Gary went to live in Haiti," said a friend when asked recently about Davidson. Whispers another friend: "I heard he tried to commit suicide."

Even as his autobiography was shuffling off the presses two decades ago, Davidson had begun taking drives into Baja, cruising from village to dusty village in search of a place to start over. By 1976 he was spending much of his time on a sisal plantation in Haiti. Ten thousand people on forty thousand acres. Among his investment partners in Dauphin Plantations was Papa Doc Duvalier, who did not believe in a liberal profit-sharing plan. The plantation was eventually sold to a group of Haitians, and Davidson was back in Orange County—not far from San Clemente. "All the people on the plantation," says Davidson as a footnote, "probably ended up starving to death."

His story was supposed to end here, horribly, but a funny thing happened on his way to obscurity. Unlike his basketballs, Gary Davidson bounced back. He found God and a new wife and revived his real estate career by developing retirement communities. At sixty he remains the same picture-of-health fitness freak who used to encourage his employees to climb five flights of stairs instead of using the elevator. He now says grown-up things about professional sports, like "Today's player salaries are a bit distorted" and "The owners have let things get out of control" and "The fans are paying too much." He has become a bona fide millionaire.

Like that Screaming Eagles check, it turns out Gary Davidson was made of rubber. "There's a famous line in Shakespeare," Davidson says. "In *King Lear* the Fool says to King Lear, 'Too bad you grew old before you grew wise.' And so the theory is, maybe I started to get wiser as I grew older."

Davidson's Shakespeare is in need of Rust-Oleum, but the important thing is that he got here, that he got to Wise. Some men go their whole lives, can't find Wisdom with a AAA road atlas. Three days after meeting Davidson, you stand in front of a Santa Monica hotel. You are waving good-bye to Dennis Murphy, who now runs a professional roller-hockey league. Abruptly, Murphy comes back to you. There is one more thing.

Smiling, he says, "You don't think Gary's interested in getting back into the sports business, do you?" No, you say. No, he isn't. Gary Davidson would rather manufacture brassieres than get back into the sports business.

CHAPTER FOUR

"Got a pencil?" Jim Brown asks when you call to arrange a visit. "Here's what you do. Call 310–652–7★★★. Ask for Rockhead Johnson. He has my calendar. You two work out the date."

"I'm sorry," you respond. "What was the first name?"

"Rockhead."

"*Rockhead?*"

"Rockhead. Rockhead Johnson."

So you dutifully dial the number and wait for Rockhead to answer, but instead you get a receptionist at Amer-I-Can, Brown's public-service organization. Summoning the most businesslike voice that circumstances will allow, you ask, "May I please speak to Rockhead? Rockhead Johnson?" A long and awkward pause follows, after which you're told that *Rock* is out of the office. *Rock* will be back in an hour. Can *Rock* return your call?

"This is Rock," Rock says when he phones back later. "Rock Johnson."

By now the full horror has hit you. You've been had—suckered, as Brown likes to say. The man's name isn't Rock*head* at all. Only one person calls him that, and only one person gets away with it. You've just been juked by Jim Brown.

He is still a familiar presence on television, an imposing bust on the small screen. His square head sits on square shoulders, a square hat sits on his square head. At fifty-eight he remains an enormous

Rock 'Em Sock 'Em Robot of a man. His arms are crisscrossed with scars, his fingers veer off at each joint in unexpected directions, remnants of the cartoon-violent NFL of the 1950s and '60s.

But that vision of a massive, muddied Brown begins to evaporate in your head while you drive, high above Sunset Boulevard, on a serpentine street that runs like a stream through the Hollywood Hills, Benzes and BMWs docked bargelike on both curbs. You turn off and plunge down into Jim Brown's driveway, where a young, besuited chauffeur, who has been dispatched by a local television studio, takes it upon himself to try to shoo you and your sorry blue Pontiac from the premises.

Moments later you are rescued, and Brown is amused. "I live in a boolshit world," he says of Hollywood. "But that's cool. When I go out, it's like, 'Put on your suit, baby, you're going down into the circus.' You go to Roxbury's, you know what you're going for: to see the stars and the girls and the boolshit—'Hey, what's goin' on, babe?' 'Aaaaay, Big Jim, what's happenin', man?' There's a time and place for that, as long as you don't buy into it. My way to cut through the boolshit is with simplicity. And when I stay here, everything is simple."

Jim Brown tolerates no boolshit. It is practically his credo. Ask him why he so unabashedly admires Muhammad Ali, and Brown tells you straight up: "He has the heart and courage to stand up for beliefs that are unpopular." Bill Russell? "Exceptionally smart, exceptionally principled, no boolshit." Conversely, in his autobiography Brown calls O. J. Simpson a "phony" and adds: "The Juice likes to pretend he's modest, but that's just the Juice being the Juice. O.J. is extremely smart, man knows how to make a buck, and his 'aw shucks' image is his meal ticket. He's not about to jeopardize it by being honest." And: "I never look at him the way I do a Bill Russell, or a Walter Payton. I talk to those guys, see them speak, I know what I'm hearing is the real man. Too often, I can't say the same about O.J." The book was published five years ago.

Today, just down the hill, lies the circus, Los Angeles, a scary riot of Simpson hearings and Menendez shootings and King beatings—an apocalyptic place of fire, earthquake, mudslide, and pestilence that only four decades ago was an Eden to Walter O'Malley. But up here at the Brown residence, all appears to be placid and predictable simplicity. He has lived in the same house, driven the same car, had the same telephone number since 1968.

That was the spring when the Reverend Dr. Martin Luther King Jr. was assassinated in Memphis. A framed portrait of King hangs in Brown's foyer. But nowhere on display in the house is a single personal memento of Brown's own varied careers—as a football superstar, as a film actor, as an activist in what he calls "the movement for dignity, equality, and justice."

Toward that end Brown has opened his immaculate home through the years to an astonishing cross section of humanity. Recently, Brown says, former secretary of housing and urban development Jack Kemp and the head of the Nation of Islam shared the couch on which we now sit. "I can have Louis Farrakhan here, you, fifteen Jews," he says. "It don't make no damn difference."

Never has. As a child he was thrown in with all races and generations, almost from the time his father, Swinton (Sweet Sue) Brown, a fighter and a gambler, abandoned him at birth. Jim Brown was raised by his great-grandmother, whom he called Mama, on St. Simons Island, off the coast of Georgia. He went to school in a segregated, two-room shack, went to the toilet in the backyard. When he was eight, Mama gave him a box lunch, buttoned him up, and put him on a train for Manhasset, New York, where his mother worked as a domestic. In that white and wealthy community Jim Brown became an athletic prodigy. At Manhasset High he was a kind of ward to a group of white professional men, doctors and lawyers and teachers, who demanded that he study and run for student government.

"Without Manhasset, without Dr. Collins and Ken Molloy and Mr. Dawson and Ed Walsh, it would've been impossible," Brown says of his remarkable existence. "These people actually saved my life, man. I would never, ever have been anything without them. And it was so pure. If kids can see honesty and interest from people of that age, that's what builds, man. So you can't fool me with all of the other boolshit, 'cause I've got an example for the rest of my life. You wanna see what goodness is? I look at those people. I know what love is. I know what patience is. I know what consistency is. I know what honesty is."

Ken Molloy was a Manhasset attorney and a former Syracuse lacrosse player who insisted that Brown select Syracuse over the dozens of schools that were recruiting him for football, basketball, and baseball. It was only after Brown arrived on campus, housed in a different dorm from the rest of the football team, eating on a different meal plan, that he first fully encountered discrimination. It made him miserable in that freshman year of 1953–54.

You have asked Jim Brown to look at his remarkable life. You are seated in his living room, which overlooks the pool, which overlooks the yard, which overlooks Los Angeles. You have come to take in the view: of race, celebrity, the real world, and the star athlete's obligations therein these last four decades. Brown has seemingly lived every issue in sport and society since he left home for Syracuse so long ago. He continues to work in places like South Central and San Quentin. You ask Jim Brown to assess this public life he entered forty years ago, and he says, "I am oh, so tired."

Just before 1 P.M. on May 17, 1954, the chief justice of the Supreme Court of the United States began to read the unanimous decision in *Brown v. Board of Education*. Legal segregation was ending. In Harlem that year Malcolm X was appointed the leader of Temple Seven for the Nation of Islam. And across the river in the Bronx, the great New York Yankees of Mantle and Berra and Stengel had still not dressed a black player.

"I came up at the crossroads of segregation," says Brown. "There were still colleges where black players couldn't play. There were teams that would go south and black players had to stay in private homes. These were very difficult times. It was a blessing on the one hand because there were opportunities, but it was demeaning because you were still looked on as inferior. It was almost as if you'd been given a favor. And you always felt you had to perform much, much better."

And so Jimmy Brown, the only black on the freshman football team at Syracuse, went from fifth-string halfback to the best player in the nation in his four years of playing for a coaching staff that—save for an assistant named Roy Simmons—initially begrudged his presence there.

By the time Brown graduated in 1957, Syracuse was eager to recruit black halfback Ernie Davis and then Floyd Little, both of whom wore Brown's number 44.

Syracuse won a national football championship in 1959 and now regularly fills that dome named for Willis H. Carrier, and much of that is directly attributable to the heroics of James Nathaniel Brown. It is more indirectly attributable to Simmons, the kind assistant football and head lacrosse coach who took Brown under his wing; with Simmons's guidance, Brown used his spare time to become, many would say, the greatest lacrosse player in history before going on to do the same, many more would say, in football.

Jim Brown scored thirty-eight points a game as a high school basketball player. He was drafted by the Syracuse Nationals of the NBA in 1957 even though he had stopped playing basketball after his junior season in college. He received a letter of inquiry from the great Stengel of the Yankees—even though, by Brown's own admission, "I wasn't that good."

On his final day as an athlete at Syracuse, Brown won the discus and shot put in a varsity track meet, returned to the dressing room to change for a lacrosse match, and was called back to the track by a student manager. Could he throw the javelin? Brown threw the javelin 162 feet on one attempt. Syracuse won the meet.

The man belonged to a higher species. Jim Brown was built like a martini glass, with a 46–inch chest and a 32–inch waist; he was an exceptionally fast man who looked slow in motion on the football field: gracefully slow, a man running in a swimming pool.

Pulling out of his stance and bursting through the line, he accumulated would-be tacklers, men hopping a moving train, until he slowed and finally collapsed eight or ten or twelve yards upfield, buried beneath a short ton of violent giants. One didn't really try to tackle Brown; one tried only to catch him, as one catches the 8:05. "All you can do is grab hold, hang on, and wait for help" is how Hall of Fame linebacker Sam Huff put it.

Brown rose slowly from the scrum after every carry and hobbled back to the huddle in apparent pain before bursting through the scrimmage line on the next play for another eight or ten or twelve yards. This was the earliest hint of Brown's acting aspirations, for he wasn't really hurt, or at least not hampered. No, in his entire nine-year professional career, he never missed a game. He played all of the 1962 season with a severely sprained wrist just this side of broken. He did not wear hip pads, ever. And so it finally became apparent to opposing defenses that Brown wasn't ever going to be hurt by conventional malevolence.

He was simply that rarest kind of competitor, who made men and women gape, whose performances each Sunday displayed the pure athlete in his prime. Jim Brown is why we love sports in the first place, the reason we tolerate the big dough, the crybabies, the boolshit.

He joined the Cleveland Browns in 1957, a year before pro football came of age with the Baltimore Colt–New York Giant overtime championship game. His coach, the progressive Paul Brown, just gave him the ball and let him run, which is all Jim Brown really wanted. "But you could never just play and not be cognizant of the social situation in the country," he says. "Every day of your life, that was in your mind. You had to question why they only put black players at certain positions, why there were positions that blacks weren't smart enough to play. They had a whole bunch of rules. You always had an even number of blacks on the team so they could room with each other. You always had six or eight. You couldn't have . . . five." Brown laughs, then immediately turns stern.

"So I was very conscious of the civil rights movement," he continues, "and very active in what I call the movement for dignity, equality, and justice. In fact, it superseded my interest in sports. Sports gave me an opportunity to help the cause. And so I did that."

He made certain that his black teammates wore suits and ties, urged them to be fiscally responsible, and saw to it that they were at all times protective of their own dignity. Whenever Brown uses the word, as he does often, he says it slowly, carefully enunciating all three syllables: DIG-ni-ty.

In the mid-1960s he enjoyed trolling the black community of Cleveland in his Cadillac convertible or walking the streets of Philadelphia with the former Cassius Clay, greeting the people in barbershops and record stores, the two greatest athletes of their time just saying hello to folks, their very presence bestowing DIG-ni-ty on a depressed and unsuspecting neighborhood.

The night Clay beat Sonny Liston in Miami for the heavyweight championship in 1964, Brown sat with him for two hours afterward in Clay's hotel, with Malcolm X waiting in the next room, as Cassius confided to Brown that he had embraced Elijah Muhammad and the Nation of Islam and had taken the name Muhammad Ali.

Brown was in London two years later, filming *The Dirty Dozen,* when Ali refused induction into the U.S. Army. "A Muslim who was managing Ali told me that they wouldn't mind him going into the service," recalls Brown, "but they couldn't tell him that." So Brown flew to Cleveland, where a group of fellow black athletes were gathering to hear Ali out in a much-publicized summit meeting. Brown, Lew Alcindor, Willie Davis, Bill Russell, and John Wooten listened as Ali said, "My fate is in the hands of Allah." The group then announced support for their friend, whose religious convictions were all they had to hear. . . .

The story continues, but Brown cannot be heard over the whine of a weed whacker, wielded by a man trimming the lawn out back. "See that man right there?" Brown asks when the noise recedes. "He's a gardener, and he's one of the best men I've ever met. I respect that man as much as I respect anyone. He does his job. He's fair. He doesn't complain. He's considerate. He's a family man. He's got principles."

The weed whacker is wailing again, but no matter. You already know how the Ali story ends: Brown flies back to London from Cleveland, never to return to football. In nine seasons he had gained a record 12,312 yards and won a championship. He got out at his peak, just before the epochal 1966 season, just before the NFL-AFL merger and the Super Bowl and the hype. His final salary in football was $65,000.

The Dirty Dozen established Brown as an actor. And while Gloria Steinem called him "the black John Wayne," his thespian talents were better described by Lee Marvin, who said that Brown was "a better actor than Olivier would have been a fullback."

Brown always played the same character, essentially himself; even the names didn't change much: Fireball, Slaughter, Gunn, Hammer, Pike. After five years the industry tired of Brown, and Brown tired of the industry—"I began to wonder," he says. "Do I have to be called 'nigger' in every script?"—and he fell back on the work he'd been doing all along.

In the late 1960s the Ford Foundation had given more than a million dollars to the Black Economic Union (BEU), an organization that Brown had helped form to promote black entrepreneurship through a network of athletes and MBAs. More than four hundred businesses were touched by the union, whose motto is splayed across the top of a battered newsletter that Brown fishes from a file in his den: PRODUCE, ACHIEVE, PROSPER, declares volume one, number one of the publication, dated April 1968. Among the items inside is a photograph of eight black high school students in Cleveland. The BEU would be funding their college educations, much as those men in Manhasset had done for Brown fifteen years before.

"It's only a drop," says Brown, suddenly putting away the file, "because what's happened is, there has been no follow-through with black athletes today."

"If I had the participation of the top twenty athletes in this country, we could probably create a nationwide gang truce," Brown is telling you, as well as a professor from the University of Iowa who is visiting Brown's house while researching a book on gangs. "These athletes represent such a great amount of resources and influence. These kids would be flattered to have their lives changed by them."

It may be little more than an accident of geography, but a trip to Brown's hillside home, up the winding drive that requires one to climb and climb, has the quality of a visit to some mountaintop guru, a man offering solutions to intractable problems. And among the most intractable of those problems—a fly in the rich soup du jour of sports and TV and money—is the notion that sports is now eating its young.

"You give the kids athletes to follow, and you give them false hope," Brown is saying. "You take the emphasis off just being a good student, getting a job and having a family. Instead, it's 'I want to be Michael Jordan. I want to have those shoes.' Kids in this area also look to the drug dealer, the gangster, the killer as a hero, which is something we didn't used to have. So these are the two sets of heroes, and both of them are bad."

Which is something we didn't used to have. Ask Brown what happened in the 1970s and '80s to create these problems, and he'll tell you it was the 1970s and '80s themselves. The seventies, the Me Decade, the Decade of Free Agency, and the eighties, with its alliterative icons, Michael Milken and Gordon Gekko, and its alliterative mantra "Greed is good." Back-to-back decades of decadence.

"The rich got richer, didn't they?" Brown says. "Well, who suffered? If you've got all the money, I'm gonna suffer. When executives are paying themselves five hundred million dollars, that's tyin' up a lotta dough. Take anything to an extreme, it will self-destruct. That's why the destruction of the Soviet Union was inevitable. . . . And this country has festered, there's an underbelly. Prisons are overcrowded, recidivism is at an all-time high, the education system is going downhill, there's this new culture of drugs and gangsters and killing without any thought. Kids are shooting each other at thirteen and fourteen, and all of a sudden it's not gonna stay in the inner city."

As if on cue, a thirteen-year-old boy from Brown's neighborhood appears at the front door. Brown says hello, asks the boy how his father has been, asks him where his mother is, then lowers the boom. "I heard you got a beeper now. You got a beeper?" he asks the kid, referring to the new totem of the urban street criminal.

The boy nods shyly.

"For what?" demands Brown.

"Messages."

"Messages? What do you need messages for?"

By now two other kids have arrived with a parent, and the whole group walks through the open house and out back to the pool.

Brown sighs tremendously, and it sounds like the air brakes decompressing on a city bus.

"The other culture's taken over," he says. "The gangsta culture. Everything is gangsta rap, the gangsta attitude, gangsta body language. Car-jackings. Drive-bys. Red, blue, Disciples. Snoop Doggy Dogg has more influence on kids than Bill Clinton does." Brown yawns enormously, like the MGM lion.

"So the teacher no longer gets any respect," he continues. "The teacher used to get respect. Athletic programs on the lower levels no longer have an effect on the general populace of schools. It used to be that athletic activity was healthy. You played, but you weren't playing to become a pro. Now, if you don't have pro potential, sports are a waste of time. Agents are now looking down to high schools to find potential prospects. So it's no longer fun. Even the Olympics are no longer fun.

"When I was playing, you weren't gonna make a whole lotta money. But you were playing the game, and playing the game at the highest possible level. And you liked that. That's why the greatest sporting event I see today is the Ryder Cup. It's about nothing except caring about competition. You can see that it means something to those guys. You can see them choking on short putts, it means so much. I don't see that in other sports.

"Now, money, period, has become the game. So the game suffers. An individual will go anywhere. The day after a team wins the World Series, the team is changed. Sure you gotta make money, but how much money, and at what cost? A person couldn't buy my house right now for any amount of money. Because it's my home. I'm comfortable here. Quality of life is what's most important."

This much is certain: By 1994 too many athletes, teams, entire franchises have long forgotten the concept of home, and too many children have never known it. As the millennium nears its end, home is just that place where you pause and pose after hitting a baseball out of the park.

"When I was growing up in Georgia, I guess we were supposed to be poor," Brown says. "But we weren't poor. We had all the crab and fish and vegetables that we could eat. The house was small and weather-beaten, but hell, I lived well. Because there was so much family there, a whole community of people who cared about each other. See, that was my foundation. I'd hate to have to come up without that."

And so, in places like Trenton and Canton and Compton, Brown teaches rudimentary life skills to gang members and soon-to-be-released convicts through his Amer-I-Can program. He directs a staff of fifty street-credentialed "facilitators," who help people learn to do things like read and get a job and manage their personal finances—which isn't to say that Brown's role is hands-off.

A visitor to one symposium on gangs in Brown's home tells the story of a punk who kept disrupting the host's efforts to establish a dialogue. After Brown repeatedly asked the young man to excuse himself, the young man challenged Brown to step outside with him. Well, Brown and the gang-banger wound up rolling out the back door in a comic-book ball of dust. Shortly thereafter they reappeared and shook hands, and the meeting resumed.

One of Brown's charges—"one of my gangsters," as Brown calls them—recently got out of his gang, got a job, and got married. The wedding was held at Brown's house.

O. J. Simpson was himself a gang member made good. He now stands charged with double homicide, having been cheered by "fans" on live television while fleeing police on the L.A. freeways. It's said we like to build our stars up just to tear them down, and in fin de siècle California, the state may deem it necessary to execute one of the greatest athletic stars it has produced. When Simpson was charged in June, Brown unbecomingly appeared on national TV to offer the opinion that Simpson was a cocaine user. In football they call what Brown did "piling on."

They are both former running backs and actors who make their homes ten miles apart in Los Angeles. Simpson eclipsed Brown's single-season NFL rushing record in 1973. Both men have histories of domestic-violence allegations. The Los Angeles Police Department has released tapes of a 911 call that Nicole Brown Simpson made when her enraged ex-husband broke down a door to her home and entered, screaming obscenities. Brown has been accused at least four times of violence against young women, most notably in 1968, when he was accused of throwing his girlfriend from a balcony. None of the charges were proved in court, and Brown denies them all. "I like sex. . . . I mess with young women," he says. "I know it's bad, but I'm bad."

Riinnnnnngg. An end-table telephone springs to life.

"Hello?" says Brown. "Mm-hmm? Oh, I'm sorry, but I'm finished. Yeah, I can't explain anything anymore. Well, I'm so sorry, but I can't. Mm-hmm . . . I wish I could. . . . No, I don't have anything to say. . . . Yeah, but I'm not interested in all that. I've said my piece, and I'm gonna let that roll. I'm gonna watch and see what happens. See, the public has to get educated. I'm already educated. I know what's goin' on. I deal with real life. I don't get into things that I don't know about. But thank you. Thanks for calling."

Yet another caller asking Brown to handicap the upcoming Simpson preliminary hearing? "Yeah, because I brought the whole cocaine thing up," says a weary Brown, who claims somewhat dubiously that he was just trying to bolster an insanity plea, that cocaine could provide a devil-made-me-do-it defense for Simpson. "They criticize me. They say I'm against O.J. I'm for him. I'm for truth. You and me and O.J., we all have our negatives and our positives. I know this is America and we like to have our heroes, but hell, Martin Luther King screwing around—people are still in denial about that. The Kennedys, Bobby and John, they womanized. I look at the good and at the bad. Do I like a lot of women? Hell, yeah. What bothers me is when people hold on to the falseness of something.

"Did you hear the [911] tapes?" he asks, by way of explaining why he has no interest in the elaborate pas de deux of the courtroom. "There's this whole emphasis on who leaked the tapes, not on the truth, not on whatever is real, not on resolving this in a real manner. Everyone is interested in the courtroom and what happens there. Well, hell, all kinds of crazy things can happen in the courtroom, and this is not necessarily going to get resolved.

"I looked at the Rodney King beating and said he got the crap kicked out of him, and I don't care what you say, I'm finished with it," says Brown. "But they turned all that around in court." Brown laughs. "Y'all can go on and talk all that boolshit. I saw the beating. That thing was ridiculous." Brown's laugh gains momentum, a ball rolling slowly downhill. "Those guys suckered that case so bad, they got everyone in doubt." Brown imitates himself watching the King tape on TV, stroking his chin reflectively: "Well, maybe he didn't get beaten . . . "

And Jim Brown sputters one more tired laugh.

Ask him how he will be remembered, and Brown offers his own epitaph. It isn't much. "On the popular level, they'll say, 'He was a football player. Controversial. Threw a girl out the window.' I don't care. Maybe they'll say, 'He was honest.'"

But he does care, all of us do, and so Brown tells one final story. When his friend Huey Newton, the former Black Panther leader, was shot to death on an Oakland street in 1989, Brown was asked to read a memorial poem at the funeral. Standing at the podium, Brown had a look at the faces sprouting from the pews: H. Rap Brown, William Kunstler, a whole team photo of sixties revolutionaries. He had an epiphany: "That these people were just like me," Brown recalls. "Different methodologies, but the same goal: to make this a better country."

His body creaks massively as he rises from the sofa and says goodbye. As you're leaving, as you approach the drawing of MLK in the foyer, you sense again that little has changed in this house since 1968. There is one thing, though. "I'm stiff," you hear Brown saying, with a laugh, as you exit the room. "I'm gettin' old."

And then Jim Brown heads for the patio, still looking for daylight.

CHAPTER FIVE

In a painting, there's a spot at which the parallel lines—a river or a ribbon of road—appear to converge. Artists call this the vanishing point, that place in a drawing where things seem to disappear into the distance, often creating the illusion of a horizon. And so

I find myself at the vanishing point of this story. I am standing, atremble, before the largest shopping mall in America. This is the horizon. All lines converge here.

So vast is the Mall of America in Bloomington, Minnesota, that the area in which I've parked is labeled P5–WEST-BLUE-NEVADA-D-6, a mantra I have desperately repeated since abandoning my rental car in the world's largest parking complex. Even by itself this would be the consummate postwar American dream: the thirteen-thousand-car garage. But the aptly named Mall of America says so much more than that about the desires of modern society.

The Megamall, as it is known locally, is built on seventy-eight acres and occupies 4.2 million square feet, but publicists prefer more grandiose international imagery to convey its knee-weakening scope. The mall, therefore, could comfortably contain all the gardens of Buckingham Palace, is five times larger than Red Square, and contains twice the steel of the Eiffel Tower. Most telling of all, it is twenty times larger than St. Peter's Basilica in Rome. For its visitors, who have come from virtually every country in the world and number a hundred thousand a day on average, the Mall of America is indeed the One True Church.

Mind-boggling sports analogies have also been employed to describe this edifice. "Seven times the size of Yankee Stadium," said the *New York Times,* adding that it has "88 football fields worth of [floor] space." Such comparisons are especially apt at the Mall of America, which was built on the site of the former Metropolitan Stadium, longtime home of the Minnesota Twins and the Minnesota Vikings. In 1982 the teams moved from the Met to the Metrodome in downtown Minneapolis. Ten summers later the mall opened, constructed as a square donut, at the center of which is an indoor, seven-acre amusement park called Knott's Camp Snoopy.

In the northwest corner of Camp Snoopy, embedded in the faux-stone floor, is a five-sided plaque that evokes home plate at the Met. In fact, it more closely resembles a tombstone, bearing as it does the legend METROPOLITAN STADIUM HOME PLATE 1956–1981. Five hundred and twenty feet away, in the southeast corner of the amusement park, affixed to a wall three stories above the floor, is a fold-down seat, looking down like a lifeguard's chair. The seat is in the approximate spot where Harmon Killebrew deposited the Met's most prodigious dinger, on June 3, 1967. If Killebrew were to hit the home run today, it would carom off Hooters.

Next to the Megamall lies the derelict rust-hulk of Met Center, erstwhile home of the Minnesota North Stars, who now play in Dallas—a hockey team in the buckle of the Sun Belt. Minneapolis officials, in the wake of the Stars' departure, are trying to lure another NHL team to the gleaming downtown arena in which the NBA Timberwolves now play. In June the NBA denied the Wolves permission to move to New Orleans, where they would have been owned, in part, by a Houston attorney named Fred Hofheinz. You will recall that he is the son of the Judge, who built the Astrodome, which spawned the Metrodome, to which the Twins and Vikings moved, thus clearing property for . . . the Mall of America.

Of course, before building the Astrodome, the Judge had planned to build an air-conditioned shopping mall on Westheimer Road in Houston. Instead he sold that property, which was developed in 1970 as the Galleria, a mall that thrives to this day with what once seemed a wonderful novelty: an indoor ice-skating rink at its center. The Mall of America, meanwhile, was developed in part by brothers Mel and Herb Simon, owners of the Indiana Pacers, late of the American Basketball Association, the first rebel league of Gary Davidson.

In America's Original Sports Bar, on the Megamall's fourth level, patrons watch games on the fifty-five televisions that pull in action from around the planet. But the most telling snapshots of sports and society today are to be seen in the Megamall's more than four hundred stores: in Kids Foot Locker and Lady Foot Locker and World Foot Locker, in Footaction USA and the Athlete's Foot and Athletic X-Press, in Sports Tyme and Team Spirit and the Sportsman's Wife, in No Contest and Golf for Her and Mac Birdie Golf Gifts, in Big Leagues and Going to the Game and Wild Pitch. A friend once counted nearly two dozen Megamall stores in which one can purchase a Starter jacket. There are, meanwhile, two bookstores in the place.

In sports-addled ancient Greece, citizens created the agora, the marketplace as a center for social exchange. Socrates said, "Having the fewest wants, I am nearest to the gods." In sports-addled postwar America, citizens created the shopping mall, the marketplace as a center for naked commerce. Social exchange? An official Mall of America T-shirt reads SHUT UP & SHOP.

It is fitting, and perhaps inevitable, that last winter's most unrelenting sports story unfolded each day from a shopping mall in America. For what are big-time sports today if not a boundless marketplace? And so there was Tonya Harding, week after stupefying week, blithely turning triple axels for the television cameras on a skating rink at the Clackamas Town Center mall in Portland. She was preparing for the Olympic Games, another invention of the ancient Greeks, suitably adapted for our times.

"Who told you you can't have it all?" So goes a lyric from the Mall of America theme song, voicing a notion as unmistakably American as the mall itself. "In our collective discourse," writes David Guterson in *Harper's,* "the shopping mall appears with the tract house, the freeway, and the backyard barbecue as a product of the American postwar years, a testament to contemporary necessities and desires and an invention not only peculiarly American but peculiarly of our own era too."

It was, fittingly, a man named Victor who developed America's first fully enclosed shopping complex, vanquishing the suburban landscape of Edina, Minnesota, in 1956. Southdale, as it is named, remains a staggering success four decades later, apparently unfazed by the Mall of America, a mere ten-minute drive to the east.

Victor Gruen's creation was quickly loosed on other inclement cities. The modest Gulfgate soon went up in Houston, and Judge Roy Hofheinz was thus inspired to explore the limits of air-conditioning for his own gargantuan mall.

Come 1960, when the Judge was newly smitten by sports and Roone Arledge was arriving at ABC, Melvin Simon and Associates, Inc., built its first shopping center, Southgate Plaza, in Bloomington, Indiana. Today the firm's $625 million megamall is the third-largest tourist attraction in America—at least according to the mall's own press kit, which claims that only Disney World and the country-music capital of Branson, Missouri, are more visited.

And yet, far more than Mickey Mouse or Mickey Gilley, it is the mall that is emblematic of our age: from the thirteen-year-old girl who went into labor here to the trailer-park marriages performed at the Chapel of Love on Level 2 to this now familiar little postwar irony: the Mall of America was financed by the Mitsubishi Bank of Japan.

Distinctly of our time and place, the Megamall is also entirely otherworldly. While strolling about the mall's four levels, I fall in behind two businessmen, one of whom produces a bleating cellular phone from his jacket. "If it's for me," says the other guy, "tell them I'm not here." In fact, no one is here, because here is . . . nowhere, a place of perpetual seventy-degree days and hospital cleanliness, a self-contained city that serves all needs, but one in which only Willis H. Carrier could feel comfortable.

At the same time the mall is . . . everywhere, with its fourteen-plex of movie theaters and its Cholest-o-Plex of fast-food counters. In the Mall of America, as in the United States of America, there is the ubiquitous Raider cap on every head, a pair of Nikes in every store window, and the presence of professional athletes everywhere—in person, on packages, in electronic pictures. They wink as we walk past, and whisper, "Who told you you can't have it all?"

It is National Fragrance Week at the Megamall, and promotional literature promises six days "filled with activities designed to stimulate your nose." There is, for example, a Smelling Bee for children. And at Bloomingdale's, "Michelle McGann, top-ranked LPGA player, will host a breakfast and speak about what fragrance means to her."

I follow my nose to Oshman's Super Sports USA, a sporting-goods concern so breathtakingly vast that one hardly notices the basketball court, the racquetball court, the batting cage, or the archery range on its premises. Not far away, the eleven-thousand-square-foot World Foot Locker is tiny by comparison. Every NFL,

NBA, NHL, and Major League Baseball jersey is available here. World Cup jerseys are on display. Every icon of international sports appears to be represented. "We sold a lot of Astros caps this spring," general manager Dan Peterson tells me. "The Brewers, the Tigers—just about any team with a new logo sells pretty well." Which is why teams now change logos like they're changing pitchers? "Yes," agrees the affable Peterson, who is attired in a referee's shirt.

On display at Field of Dreams, a sports-memorabilia store, is the cover of SI's thirty-fifth-anniversary issue. Framed—and autographed in the enfeebled hand of Muhammad Ali—the cover can be yours for $149. A 1954 Topps Hank Aaron baseball card from his (and our) rookie year goes for $900. This same week, on a home-shopping channel, I have seen Stan Musial peddling his signature for $299.95, "or three monthly payments of $99.98." Children once got Musial's signature on a game program. Now they get it on the installment plan.

An Orlando Magic jersey signed by Shaquille O'Neal is available for $595 at Field of Dreams. I want to ask the manager how many of those the store sells, but I am reminded of the advice proffered by the Mall's T-shirt: SHUT UP & SHOP. The shirt sells, if you're interested, for $14.95.

Beneath the fronds of a potted palm, a doleful black man waits on a bench. His is the hundred-yard stare of the Mall Widower, a man whose wife was swallowed by Macy's much as sailors are claimed by the sea. The mall has a two-story miniature golf course to alleviate the Widower's ennui, but this potbellied man is a good mile away from Golf Mountain. And so he waits, in his replica NFL jersey, a three-quarters-sleeve Cleveland Browns shirt of a 1960s vintage. The number on his chest, naturally, is 32.

This corpulent Jim Brown reminds me of the corporeal Jim Brown, who would probably not be surprised to learn that six months after the Megamall opened, gunplay crackled in Camp Snoopy and three people were wounded in a struggle for a San Jose Shark jacket. This was an address on the appalling state of society, to be sure, but the shots were more than that. They were literally a ringing endorsement, a one-gun salute to the San Jose Sharks and the wild, worldwide popularity of their logo.

I am reminded of the fact that this hockey team in San Jose is a direct descendant of Gary Davidson. So is the hockey team in Orange County, California. The Anaheim Mighty Ducks are the first postmodern pro sports franchise, a mere merchandising venture owned by Disney, a logical line extension derived from a film. And as the Pepsi Ripsaw roller coaster ratchets up a hill overhead, I am further reminded that *The Mighty Ducks* sequel was filmed, in part, here, in Camp Snoopy.

A columnist once described Davidson as "always eager to meet the demand for something nobody asked for," and it occurs to me now that the same might be said for the Megamall. You can buy a synthetic human skeleton here or a sign that reads PARKING FOR LITHUANIANS ONLY or the children's book *Everyone Poops*. In this state of reverie I find my reflection in a beer at America's Original Sports Bar, twenty thousand square feet of tavern, fifty-five televisions flickering like lightning through windows at night. As ESPN parcels out the evening's highlights, I recall something Roone Arledge said as we sat in his network office. "It used to be common practice in tennis that if a tough call went against your opponent, you hit the ball into the net on the next point if you were a gentleman," he had said. "You didn't want to win because of a bad call. I can't conceive of a top tennis player doing that today. Could you see McEnroe? Connors? Andre Agassi?"

And while watching *SportsCenter,* I cannot conceive of a player today hitting a home run and running the bases with his head down. Or imagine a halfback simply handing the ball to an official after a touchdown. Why would a man merely lay the ball off the glass when he could dunk on some fool and then bark into the baseline camera, sure, like Narcissus, to see his own reflection on the cable network that night?

Only a few weeks have passed since Chicago Bull captain Scottie Pippen refused to enter a playoff game when his coach designed a play giving someone else the last-second shot. Pride and insecurity, the prospect of embarrassment, and the perception of disrespect. It is why children shoot children for their Shark jackets; it is why Derrick Coleman turns down a $69 million contract offer from the New Jersey Nets; it is why Barry Bonds demands the same obsequious deference given to the supernovas of the movie and music industries. As Agassi says in a famous TV commercial, "Image is everything."

All of which makes it devilishly tempting in 1994 to look beyond the beauty of athletic competition and see only the off-putting backdrop of marketing and money, money in amounts unimagined in 1954. "Everyone is more interested in money in most cases than they are in sport," Arledge said. "And a lot of fun has gone out of it. The original motivation a lot of us had for wanting to be a part of sports—that no longer exists." Pause. Sigh. "On the other hand, the level of performance is so high today, who could have ever imagined that?" And it became clear as he talked enthusiastically about the Stanley Cup playoffs that the harried Arledge hadn't shaken sports at all, and couldn't if he wanted to. "I'm so happy to see him talking about sports again," his assistant said while ushering me out. "I really think he misses it."

Cynicism is a sine qua non of modern citizenship, and as I continue pacing the Megamall's terrazzo floors, past the Carolina Panther beach towel beckoning from the window of Linens 'n Things, I am given to seeing sports only as the multinational business that it is. Then I think of the unfailingly upbeat baseball writer I know. He checked into a drafty old hotel in Cleveland at three o'clock in the morning a few years ago, preparing to cover the miserable Indians that afternoon. "Business or pleasure?" the desk clerk asked him, and the scribe was forced point-blank to describe the sports industry. "Business," the writer finally said, smiling, "but it's a pleasure."

Sports are a swirl-cone mix of capitalism and entertainment (it occurs to me at Freshens Yogurt), and forty years after the Army-McCarthy hearings, fourteen years after Lake Placid, four years into the post-Soviet nineties, America remains the world's leading exporter of both commodities. Ray Charles opened the Mall of America by singing a single song: "America, the Beautiful." His rendition raised gooseflesh. His reported fee for doing so was $50,000.

America, the beautiful, indeed.

★ ★ ★

They stand as twin towers of postwar American ingenuity—the fast-food emporium and the suburban shopping mall—and the two concepts are conjoined in connubial bliss in a Mall of America food court, where I am ingesting a Pepsi-Cola: "The Official Soft Drink of the Mall of America," the press kit reads. "2.6 million cups served in 1993." My "cup" is roughly the size of a nuclear-waste drum.

Pensively sipping, I cannot help but recall the two Pepsi spokespeople I had seen a day earlier, two tall-drink celebrities conversing on MTV. Orlando Magic center Shaquille O'Neal was sitting for an interview with supermodel-journalist Cindy Crawford. Shaq was demonstrating the different smiles he will rent to interested advertisers. "This is the 2.9," he began. And though a small fissure appeared across his face, Shaq was speaking not in Richter-scale figures but in millions of dollars. "This is the 5.3," he continued, grinning amiably. "And this is the 8.9." O'Neal beamed enthusiastically.

"And if somebody offered you twenty million dollars?" asked Crawford.

A ridiculous smile-for-hire engulfed O'Neal's head; he held the pose, a ghoulish grinning Shaq-o'-lantern.

You can't spell Shaquille without the letters S-H-I-L-L. Stoked by this realization, I take a stroll, attempting to count the stores in which one can purchase an item bearing the euphonious name of the seven-foot spokescenter. When the toll hits nineteen (stores, not items), I realize the laughable inadequacy of my count. I have not looked in video-game stores or in department stores. A pasty fat boy wearing an O'Neal road jersey pads past me in Shaq Attaq shoes by Reebok. I have even neglected, somehow, to count the shoe stores.

How could I have forgotten? An unmistakable size-twenty Shaq shoe stands sentry in front of World Foot Locker. One cannot handle the autographed shoe, for it reposes under glass like the Star of India. What the shoe really is, is the star of Bethlehem, drawing mall-walking magi into the store. "Shaq," the manager needlessly informs me, "is quite popular."

In Babbage's, an electronics store, I ask the manager, "Is there a video game that Shaquille O'Neal—"

"The rumor is they're working on one," the guys says, anticipating my question. "Look for it the beginning of next season." I am given to understand that the much-awaited game will have a martial-arts mise-en-scène and that it will be called . . . Shaq-Fu!

Fu, Fi, Fo, Fum: Sam Goody stocks the rap album. *Shaq Diesel,* while allegedly unlistenable, is nevertheless available on cassette and compact disc. At Toy Works, I adore the Shaq action figures by Kenner. Shaq's film debut, *Blue Chips,* has come and gone at the movieplex. *Shaq Attaq!* and *Shaq Impaq* beckon from bookstores. Shaq-signature basketballs line the shelves at Oshman's. Field of Dreams stocks wood-mounted photos of O'Neal: Shaq-on-a-Plaque. I stagger to the Coffee Beanery, Ltd., looking for Swiss Shaqolate Mocha, vacuum-Shaq-Packed in a foil Shaq-Sack. The mall's walls are closing in. T-shirts seem to be telling me to SHUT UP & SHAQ.

In addition to harvesting these golden eggs, Shaquille O'Neal is paid $48,000 per game to play a fearsome brand of basketball in Orlando. Fifteen thousand fans happily pay to watch him do so forty-one nights a year. He may yet revolutionize the game. Who told you you can't have it all?

"You can't have everything," comedian George Carlin likes to say. "Where would you put it?" It appears they've put everything here, in Champs Sports. Surrounded by officially licensed merchandise, seated in a director's chair embossed with a Mighty Duck, thirty-two televisions arrayed before me and each one of them playing NBA highlights, I rest my Niked feet at last.

For weeks I've been wondering how we got here in sports—from primitive to prime time, from the invention of the wheel to the invention of Shaquille—without ever pausing to ask, "Where are we, anyway?" Yet the information kiosks at the Mall of America make it perfectly clear. "You Are Here," all the map arrows say. "You Are Here."

(August 16, 1994)

THE SWEET SMELL
OF INNOCENCE

I nnocence survived September 11. Its walls shuddered and its windows rattled and its switchboard was silenced. But the day didn't mark the death of innocence, whose headquarters still stands, six blocks from ground zero, at 1 Whitehall Street, where the Topps Company continues to conjure up baseball cards, bubble gum, and Bazooka Joe comics for a nation in need of summer.

Step inside. The hallways are redolent of rectangles of pink bubble gum, the kind still inserted in Topps's Heritage line of baseball cards. The gum is still pressed, to judge by its texture, from the same cardboard used in the manufacture of the cards.

"People's eyes roll back in their heads when they smell the gum," says Scott Silverstein, a company vice president, his office festooned with cards and candy. "Males of a certain generation are transported back to childhood"—and here the executive gets lost in his own Proustian reverie—"and carefree days."

In an age when athletes decline White House invitations, virtually every professional baseball player, from A ball to the bigs, still signs a ridiculously unremunerative contract to appear on a Topps baseball card. For decades the deal was $5 upon signing plus $250 when the card came out. (The latter fee is now $500.) "And many times," says Silverstein, "a player has said, 'Five dollars? Great! Just let me get my wallet out of the car.' We've had to tell them, 'No, you don't understand: We pay you.'"

If the Smithsonian is America's attic, then the Topps building is a nine-year-old's bedroom. Cubicle floors are littered with laundry. The game-worn uniforms of Jeff Bagwell, Chipper Jones, and Curt Schilling will be cut into nickel-sized patches and inlaid into baseball cards. Topps' hockey honcho, Mark Sakowitz, holds a cross section of a game-used NHL puck—sliced as thin as deli salami—and says, "We're thinking of putting these into packs of hockey cards." Says an officemate, Clay Luraschi, "It's like working in Willy Wonka's factory."

"It is not unusual to be in a roomful of adults here who are blowing bubbles and sucking on [Topps] Ring Pops," says Silverstein. "It's a combination of a board meeting and the movie *Big*."

The Topps Company was founded in Brooklyn in 1938 by the four Shorin brothers—Abram, Ira, Joe, and Phil—whose first product was adult chewing gum. "During the war," says Topps CEO (and Joe's son) Arthur Shorin, a small man in a large cardigan, "our slogan was, 'Don't talk, chum, chew Topps gum.' It was along the lines of 'Loose lips sink ships.'" When the war waned, sales of Topps gum did likewise. That's when the Shorins created Bazooka, whose eye-patched mascot—Bazooka Joe—may have been named for Arthur's father. The comics that come in every nickel piece of Bazooka remain, to this day, borscht belters. (Mort: "I'm thinking of taking driving lessons." Joe: "Well, I won't stand in your way!")

The gum is still chewed by nearly every player in the big leagues. When Luis Gonzalez hocked up a gum wad that sold at auction for $10,000, that wad was Bazooka.

In 1951, to bolster candy sales, Topps began to insert baseball cards into its packs of taffy. The next year, cards were sold with gum. The modern-day baseball card—standardized in 1957 as a 2½-by-3½-inch rectangle of cardboard—was invented by a Topps employee named Sy Berger. (Card number 1 was Brooklyn's own Andy Pafko.) It was Berger who, around 1960, dumped thousands of unsold '52 Mickey Mantle cards (the most valuable Mantles) into the Atlantic Ocean.

The two worlds of Topps—baseball cards and Bazooka—realized a remarkable synthesis in 1976 when a Topps card featured

Milwaukee Brewer Kurt Bevacqua winning the 1975 Joe Garagiola/ Bazooka Bubble Gum Blowing Championship, monitored (as memory serves) by a man measuring the bubble with a caliper.

In addition to career stats, the flip side of many Topps cards features stylistically unmistakable line drawings of ballplayers, say, pumping gas in full uniform. ("Bobby works at a service station in the off-season.") The subversive American artist Robert Crumb got his start at Topps. "All the old guys are gone now," says creative director Shu Lee, referring to the masters whose canvas was the card's back, "but we have a couple of artists who studied under them."

"Before SI and *SportsCenter*," says Silverstein, "a primary conveyor of information on an athlete was the back of his baseball card." Indeed, all I ever knew of Jim Fregosi was on the back of his Topps card: "Jim is a sales executive in the off-season." Fregosi was, to go by his line drawing, a door-to-door salesman of Fuller brushes, and he rang doorbells while wearing his baseball uniform.

The other day I bought a pack of Topps at Target, peeled back the wrapper with a tingle of anticipation, and felt the hair on my neck stand at attention before I saw—staring back at me, on top of the stack—not Barry Bonds or Sammy Sosa or Pedro Martinez but (sigh) Giants pitching prospect Boof Bonser.

Then I pressed the gum to my nose and—for a moment, anyway —all was forgiven.

(May 13, 2002)

PLANET NAGANO
1998 Winter Olympics

Japanese men eat squid jerky. They buy underwear from vending machines. According to an actual survey, 78 percent of Japanese men would select, as their sole female companion on a desert island, U.S. Attorney General Janet Reno. So the indelicate conclusion is inevitably drawn: Being branded a misfit in Japanese society is, in fact, a certification of one's sanity.

No other nation walks so fine a line between what is normal and what is perverse. Japan is all fine lines. When trying to procure aspirin in a Japanese hotel, never tell the concierge, "*Atama ga itai* [my head aches]," for he might mistakenly hear an almost identical phrase, "*Kintama ga itai* [my testicles ache]." I assure you, the silence that ensues is excruciating.

The point is, Japan can be "a little difficult for the unaccustomed," which is how a Nagano restaurant called Fu-Ru-Sa-To describes the "squid guts" on its menu. Japan is nearly as difficult for the well accustomed. So on a ten-day flak-finding mission to the host nation of the 1998 Winter Olympics, one meets countless citizens who feel they somehow fail to fit into Japan. When you consider that 125 million Japanese live on four main volcanic outcroppings collectively smaller than California, they might just be speaking literally.

But probably not. For it's easy to feel out of place in a country where convention is so unconventional, where the mundane is often bizarre. "Other nations have mocked this country, saying, 'Japan's rationality is the world's irrationality,'" read a recent editorial in the *Sankei Shimbun* newspaper. "The Japanese sports world is no exception to this view."

In which case the forthcoming fortnight will be interesting, to say the least. Welcome to the Olympics. Smoking is compulsory.

The man who secured the Winter Games for his native Nagano smokes Mild Sevens through a tortoiseshell holder, which he carries at an imperious angle, in the manner of Franklin Roosevelt. "[Juan Antonio] Samaranch doesn't like me to smoke," says Soichiro (Sol) Yoshida, blowing Olympic smoke rings with each exhalation, chain-defying the president of the International Olympic Committee.

He is in his driveway, leaning rakishly on a phlegm-colored '54 Mercedes 300 rolltop sedan that once served as the limousine for West German chancellor Konrad Adenauer. The Benz now belongs to Yoshida, who has a collection of fifty classic cars that he drives only after midnight, when the rest of Nagano has gone to bed. "Japanese jealousy," he says with a sigh, by way of explanation. "I have to tell you, after we got the Games, I experienced a lot of what we call 'high-poppy syndrome.'"

Among Nagano's 360,045 residents, there is no tall poppy riper for pruning than Yoshida, the zillionaire owner of sixty-six gas stations, thirty-four Kentucky Fried Chicken franchises, and one diabolical biodiesel plant that converts used KFC oil into automotive fuel that is then sold at his gas stations.

By day Yoshida, fifty-two, drives a Land Rover that runs on old cooking oil and emits fumes that smell like Original Recipe. As the Rover belches out fried-chicken emissions, salivating pedestrians subconsciously seek out one of his ever-near KFCs.

Says Yoshida, grinning like a Batman villain, "All conditions are working perfectly for me."

Or they were until he did a dumb thing like land the Olympics. From 1988 through 1991, in eighty countries, Yoshida personally charmed, and imbibed Jack Daniel's with, each of the IOC's ninety-two voting members. He glad-handed world leaders and mingled among tenors. "I met the opera singer, what's his name, not Pavlov, the other one," he says. "Domingo!"

When Nagano was at last awarded the Winter Games, in June '91, a rival Salt Lake City representative was quoted as saying, "We did not lose to Nagano, we lost to Yoshida." The Japanese were less impressed. "People thought we were too extravagant [in courting the IOC]," Yoshida says one afternoon over steaks and wine in an exclusive Nagano restaurant—so exclusive that Yoshida and his guests are the only patrons. "We spent two billion yen. That's twenty million dollars. In Japan you cannot be so much more outstanding than other people."

This also presents a conundrum for Manabu Horii, who is imprudently distinguishing himself as the world's finest speed skater. The former world-record holder in the 1,000 meters and his nation's best hope for a kin-medaru (gold medal) in Nagano, Horii stands out among his countrymen in every way, from his skate blades (they're gold) to his scalp (it's bald).

Last year Horii found himself at the epicenter of an entomological earthquake when the governor of Nagano Prefecture, Goro Yoshimura, publicly dismissed speed skating as "uninteresting." Worse, Yoshimura likened speed skaters on an oval track to "water beetles on a whirligig." Whatever in god's name that means, the comment was presumed to be unflattering, and the guv was made to give the most abject of public apologies, serve a cruel and unusual penance of attending thirty-nine speed-skating races, and restore honor to the water beetle by praising it as an "admirable insect."

Such public embarrassment is to be avoided at all costs in Japan, which is why the country has karaoke practice booths. In any event, Horii is too good-natured to rise to the "water beetle" bait.

Seemingly every article on the interview-shy athlete, who won the 500-meter bronze medal in Lillehammer, claims he shaved his head to intimidate opponents, a fiction that is rather humorous to anyone who has met this unassuming absentee employee of the Oji Paper Company.

"I shaved my head before one race," says Horii, twenty-eight, between sips of coffee in the lobby of a hotel in Obihiro, on the northern Japanese island of Hokkaido. "It felt good, so I kept doing it. I didn't do it for an image, I did it for myself. It's normal in North America for athletes to shave their heads, like Michael Jordan. Or in ice hockey, what is his name, Mark Messier? But in Japan, it is not what the group does, so people must come up with an explanation."

That's the trouble. Japan defies explanation. Guns are legal, but bullets are not. This is a nation that produces and distributes pornographic movies that show no private parts. (Or so I am told.) By Japanese law, images of private parts are pixeled, which seems rather to be missing the whole point of pornographic movies.

Then there is the men's Olympic downhill ski course in Hakuba. The Japanese set the starting gate 1,650 meters from the finish line, rather than the 1,800 meters requested by FIS (skiing's world governing body), so that the course would not infringe on a national park farther up the mountain. That would have been admirable, except that the park is open daily to thousands of non-Olympic skiers during the rest of the ski season, raising the question: What's the point, exactly?

"No one knows the reason," Chiharu Igaya, a silver medalist in the slalom in the 1956 Games, told the Kyodo News Service. "No one can understand the explanation." After five years of resistance on the issue, Japanese Olympic officials abruptly raised the start to 1,750 meters in December. But Igaya's statement amounts to a national mantra on a multiplicity of issues in Japan: No one knows the reason.

Vending machines (*jido hambaiki*) are on every corner, selling everything from forty-ounce beers to AAA batteries. I asked a Canadian who lives in Nagano what is the oddest item he has ever seen on display in a Japanese vending machine, and he said without hesitation, "Underwear and dress shirts." In Tokyo there is now a clerkless department store containing row after row of vending machines. Why? No one knows the reason.

Yet a funny thing happens to a tourist after a week or so in this bewildering, nonsensical, Nagano-a-go-go. Just when you become convinced that Japan's rationality really is the world's irrationality, the country inexplicably begins to inspire not frustration or dread, but something close to awe.

I refer not to the nation's gratuitous technophilia, though some of Japan's solutions to problems that you didn't know you had are indeed wondrous: traffic-signal clocks that count down the seconds remaining until the light changes, or the glorious electronically heated toilet seats of Japan's upmarket hotels (rump-roasting, bum-toasting delights that ought to be made code for all new construction in North America).

Rather, I am talking about the people of Japan. Yes, their sense of humor can be obtuse. When Yoshida said he recently played a match with the crown prince of Japan at the Tokyo Tennis Club, I asked, "Did the prince use a Prince?" and Yoshida replied, "No, he used a Mizuno."

This opacity, one soon discovers, is often deliberate, and little more than a veneer. In that sense Naganoans are not unlike Nagano, whose narrow and mazy streets were designed to prevent invading hordes from ever reaching the city center. With sufficient time and chicken gas, however, you will reach central Nagano, and with similar perseverance you will likewise reach Naganoans. Know this: When you arrive at the heart of either, you will not believe your eyes.

In Nagano's small but intense nightlife district, there is an obscure bar called Police 90 that is owned and operated by ponytailed forty-six-year-old Yosio Matuzaki, who insists that you call him Machan, or "friend." Machan has a face that could stop a clock. In fact, I watched him halt the second hand on a tourist's Tag Heuer wristwatch simply by staring at it.

Nine years ago, when he was working at a Nagano hotel, Machan awoke one morning with the unaccountable abilities— paranormal, supernatural, call them what you will—that burden him to this day.

Or so I discover when I sit down to dinner at the bar one evening. Lightly applying his thumb and forefinger to the tines of the stainless-steel fork I am eating with, Machan bends them into coils. He then ties each tine into a knot. Later, he holds his hands an inch from mine, closes his eyes, and radiates a pulse of heat that feels as if he has opened an oven door. A patron puts his rental-car keys on the bar, and they violently swing toward Machan, pointing to him like a compass needle finding north.

Machan asks for a disposable lighter. When one is placed in his palm, he closes his hand and instantly reopens it, revealing a lump of melted plastic in a puddle of butane. Even Machan appears powerless to comprehend these powers. He makes celebrity spoon-bender Uri Geller look downright dilettantish, but Machan is neither rich nor famous, all but unknown even in Nagano. When I suggest he might make millions in Las Vegas, Machan and his patrons howl with laughter. "Vegas!" he says, offering his best Michael Buffer impression: "Lllladies and gentlemen . . ."

Years ago Machan made a single appearance on Japanese TV, during which he took a lie-detector test. He passed, but then he demonstrated the unreliability of the exam by using his mind to manipulate the polygraph needle.

How the hell does he do these things? With furrowed brow, Machan utters the only phrase I have ever heard that adequately explains anything in Japan. He says wearily, "I cannot explain."

Sixty-six days before the Olympics begin, countdown billboards all over Nagano reveal that there are sixty-six days before the Olympics begin. "When do the Olympics begin?" a reporter from a Nagano television station asks me in a man-on-the-street interview.

"In sixty-six days?" I venture.

The reporter nods, then says in Japanese, "Many local residents we have asked do not know the answer."

In December speed skater Hiroyasu Shimizu, who will carry Japan's flag in the opening ceremonies, tells me, "I am worried that people are not very excited yet."

Where there isn't apathy, there's antipathy. The cost of the Olympics, which could reach as high as $1.5 billion, will be borne largely by residents of Nagano Prefecture, where public debt has increased by $30,000 per household. That's a lot to pay for the privilege of watching water beetles on a whirligig.

"But without the Games," protests Yoshida, "there would be no bullet train to Nagano. There are now two major highways coming here from Tokyo, which is very rare for a Japanese city of this size."

There is indeed a bullet train, which became operational last October. It serves an exquisite squid jerky, covers the 120 miles from central Tokyo to Nagano in seventy-nine minutes, and cost a mere $7 billion.

There is, likewise, a new superhighway from Tokyo to the Nagano region. It ends at the doorstep of Shiga Kogen, a ski resort owned by Yoshiaki Tsutsumi. He's the reclusive, richer-than-Buddha president of the Japan Ski Association, a vice president of the local Olympic organizing committee, and the owner of the gargantuan Seibu corporation, whose holdings include the Prince Hotel chain and baseball's Seibu Lions, last season's Pacific League champion.

More troubling than the perception of political favoritism in Nagano is the notion that there is no snow in Nagano. The very first question at the very first press conference, in 1989, to announce Nagano's bid for the Olympics came from a Tokyo-based reporter who inquired of Yoshida, "Uh, do you have snow in Nagano?"

This winter, until early December, the answer was no, and the southernmost city ever to host the Winter Olympics was in danger of having its Games called on account of El Niño.

"I think the Games will be a success, but I am worried about the traffic," says speed skater Horii, voicing another mass concern but one that he need not worry about personally. During the Olympics, vehicles ferrying around twenty-five hundred athletes and bigwigs will be equipped with infrared sensors that instantly change red lights to green.

Rest assured, the devices will work. If you have ever gone virtual deep-sea fishing in a Nagano amusement arcade, or shopped for inch-thick TV sets in Tokyo's Akihabara electronics district, or waved to a road construction worker who turns out to be a robot, you know that Japanese society is a monument to all things man-made. Which explains why the slogan for these Olympics is "Respect for the beauty and bounty of . . . nature."

Nature? To be fair, Nagano is endowed with breathtaking natural beauty, from the perhaps too ambitiously named Japan Alps to the enviable monkeys at the Shiga Kogen hot springs, where 265 simians live out their days enjoying one long monkey shvitz.

Precisely because there is so much beauty, environmental activists have been going monkey-shvitz ever since Nagano announced its bid. Yoshida occasionally encountered anti-Olympic eco-protesters from Japan during his bid-related overseas travels. "Fortunately they would chant in Japanese, so only I understood them," he says. "They didn't have much money, so they couldn't follow me to many places."

The irony is that Japanese Olympic officials are now the folks without much money. They made their bid at the late-eighties apex of Japan's bubble economy. It was a giddy time when—according to at least one newspaper account—people thought nothing of "spending thousands of dollars on funerals for their pets."

That was then. Today, of course, the whole of Asia's economy is going down the electronically heated toilet. "The Japanese [economic] system was built after World War Two and never checked very closely," says Yoshida, who earned his MBA from Michigan State in 1969. "What we are seeing now is like metal fatigue in aircraft." Only days earlier, Japan's giant Yamaichi securities company failed, prompting its silver-haired chairman to appear on national television and dutifully weep in shame.

There is unlikely to be such a denouement to these Olympics, though officials do have some explaining to do. Nagano won the Games in part by promising to pay the travel expenses of all visiting athletes. They can now afford just $1,000 per athlete. A promised twelve-thousand seat hockey arena will in fact hold fewer than nine-thousand spectators, some of whom will have to stand.

Blame everything on the Japanese bureaucracy. Everyone in Japan blames everything on the Japanese bureaucracy. It is a favorite target of Yoshida, a maverick who is married to a Minneapolis-born woman named Carole. ("With an *e*! I don't know why she spells it this way," Yoshida says.) Their son and daughter both live in the United States.

"*Wa* means harmony," says Yoshida. "When we make a team in Japan, we must have *wa*. The Japanese concept of *wa* is, if there are four of us working together, and you have four units of competence, and someone else has three units, and I have two units, then we all work together at two units of competence. This is the kind of teamwork respected in Japan."

Wa went out the window in Nagano's pursuit of the Olympics, he says. "If we tried to get the Olympic Games by *wa* system, we wouldn't have cared about the outcome," says Yoshida. "Under *wa* system, if we lose to Salt Lake City, we should just cry and say, 'Well, we worked very hard.'"

In parting, he adds his hope that these Olympics will become a global group hug. "If the Japanese people think the Olympics are our success, that we won over other international communities, then this is not good," he says. "But I think these Games will be the beginning of a good change."

Sports are an engine for change in the world because they transcend cultural and religious differences. They are Esperanto, as catholic as the life-sized Colonel Sanders outside the Kentucky Fried Chicken on Chuo-Dori, the bustling street that leads uphill to the stunning centerpiece of Nagano Zenkoji temple.

On this morning, before a lapis lazuli altar, a blue-robed Buddhist priest sounds a silver gong in a solemn ceremony inside Zenkoji. The temple is fourteen hundred years old and has burned to the ground eleven times, most recently in 1707. The priest is forty-one years old, and his name is Katsuhika Ito. When he smiles without his false front teeth, he looks alarmingly like former Broad Street Bully Bobby Clarke.

That is no coincidence. The priest's teeth have been knocked out repeatedly by the butt end of a hockey stick. "I have given up trying to have them fixed," Ito says that evening at the Nagano Skate Center, a dilapidated indoor rink where the player-coach-goon of the Nagano beer-league Polar Stars is conducting hockey practice. He has shed his priestly vestments for a pair of Philadelphia Flyers breezers and a Los Angeles Kings practice jersey, which he obtained when playing with members of the Kings at their practice center in L.A., where Ito's sister lives. Ito is an ardent fan of the NHL. The Polar Stars' game jerseys are modeled on the Pittsburgh Penguins'. He will work as a volunteer at Olympic hockey games. When I ask him whom he admires in hockey, he looks at me to make sure that the question is not rhetorical, then gives the inescapable answers. "Gretzky," he says, "and Messier."

As a player Ito is more Messier than Gretzky, a hard-knuckled forward unafraid to drop his gloves. "I think I know him," Yoshida says, when told of Zenkoji's hockey-playing priest. "He drinks at my bar. He is a tough guy, yes?"

Ito has been skating since fourth grade, when the Nagano Skate Center opened. He has been a priest since he was twenty-three. He sees no conflict in his twin passions; to him, they complement each other. "In sport and religion, I believe in doing one's best," he says. "Believe in the god that you believe in in the best way that you can. I tell this to schoolchildren in motivational speeches."

He is pleased that CBS has built a makeshift studio on the grounds at Zenkoji, from which the network will broadcast the image of the temple around the world for sixteen days. "Of course there are problems," says Ito, leaning on his stick. "But we hope to have the best Olympics possible. I think it is great that people will identify Japan with religion and with Zenkoji temple."

In the winking fluorescent light of the ice rink, Japan suddenly seems not so very foreign after all. You say Zenkoji, I say Zamboni. Why call the whole thing off?

I have breakfast with Koji Aoki, a Japanese sports photographer who is as callous as the rest of us in this business, and talk naturally turns to . . . ice dancing. Aoki remarks that his favorite Olympic moment came at the 1984 Sarajevo Games, when British ice dancers Jayne Torvill and Christopher Dean scored a string of perfect 6's.

The photographer saw the twosome ten years later, after the Lillehammer Games—they were gnawing on stale cinnamon rolls in the Oslo airport. Aoki approached them and said evenly, "I saw you in Sarajevo. I was there. And I want to thank you. It is rare in life that one gets to witness such a . . . "—he paused, then lit upon the appropriate phrase—"such a moment of perfection."

Then, as now, Aoki's eyes went slick, like resurfaced ice, and so did the eyes of Torvill and Dean. "I could see," says Aoki, recalling the scene, "that this touched them."

Isn't that all you can ask, from life or from the Olympics: amid all the manifold problems, a moment of perfection?

Nagano has already given me one. It transpired in the Police 90 pub, with its multiple portraits of Marilyn Monroe, whom Machan admires because, as he puts it, "hers is a story that could never happen in Japan." I took him to mean all of it, the good and the bad, the blond hair, the drug overdose, the marriage to DiMaggio, the peculiarly American miasma of superstardom.

Anyway, police paraphernalia (and the year of its grand opening) give Police 90 its name. There is an arsenal of weaponry on the walls and an AK-47 behind the bar. "I can own the guns but not the bullets," Machan says. It is a concept that now makes sense to me. Machan was fascinated when an FBI agent popped into the pub last year, sweeping Nagano in advance of a visit by Hillary Clinton. "We have nothing like the FBI in Japan," he says. "It simply isn't an issue here." Imagine that.

As I did, Machan was behind the bar, mixmastering this little moment of perfection. In one flourish he broke a spoon into pieces with his gaze, poured a pair of Suntorys from the tap, and answered the bar phone with the harried *Moshi-moshi* of a Japanese publican. I sat by, slack-jawed, with a British photographer, a Canadian interpreter, a German editor, and a Japanese blues guitarist named Sam.

On the bar, our drinks had left five linked rings that resembled the Olympic logo. An authentic CHiPs motorcycle stood sentry by the doorway. Someone taught me the proper phrase for aspirin-procurement in Japan (*futsuka yoii*: "hangover"). A man at the bar sang the Sex Pistols' "Anarchy in the UK" on karaoke. At that moment I felt precisely the way the Olympics are supposed to make you—and me, and everybody else—feel: like nothing less, and nothing more, than a citizen of planet earth.

(February 9, 1998)

EMERALD ISLE HOPPING

I n Ireland, when a caddie says, "Yer too farty," he does not mean
that you're excessively flatulent but rather that you're 240 yards
from the green. Unless you're my brother Tom, in which case he
means both. Or so my family and I learned during seven swelter-
ing days in Ireland, playing golf courses that sounded like draft
beers (Old Head) and drinking draft beers that sounded like golf
courses (Smithwick).

In truth, not all our time was spent golfing or drinking. No,
much of it was spent golfing *and* drinking. In Tralee, I abstained
while my caddie shotgunned cider. An older man with twin
mushroom clouds of white hair billowing from his ears, he had
to be chauffeured, by a ranger on a golf cart, over much of the
back nine. This allowed him to do drive-by readings of my putting line. On most shots he simply sighed on impact, "Oh, *Jaysis,*
no."

Not that I could blame him. Over the week I sprayed more
balls than Cruex. When I asked my caddie at Old Head what the
course record was, he said, "Safe." In the evening my brothers
and I sneaked onto the course at the Killarney Golf and Fishing
Club, pulling a cooler full of Harp packed, in ice-bereft Ireland,
in frozen bags of Birds-Eye garden peas. We played until dark, at
which time we could just make out, circling us in the gloaming,
a dozen predatory pack animals. When a bus made a U-turn in

the parking lot, sweeping the course with its headlights, we saw, to our horror, what these creatures really were: twelve other cheap bastards, also playing Killarney for free, their beers packed in frozen-broccoli bags.

Mostly, they were other Americans. On the hottest day in a decade in Ireland, the locals were all on the beach at Ballybunion, where the only thing bronzed was the statue of Bill Clinton, driver in hand, in the center of town. The alabaster natives were turning pink, shellacked though they were in sunscreen.

Rounds of golf succumbed to rounds of Guinness. At Oscar Madison's in Kinsale we drank to America's greatest sportswriter. (And, in a manner of speaking, *with* him: the bar is festooned with photos of Jack Klugman.) In every pub we found ourselves playing—in time to the music, against our better judgment—air accordion.

With a hired bus and driver the eight of us traversed the breadth of counties Kerry, Clare, and Cork, from which my great-great-grandfather, James Boyle, emigrated to Cincinnati 150 years ago. And so, if you riffle past ALOU and just beyond BOYER in *The Baseball Encyclopedia,* you'll find another big league baseball family: the two sets of Boyle brothers, Jack and Eddie and their nephews Buzz and Jim. Jim Boyle, my grandfather, played catcher for a single inning of a single game at the Polo Grounds for the 1926 New York Giants.

His sixty-two-year-old son, my uncle Pat, came with us to Ireland, but Pat's wife, my aunt Sandy, did not. Nor did any wives. "It gets real old saying, 'Nice shot,' one hundred fifty times a round," explained Uncle Pat, who still parties like it's 1899.

Uncle Pat bunked all week with my dad, who unburdened himself at breakfast on the third day, whispering to us—with a deeply disquieted look on his face—"Pat sleeps in the nude." This was not a good swing thought to take to Old Head. Eight miles off its fairways, along with countless souls and a few hundred thousand Maxfli Noodles, rests the *Lusitania.* One of its three salvaged propellers was bought by a company in the British Virgin Islands and forged into thirty-five hundred sets of golf clubs.

In Ireland money and sports remain strange bedfellows, not unlike my dad and Uncle Pat. Each of the Irish football quarterfinal matches last week drew—in a nation of 3.9 million—seventy thousand spectators to Croke Park in Dublin. It's the per capita equivalent of five million Americans attending an AFC wild-card game. And yet the players—national celebrities—aren't paid. "They play for pride of county," said Johnny, my caddie at Waterville, "and they go back to work on Monday morning."

In one quarterfinal, Laois manager Mick O'Dwyer screamed so hard at his squad that his dentures flew out, tracing a perfect parabola in midair, a photograph that ran in all the Irish dailies the next day. For all I know, the disencraniumed teeth are still going, like those novelty windup chattering choppers, chewing on the ass of some poor Laois midfielder even now.

"I'd like to see yer man, the average American footballer—guy six-tree, tree-turty-five, wit all tem pads and whatsit—have a go at one of our lads," said Keith, our diminutive bus driver from Tipperary, with a sardonic laugh. Our padded NFL behemoth, Keith suggested quite convincingly, would be turned into lumpy mashed pot*ay*toes by his boys.

Even so, the toughest man in Ireland last week was Jim Rushin —my bunkmate and brother, twelve weeks removed from a bone-marrow transplant—playing seven rounds in six days in ninety-degree heat on a cruel, doctor-imposed ration of one beer a day. No matter. Guinness is good for you. But golf, it turns out, is even better.

(August 18, 2003)

THE NEW PERFESSER

Beautiful blue-rinsed Tiger Stadium, home of the Detroit Baseball Club, is directly across Trumbull Avenue from the Checker Cab Company, whose telephone number is displayed on the front of its building: WO3-7000. In Detroit there are still Checker cabs and a Woodward exchange and old Tiger Stadium, where members of the Detroit Baseball Club still play for manager George (Sparky) Anderson. Things should forever be this way: a timeless painting, "Sunday in the Park with George."

"I wish there was such a thing as 'You could do this forever,' and there ain't, let's face it, it don't work that way," says Sparky himself, the words tumbling forth in one Stengelesque exhalation. When Sparky opens his mouth, words fall out like items from Fibber McGee's closet.

He seldom brakes for periods. Sparky believes in punctuation, he just thinks the word means being on time. "I truly don't know the language," he is happy to concede. "I wish I could know the difference between a noun and a pronoun and an adverb and a verb, but I don't know, and you know, I don't wanna know. Why do you have to know English? It's like 'two'. There's three twos! There's tee-oh, there's tee-doubleya-oh, and there's tee-double-oh! Three twos! Now, if I put any one of those down in a letter, you know which one it is I'm talkin' about. It's like 'there' and 'their.' What's the difference, as long as you know there's a *there* there?"

Hear, hear.

It was Gertrude Stein who once said of Oakland, "There's no there there." It was Sparky Anderson who once said of nostalgia, "I've got my faults, but living in the past isn't one of them—there's no future in it."

As usual, he is right. Why live in the past when you have a first-place team in the present? His Cincinnati Reds finished in first place in the National League West in Sparky's first year as a Major League manager. Twenty-three years later his Tigers are in first place in the American League East. While all about him skippers have come and gone and often come again, Sparky alone has managed a Major League club every summer since 1970. Out of chaos . . . order. Out of Stump, Stick, Doc, Buck, Bucky, Bambi, Jimy, Yogi, Whitey, Blackie, Jackie, Dusty, Cookie, Frenchy, Sherry, Salty, Smokey, and Stanky . . . *Sparky*.

Why brake for periods when you've raced through life as if the light were yellow? Sparky's hair turned white when he was in his twenties. He was a big league manager at thirty-five. Already this season, at the relatively youthful age of fifty-nine, Sparky has won the two thousandth game of his magisterial managerial career.

Already this season he has passed Leo Durocher and is on the verge of passing Walter Alston to take fifth place on the list of baseball's all-time winningest skippers, disproving what the Lip once said about nice guys. Within two years Sparky will pass Joe McCarthy and Bucky Harris to take third place, behind untouchables John McGraw and Connie Mack. "It just means I'm gettin' old," says Sparky. "I was tellin' Lou Piniella the other day, a guy hangs around the bar long enough, he'll get drunk."

Nonsense. Sparky's teams have won seven division titles, five pennants, and three world championships. One of each would be enough for most men, but Sparky Anderson likes redundancy. Thus, "Stengel is my all-time favorite in the history of baseball," Sparky will say. Or, "I've never had a complaint on an airplane ever." (Which is true—you could look it up.) In Sparkyese, "stats and statistics" may be manipulated to perpetuate "fallacies and falsehoods," the opposite of which happen to be "true facts."

In any event, "When you win, you sleep better, everything's better, and that's a true fact," says Sparky, whose team has put him in an especially wonderful mood in his wood-paneled office at Tiger Stadium this day. Three pipes and a silver tamp are arrayed neatly on an ancient wooden desk. Folds of skin hang from his cheekbones like curtains drawn open on his brilliant white smile. He has those white eyebrows as well, and that white head of hair. Yessir, George Lee Anderson has the matching set, much like that other tactical and syntactical adventurer, the Ol' Perfesser, Charles Dillon Stengel.

It is a beguiling package. Hence this informal study of the man, this Sparkaeological expedition, which begins with our subject about to address reporters. Full-volume heavy-metal music coming from the clubhouse threatens to blow Sparky's closed office door from its hinges.

How are ya, Sparky?

"If they'd turn that noise down, I'd be fine," he says. "But go ahead, gentlemen, with whatever maaarrrvelous questions you have."

In response to an inquiry about Rob Deer's condition, Sparky mentions that the Tiger right fielder is being placed on the disabled list. "He moved his neck yesterday and it hurt in the bottom of his back, and that's not good, no-hooo," explains Dr. Anderson. He then acknowledges that a certain Tiger is indeed unhappy on the bench. Admits Sparky, "He don't wanna not play."

A man delivers the mail. Sparky rescues *The Sporting News* and *Golf World* from the teetering pile, then puts on his black-framed reading glasses. Hideous human screams, independent of the stereo, come from beyond his door, followed by the crashing of clubhouse furniture.

"It's never lonesome here," Sparky says without looking up from his *Golf World*. "That's the nice thing."

Lonesome? Sparky would need a Rolodex the size of a riverboat paddle wheel to catalog his friends. If you went to third grade with George Anderson, he probably remembers your name. It's the names of opposing players that occasionally elude Sparky. He is aware of this dread affliction, which is why the other day he said apologetically of a California Angel catcher, "I call him Tingley." (The catcher's name *is* Tingley.) Sparky gets no help from Detroit's famously malaprop scoreboard, on which Chicago White Sox center fielder Lance Johnson once became LANCE LANCE and Seattle Mariner relievers Russ Swan and Dwayne Henry were gene-spliced into one ambidextrous man named SWAN HENRY.

For a moment during one game last season, the Tiger Stadium scoreboard actually read AT BAT NUMBER II SPARKY ANDERSON. Given Sparky's maddeningly Byzantine lineup changes, this could actually come to pass. While making a substitution the other day, Sparky told an umpire, "I'm puttin' only one guy in here, but there'll be five movements out there, don't pay no attention to 'em."

Even as he is calling the Cleveland Indians' Paul Sorrento "Sarmiento," precise details of his own life remain stuck in Sparky's brain like lawn darts. Thus, George Anderson was raised at 1087 West 35th Street in Los Angeles. He was fired by "Cincinnatuh" team president Dick Wagner on November 28, 1978, in room 1118 of the airport Marriott in Los Angeles. He was hired by the Detroit Baseball Club on June 12, 1979. He went to bed at 12:27 last night and arose at 7:45 this morning.

Sparky has a prodigious memory in many areas. The only thing that has acquired more lines than Sparky's face is Sparky himself. He remembers every felicitous phrase he has ever heard. In this regard he envies his friend and former minor league teammate Tommy Lasorda. "Tommy said in his book that he was so poor growing up that he could tell when he stepped on a nickel if it was heads or tails," says Sparky. "Man, how great. How he comes up with 'em, I don't know."

To apply an old line to an old manager, Sparky Anderson doesn't have to be naked to count to 21. We know this because just the other day he mentioned the importance of mathematics. "You have to know your math," he said. "In school, I used to be finished with my math so early, I'd go to the bathroom, come back, and they'd still be workin' on it. Now, when a contractor's throwin' numbers together, I know if they add up." Sparky looks you square in the eye and taps his right index finger to a snow-white temple.

"But English?" he continues. "What's the difference? If you're a writer, yeah, you gotta put it all in there or you'll get letters from teachers. But I see now they're even puttin' 'ain't' in the dictionary, so I'm good, man." Sparky beams. "I'm covered."

He is a learned man. Sparky frequently precedes his serpentine sentences with the phrase "There's one thing I've learned." There's one thing he's learned . . . and that one thing is something different every time. "There's one thing I've learned," says Sparky. "Live today the way today's lived. Every father walked through snowstorms to get to school. That's not today. Things change, so change with 'em."

"He's changed with us and the times," confirms shortstop Alan Trammell, a Tiger since 1977. "He changed the dress code this year. He now lets us wear nice jeans—*nice* jeans—on the road. But not on airplanes. You still have to wear slacks and a sport coat on airplanes. For the first time in my lifetime, except for the World Series, wives were allowed on one of the road trips. It's the nineties, and he understands that."

"I wish that when I started managing, I understood the needs of the players," says Sparky. "My first concern now is them. When I started managing, my first concern was me. Meeee. I don't know why you can't put it all together when you're young."

Life should be lived backward. ("Thaaaat's right," agrees Sparky.) If it were, think of all that this man would have to look forward to: managing the Tigers, then the Reds, then nine years of playing and managing in the minor leagues. A big break comes in 1959 when Sparky is called up to the last-place Philadelphia Phillies and hits .218 in the only 477 Major League at bats of his career. After six more years in the minors, it is off to L.A.'s Dorsey High, where Sparky and the baseball team win forty-two consecutive games. By 1951 he is playing shortstop for Crenshaw Post No. 715, which wins the American Legion national championship at Briggs Stadium in Detroit, the ballpark now called Tiger Stadium.

"When I'm here, I'm at home," Sparky says while sitting in the Tiger dugout, the very same one the Crenshaw Post team used forty-two years ago. "There are days when I'm at home and I say, 'Oh, Christ,' I say to my wife, 'I don't mean this against you, but when I'm here'"—Sparky is back at the ballpark now—" 'I'm home.'"

"You have to realize that everything revolves around baseball for George," says Tiger coach Billy Consolo. "It is the only thing he has ever wanted to do. Other kids had hobbies. For George it has always been baseball."

When both boys were eight years old, George Anderson met Billy Consolo on the Rancho playground in Los Angeles. The Andersons had just moved west from Bridgewater, South Dakota, and the Consolos had come from Cleveland. George and Billy were best of friends through high school and Legion ball, and a lifetime later, in June 1979, Sparky asked his friend to join his staff in Detroit.

"I'd been out of baseball for so long at that point that I really wanted to be around for a while," says Consolo, who played for ten years in the Major Leagues. "So before the press conference that announced George as manager, I asked him not to make any statements that would put us in a hole."

Sparky cleared his throat that day and announced to a throng of reporters, "We'll win it all in five years."

"And I thought, I'm back to barbering in five years," says Consolo, who had a world championship ring exactly five years later.

Postscript: For the sheer euphony of the phrase, it should be noted here that Sparky played with Spanky. The Rancho playground was next to the MGM studio lot, and the "Little Rascals" and other child stars of the day often played sandlot ball there with George and Billy. Billy cannot confirm with certainty that Spanky played with Sparky. "But," he says, "I know we did play with Buckwheat."

Sparky hates to travel. Those who know him say he remains in his hotel room on road trips, bingeing on CNN's *Headline News.* It is one of the little joys in his life. Sparky goes "Around the World in 30 Minutes" several times a day, and that is enough travel for one man. When Carol Anderson recently asked her husband of forty years if he would like to experience the breathtaking sweep of the Grand Canyon, Sparky issued the only one-word answer of his life: "No."

If Sparky were a test, he would have no short-answer section. Sparky Anderson is all essay. It is a rainy Monday afternoon in Chicago, and Sparky sits tugging on a pipe in the visiting manager's office at Comiskey Park. He is staring trancelike at the portable TV that rests, on a desk, two feet from his face. But Sparky looks up from the College World Series on ESPN to consider this question: You don't enjoy traveling anymore, do you?

"When you first start out young," says Sparky, throwing out a triple redundancy for openers, "you enjoy all of the travel. The first time I had a suite, my God! But as time goes on, you get spoiled. You're spoiled in the Major Leagues, let's face it. Phil Niekro said it best. They asked him why he continued to play on and on all those years, and he said, 'Nobody ever gives you meal money in real life.' And it's true. The air travel is first class. The hotels, outstanding. We're spoiled, and it's as simple as that. Half of us wouldn't know how to get a plane ticket in the wintertime.

"In twenty-four years I've learned something, a trick, I do this religiously. When I'm on the road, nobody sees me. Period. I do not socialize at any time on the road. I'm up at a quarter to eight, and I do the little radio show I have. Most of these hotels have a room with coffee, juice, fruit, and sweet rolls, and sometimes I take that back to my room. I watch CNN. I'll watch CNN for four trips around. I'll know every single thing that's happening in sports and business, the world. I watched the news from Bosnia four times today. Then I'll go back to bed and cut off the phone. I went back to bed at ten-oh-seven this morning and got up at five after one."

He has been known to exhaust entire stenography pools with a single answer, but Sparky refuses formal speaking engagements. In Cincinnati in the 1970s folks said grace before every meal, and the manager of the Big Red Machine made a few remarks after the meal. But no more. Because now he is certain of who he is. "The biggest misconception about me is that I'm an extrovert," he says. "I'm an introvert. My real name is George, and that's the name I like best, and it's who I am. 'Sparky' was given to me as a player, and it stayed with me. It's great that people recognize me for that. But 'George' is who I am, and when I hit spring training, it takes me four or five days to become Sparky again. My wife, she always knows when I switch over from George to Sparky."

But even after he blooms each spring, not everyone calls him Sparky. Consolo calls him George year-round, and Consolo is not alone. "If he hears someone in the crowd say 'Sparky,' he might not turn around," says Consolo. "But if he hears someone say 'George,' he'll turn around, because he knows it's someone he went to school with." Another man who calls him George is American League umpire Al Clark, who explained three years ago, "I refuse to call a fifty-six-year-old man with white hair 'Sparky.'"

"The job is like any other job," says Sparky. "It's a selling job, and I have to be extroverted to sell the players I want to sell."

He never met a Tiger he didn't want to sell. Chris Pittaro? "He has a chance to be the greatest second baseman who ever lived," Sparky once said, adding that the youngster was "the best rookie infielder I've seen in fifteen years of managing." Rico Brogna? "The finest young player I've seen since Johnny Bench." Torey Lovullo? "I'll die," said Sparky, "before he comes out of the lineup." Sparky lives. In Detroit, Lovullo does not.

When you are a veritable Mount Pinatubo of enthusiasm and kindness, you simply cannot help yourself. In 1982 Sparky publicly proclaimed that he would not make any more predictions (which of course was itself a prediction). Hours after the story rolled off the presses, Sparky approached Boston Red Sox hitting coach Walt Hriniak at the Tiger Stadium batting cage. It was June. The Mariners were hot. "Watch Seattle," Sparky said, arching those eyebrows meaningfully. "They're gonna win the whole thing."

In 1989 Sparky took seventeen days off in the middle of the season for what he describes as "personal reasons." Sparky is old enough to remember when there were such things as "personal reasons," and, admirably, his personal reasons remain personal. Sparky is the last American celebrity not to gleefully fly his dirty laundry from a flagpole in the town square. In fact, he has no dirty laundry. Sparky is said to spend most days in the off-season padding about his Thousand Oaks, California, home in a sweatsuit.

"My wife and I, we're like old farmers," he says. "We're not party people. I don't care about celebrities. I ain't awed by 'em, and if I'm one of 'em, I ain't awed by me. The word 'celebrity' and the word 'VIP'? *Ha ha heh heh hgggh.* I die laughing when I get a letter marked VIP. It says call this number to say whether you're coming or not. I don't wanna go to the White House. I don't wanna go nowhere.

"Show-business people, that don't thrill me. I just wanna be around old friends who don't wanna talk about baseball. People think I'm outgoing, I'm not at all. If our general manager wants to talk to me in the wintertime about a deal he's got going, we'll talk. But otherwise the office doesn't call me, and I don't call the office. I want four and a half months to be a grandfather.

"I have nine grandchildren. Three children and nine grandchildren. My wife and I, we're in the same house in Thousand Oaks we bought twenty-seven years ago, and I'll be there when I die because that's where our children were raised. If they don't want the house when I'm dead, it'll be up to them to sell it, not me."

It is a wonderful, Sparkyrific sentiment, and he is adamant about it: He will not sell the house when he's dead.

"They used to plunk ya regular."

Sparky is holding forth this Thursday in front of the Tiger bat rack. The subject is the lost science of beanball pitching. Someone has informed Sparky that the Angels and the Toronto Blue Jays engaged in an eighteen-minute brawl late last night on the West Coast. This gets Sparky going on the sundry atrocities that pitchers once perpetrated on hitters.

"What's this?" asks Tiger designated hitter Kirk Gibson, sidling over to his manager, surveying the audience, his interest clearly piqued. "We got the Thursday court here. Really feedin' 'em the shit today, huh?"

In reply Sparky gushes to Gibson the news he has just heard about the brawl in Anaheim. "They said there were something like eighteen different fights," sputters Sparky. "No, no, an eighteen-minute fight. They said it was great! And it was Ball Night, and the fans were throwin' the baseballs at 'em!"

"Always happens with Ball Night," says Gibson, a grin curling in one corner of his mouth. "Be a shaaame if that happened here, wouldn't it?"

Two hours later, before 16,532 fans, Sparky is on the third base line, giving home plate umpire Dale Ford the international up-yours sign: clutching his right biceps with his left hand, Sparky thrusts his right fist upward. Ford, who has just made an egregious call behind the plate, sheepishly ejects Sparky. As he leaves the field, Sparky stops to greet a friend of his who happens to be umpiring third base. "You're outstanding, Richie," he tells Richie Garcia, apropos of nothing. "Outstanding."

That's Sparky. He can't help himself. There's one thing he has learned, and his father, Leroy, taught it to him when he was eleven years old: Being nice doesn't cost anything. "Doesn't cost a dime," says Sparky. "Look at Alan Trammell. I call him Huckleberry Finn. You would never know to talk to him that he's accomplished all that he has."

"He taught me that," says Trammell. "He taught me that when I was twenty-one and looking for direction, when I thought I knew it all and didn't. And I still appreciate that. It is a pleasure to play for him, not just because he'll be in the Hall of Fame as a manager, but because of the kind of person he is."

A flight attendant drew Sparky aside as the Tigers were deplaning from a recent charter flight. She told him that she and her crew had just flown a National League team into St. Louis, and the players had turned that trip into an ugly airborne bacchanal. She thanked this skipper for his tight ship.

"Thank me?" responded Sparky. "Let me ask you something. Isn't this the way it's supposed to be? Why not be nice on an airplane? Why not be nice when you're out in society? Why give me credit for acting the way people are supposed to act?"

Leroy Anderson died during the historic 35–5 run that began the Tigers' championship season of 1984. But Sparky's mother, Shirley, is still alive. "And I wouldn't embarrass her for the world," says

Sparky. "I'm in a restaurant, that waitress could be my mother, could be my sister. If the food stinks, don't go back. But don't get all worked up and take it out on the waitress. Treat everybody as if they're somebody, because they are. That's one thing I've learned."

A homemade sign in his office reads EACH 24 HOURS, THE WORLD TURNS OVER ON SOMEONE WHO IS SITTING ON TOP OF IT. That is Sparky. Another sign says A MAN NEVER STANDS SO TALL AS WHEN HE STOOPS TO HELP A CRIPPLED CHILD. That is also Sparky. The sign above the office door through which Sparky passes most days reads ATTITUDE. Every week when the Tigers are at home he takes his extraordinary attitude to Henry Ford Hospital in Detroit, spreading joy among ailing children like some antidisease.

On his last visit Sparky tried to cheer a boy who was awaiting skin grafts to his face. The child had nearly been electrocuted. Ten thousand volts had surged through his body. Seven days later, two hours before a game three hundred miles from Detroit, Sparky still can't shake thoughts of the kid.

"You and me," he says, "we wake up tomorrow, what's our biggest problem? You might have a few bills? I might have a loss? This little boy and his parents—he lived, he's doing fine, he'll be okay, but . . . People feel bad for a baseball player having a bad year? Our values are so messed up it's unbelievable.

"I was watching this thing on the Chinese immigrants on CNN. They went a hundred and forty some days on a boat. Without a bathroom. And I'm laying myself down in a suite tonight? If you don't recognize what you have, man, something is wroonnng."

What Sparky has this day is a one-game lead in his division. The Tigers finished in sixth place last season. Many fans wanted Sparky fired, but many more grieved needlessly for this endearing Casey Bengal.

"People say"—and here Sparky affects an old lady's voice—"'Oh, I feel so sorry for Sparky and his club.' All the years I've had? All the luck I've had? Jesus Christ, feel *sorry* for me? Don't feel sorry for me. In fact, root *against* me. I've had too many good ones. If I manage five, six more years, I could have an El Stinko every one of 'em, all the luck I've had. Don't feel sorry for me."

★   ★   ★

As Sparky imprudently attempts to moonwalk in his office, one fears he will stumble on the blue carpet, like Carnac the Magnificent, and go crashing through his desk. Sparky is doing a ridiculous impersonation of the slapstick, showboating umpire in the film *The Naked Gun*. Because his Tigers strike out so frequently, Sparky perversely appreciates the punch-out techniques of the league's most flamboyant umpires.

"You know what I'm waitin' for?" Sparky asked a moment ago. "Someday we're gonna see the cat really put it in for us, like that guy in the movie, what the hell's his name, Leslie Nielsen. We're gonna see the ump doin' this." And then, his eyes glinting impishly, Sparky stood. On one foot. He started hopping. Backward. With his arms, Sparky began doing what disco instructors once called "rolling the dough" and what NBA officials do to signify a traveling violation. He pirouetted. And, suddenly, the precarious moonwalk attempt. Now Sparky is laughing that wonderfully contagious laugh, the one that sounds like a power sander, and hanks of hair have fallen over his watering eyes.

"Oh, God!" Sparky shouts over the heavy metal. "That's what I'd do if I was umpirin'! I'd be in your dugout!" He presses his face to within inches of a writer's and then punches an invisible speed bag repeatedly with his right fist. "Yooo-oooo-ouurrre OUT!" Sparky trills polysyllabically, and with that he is out the door himself, cackling maniacally in the clubhouse.

Four witnesses exit wheezing before one of them can finally speak. "We are blessed," says a Tiger beat writer, shaking his head. A cynical old scribe like the rest of us in this racket, and he actually says that. By George, "We are blessed."

(January 25, 1992)

THE RIGHT STUFFING

I t would have none of the fanfare, and few of the table manners, found at the G8 summit of economic superpowers. But the G8 summit of gastronomic superpowers would be no less momentous, as eight world champions of competitive eating gathered for a Thanksgiving EatOff at Mickey Mantle's sports bar, a New York City shrine to competitive drinking.

The Group of Eight included four wafer-thin men. Crazy Legs Conti has eaten three and three quarter pounds of pancakes and half a pound of bacon in twelve minutes and run the New York City Marathon, though not consecutively. Joe Menchetti once consumed forty-five conch fritters in six minutes. Oleg Zhornitskiy laid waste to seventy-four buffalo wings in twelve minutes. And the hundred-thirty-pound Rich LeFevre, in six hundred seconds, inhaled one and a half gallons of five-alarm chili. Though slight of stature, these men are, in the dog-eat-chili-dog world of competitive consumption, larger than life: four faces on eating's Mount Flushmore.

Yet these Four Forkmen of the Apocalypse reflect a larger, and disturbing, trend. Have you noticed? Once peopled with literal giants like Babe Ruth and Art Donovan, sport makes less and less room at the table for fat guys, who are increasingly consigned to society's margins, if not its margarines. Competitive eater Don Lerman, in five terrible minutes last year, ate seven quarter-pound sticks of butter, inserting them lengthwise into his maw—one after another—like a man dispatching logs into a woodchipper.

Indeed, the Tiger Woods of competitive eating, Japan's Takeru (the Tsunami) Kobayashi, weighs all of 113 pounds. (Before competition.) "To call Kobayashi the Tiger Woods of competitive eating," says Rich Shea, president of the International Federation of Competitive Eating, "is to slight Kobayashi." Last Fourth of July, Kobayashi ate fifty and a half hot dogs and buns in twelve minutes. The next closest competitor, three-hundred-plus—plus—pound Eric (Badlands) Booker, ate twenty-six and a half. So guess what he's doing? "Right now I'm trying to lose what Kobayashi weighs—a hundred and thirteen pounds—for next July Fourth," says Booker, who once ate, while in a self-described "zone," forty-nine glazed doughnuts in eight minutes. "If I can then expand my stomach to meet my [stretched] skin, the sky's the limit for me."

In all sports it now, literally, pays to be thin. The Tsunami is rumored to make a quarter of a million dollars a year by eating professionally. Boosters have pledged $1,000 for every pound that Maryland football coach Ralph (Fridge) Friedgen loses, and at last report the Fridge, who began his regimen at 355 pounds, was forty pounds—and boosters were forty grand—lighter.

Fat is costing Chris Childs money. Last month the six-foot-three New Jersey guard, who was a swollen 230 pounds, was suspended by the Nets, packed off to the Duke Diet and Fitness Center, and ordered to lose twenty pounds. Inspired, Childs began to drop weight that very day, surrendering $30,000 in jewelry and cash to armed men outside P. Diddy's Manhattan nightclub.

Believing that no NFL team would hire an obese head coach, New England Patriots assistant Charlie Weis had his stomach stapled last June. In July, six-one, 286-pound Sanford Rivers, a highly respected NFL head linesman, was suspended for the entirety of this season. His vertical zebra stripes were deemed, in the image-obsessed eyes of the league, insufficiently slimming. Which is odd, as the NFL—along with sumo wrestling—is the last refuge of the overweight in sports. Ten years ago there were sixty-six three-hundred-pounders in the league. Today there are well over three hundred who are well over three hundred.

To be sure, the competitive eating circuit still has its behemoths, like Atlanta's 360-pound Dale (Mouth from the South) Boone, who has speed-eaten more Russian dumplings (274 in six minutes) than any man on earth. Boone was planning to stay at Crazy Legs Conti's apartment in New York City during the G8 summit. "And we'll have our own Macy's parade," Conti said last week. "Dale is the size of one of the smaller blimps."

But Conti's hero and mentor is the legendary, 400-pound Hungry Charles Hardy, with whom Crazy Legs used to haunt an all-you-can-eat Greenwich Village sushi joint. "Charles eats a California roll the size of California," says Conti, whose friend was barred for life from that depleted establishment. But not before he taught Conti everything he knows. Last Super Bowl Sunday in New Orleans, Conti ate 168 oysters in ten minutes to defeat heavy favorites like Mo' Ribs Molesky and Crawfish Nick Stipelkovich.

In eating as in everything else, thin is in. The heavy man is a dinosaur, in every conceivable way. "Bigness helped the dinosaurs thrive," says Shea, who has no formal training as a paleontologist. "But ultimately it hurt them, and it was the birds and stealth lizards that survived. Not to take anything away from Booker"— and any busboy will tell you, you can't take anything away from Booker—"but tomorrow's competitive eater is likely a physically fit guy."

Thus, on Thanksgiving eve at Mickey Mantle's, nothing short of sport's future would be at stake. Does it belong to skinny marathoners like LeFevre, who once scarfed down two seventy-two ounce steaks in fifty-eight minutes on Donny & Marie? Or to full-bodied fullbacks like Badlands Booker, who did away with thirty-eight hardboiled eggs in ten minutes on Fox's Glutton Bowl?

Both men say the thrill of competition is enough for them. Everything else is gravy.

(December 2, 2002)

WINTER RULES

Into Thin Hair: A Personal Account of the Greenland Golf Expedition, in Which Aging White People Braved Arctic Cold, Dog Hazards, Whale Jerky, Beer Famine, Clowns, Clinical Madness, Walrus Genitalia, and a Moldavian Rock Band Singing "Mustang's Alley"—All in Pursuit of a Timeless Dream: To Ascend to the Top of the World and Break Ninety.

I.

"I couldn't care less about Greenland," William C. Starrett II said with disarming candor shortly after arriving in the northernmost country on earth. "I'm here for the golf."

Sixteen empty beer bottles were lined up in front of the retired California bankruptcy lawyer, so he looked like a contestant in a carnival midway game. It was the last week of March, and Starrett, two photographers, and I were passing a five-hour layover inside the modest air terminal in Ilulissat, a southern suburb of the North Pole, by systematically divesting the bar of its biennial beer supply. We began by drinking all the Carlsberg and then depleted the Tuborg reserves, and we were grimly working our way through the supply of something called Faxe, evidently named for the fax-machine toner with which it is brewed, when Starrett began recounting his life's memorable rounds. Rounds of golf, rounds of beer—the distinction was scarcely worth making.

"Livingstone was an interesting course," he said. "It's in Zambia, near Victoria Falls. The greens fee is thirty-five cents, and the pro shop has one shirt. At Rotorua, in New Zealand, the hazards are geysers. Sun City, in South Africa, has an alligator pit, and you don't play your ball out of that." This summer, Starrett said, he would rent a house in County Cork ("Walking distance to the Jameson's distillery") and travel from Ireland to Iceland for the Arctic Open, played in twenty-four hours of sunlight. He was, on the other hand, unlikely ever to return to the Moscow Country Club. It has gone to seed, don't you think, after expanding hubristically from nine holes to eighteen?

I feigned a look that said, You're telling me, and shook my head world-wearily.

"It is said that once a traveler has seen the world, there is always Greenland," says the Lonely Planet guidebook *Iceland, Greenland, and the Faroe Islands,* which only partly explains Starrett's presence here, 250 miles north of the Arctic Circle in Ilulissat, at the exact point at which mankind's appetite for golf exceeds the capabilities of fixed-wing aircraft.

Our profane party of golfers and journalists had flown five hours to Greenland on its national airline, Gronlandsfly, after first laying waste to the duty-free liquor shop in the Copenhagen airport so that its ravaged shelves resembled those of a 7-Eleven in the hours immediately following a hurricane warning. After alighting on Greenland, the world's largest island, we required two more northbound flights of an hour each to reach Ilulissat. This was the end of the line for the four-prop de Havilland DHC-7, and we now awaited the arrival of a Vietnam-vintage Sikorsky military transport helicopter to take us the last hour-and-twenty-minute leg north, to the frozen coastal island of Uummannaq, for the first—and possibly last—World Ice Golf championship (hereafter known as the WIG).

The WIG was open to anyone with $2,000, a titanium liver, and a willingness to spend a week 310 miles north of the Arctic Circle, in one of the northernmost communities in the world. Who could resist such a powerful come-on? Every citizen of planet earth save twenty, it turns out.

Still, though the tournament was a sponsored contrivance designed to promote Greenland tourism—and a Scottish liqueur company, Drambuie—winter golf on Greenland promised to have singular benefits for the high handicapper. For starters, the island's 840,000 square miles are virtually unblighted (from a strictly golf-centric view of the ecosystem) by trees. Nor would water come into play, as 85 percent of Greenland is covered by a permanent icecap, which in places is two miles thick. Most significant, the Greenlandic counting system goes only to *arqaneq marluk,* or twelve, after which there is simply *passuit,* or "many"—an idiosyncrasy surely to be exploited to my advantage on a scorecard.

The incoming Sikorsky at last set down in Ilulissat like a great Mosquito of Death. The vehicle was so old, a Dane living in Greenland told me with perverse pride, that its manufacturer wants the relic returned for display in a museum when Gronlandsfly retires it. At this news I signaled the bartendress for a final round of Faxes, but she gestured to her glass-fronted refrigerator, now empty, and said accusingly, "No more beer."

With growing dread, I returned to my companions in the waiting area. In the lounge chair facing me was a London-based sports photographer named Gary Prior. A janitor who moments earlier had been cleaning the men's room approached Prior from behind and began massaging his scalp, and a look of supreme serenity spread across his—the janitor's—face. Prior prudently avoided any sudden movement as he mouthed, "This bloke's gone mad."

So it was with a profound sense of foreboding that we boarded the Sikorsky, its belly filled with golf clubs, and set out to defy Robert Louis Stevenson, who wrote, "Ice and iron cannot be welded." Would this prove to be a prophecy? With a terrible shudder, the rotored beast rose above the icebergs, carrying us, its human prey, deeper, ever deeper, into a golfing Heart of Darkness.

II.

I had first heard of ice golf two summers earlier, while traveling under the midnight sun in northern Scandinavia. "You must return in the winter," implored the deskman at the Strand Hotel in

Helsinki, "when we play ice golf on frozen lakes and snow, in freezing temperatures, with balls that are purple."

"Yes, well, I imagine they would be," I stammered, but truth be told the idea intrigued me. Greenland was among the last outposts—on earth or in its orbit—to resist golf's colonial overtures. Man first walked on the moon in 1969, and within two years he was golfing there. Greenland was first inhabited five thousand years ago, yet it had only a nine-hole track near the main airport, in Kangerlussuaq, to show for it. Until two months before our arrival, the game had never been seen in Uummannaq, and when the Sikorsky touched down outside the village, I had an irresistible impulse to plant a numbered flagstick, as if landing at Iwo Jima.

A week before our visit, two hundred of Uummannaq's fourteen hundred residents had turned out for a golf clinic conducted on a makeshift driving range: the frozen fjord waters that surround the island. "I think it is very difficult to hit this ball," said Jonas Nielsen, a fifty-eight-year-old resident, after taking his hacks off a rubber tee. "But the young kids, they are very interested and would like to learn more about this game."

As well they should. Greenland's fifty-six-thousand residents, 80 percent of whom are Inuits (the word *Eskimo* is best avoided), are said to be temperamentally suited to golf. "One thing about Greenlanders," wrote Lawrence Millman in his Arctic travelogue *Last Places,* "they tend to find misfortune amusing."

You have to, on Greenland or in golf. "When they contacted me many months ago to attend this event," said Ronan Rafferty, referring to the tournament's sponsors, "I thought it was a joke." Rafferty, a thirty-five-year-old native of Northern Ireland, was the leading money winner on the European tour in 1989 and a member of that year's Ryder Cup team. He was paid by sponsors to attend the WIG, but a wrist injury would prevent him from actually playing. Mercifully he had his own wines shipped to Greenland, and he was toasted at dinner by the mayor of Uummannaq as "Ronan Rafferty, the famous golfer which I never heard of."

Rafferty arrived the night before I did with another party of golfers and journalists. All told, twenty competitors and twenty noncompetitors, representing six nations, attended the WIG. From Holland came Lex Hiemstra, who won the trip in a contest and was often asked if second prize was two tickets. Joining me from the United States were Starrett and Mark Cannizzaro, a *New York Post* golf columnist who turned up some instructive literature on local custom. "The stomach of a reindeer is like a large balloon, and the green substance in the stomach has a very particular smell," read the section headed "Food and How We Eat It" in a Greenland publication. "It is neither delicious nor revolting, but somewhere in between." This would prove useful, as our menus for the tournament would include whale jerky, blackened musk ox, and battered auk.

Jane Westerman joined my table at the welcoming dinner in the Hotel Uummannaq. Westerman, a widow from England with a newfound love of golf ("I'm quite keen, really"), is a member of the Roehampton Club in southwest London. "We have bridge, croquet, and golf," she said. "But hardly any ice golf a-tall."

Peter Masters, also English, asked Westerman where exactly the club was located. "It's near the Priory," she replied. "Do you know the Priory? The upmarket psychiatric hospital?"

Masters did not know the Priory, but soon enough, surely, we all would. Outside the hotel, hundreds of Greenlandic sled dogs—frightening creatures resembling wolves—wailed all night at the moon. A message posted in the hotel said that alcohol was forbidden in guest rooms. A man explained that a drunk once wandered out and lay down among the dogs. In the morning all that was found of him was a button. A single button.

"What's the saying?" Masters asked, with more portent than he could possibly know. "Mad dogs and Englishmen . . . ?"

III.

It was fifteen degrees below zero when I rose to play a practice round with Starrett. On the course he stood up his stand-up bag, and its plastic legs snapped in half. The bag collapsed to the ice, legs dangling at odd angles, like Joe Theismann's.

My own legs buckled at the beauty of the layout. The course was constructed entirely of ice and snow, nine holes laid out like a bracelet of cubic zirconiums on the frozen fjord waters surrounding Uummannaq. Fairways doglegged around icebergs ten stories tall. This is what Krypton Country Club must look like. My disbelieving eyes popped cartoonishly, and I had half a mind to pluck them from my face, plop them in a ball washer, and screw them back into their sockets to see if the scene was real.

The fairways were snow-packed and groomed and set off by stakes from the icy rough. The greens, called whites, were smooth ice, like the surface of a skating rink. No amount of Tour Sauce could get a ball to bite on these whites; bump-and-run, I could see, was the only way to play.

The hole itself was twice the diameter of a standard golf hole, and players were allowed to sweep their putting lines clean with a broom. Other winter rules were in effect. All balls in the fairway could be played off a rubber tee, while balls in the rough could be lifted and placed within four inches of where they landed, on a line no closer to the hole. My own balls, alas, were not purple, but rather optic-yellow low-compression Titleists, replete with the WIG logo.

I discovered many things during my practice round of ice golf. I discovered that any given golf shot is 30 percent shorter in subzero temperatures than it is at seventy-two degrees. (The course was appropriately abbreviated, at 4,247 yards for eighteen holes.) I discovered that it's difficult to make a Vardon grip in ski gloves, to take a proper stance without crampons, and to find a ball that had landed in fresh powder. But mainly I discovered that, with suitable clothes, no spouse, and no desire for country club indulgences—caddies, shoeshines, combs adrift in a sea of blue Barbicide—there is nothing to prevent you from playing golf anywhere on earth, in any season, any day of the year.

That alone seemed a more worthwhile discovery than anything Admiral Peary had stumbled on in the Arctic.

IV.

The WIG had a shotgun start. Except that a cannon was used instead of a shotgun, and the cannoneer reportedly suffered powder burns on his face and had to be treated in the village hospital. The next shotgun start employed an actual shotgun.

I was playing with Masters, an editor at the British magazine *Golf World* and a seven handicapper. On the second hole, a 284-yard par four with an iceberg dominating the right rough, Masters uncoiled a majestic drive. As he did so, a team of speeding dogs pulling a sled abruptly appeared to our left, two hundred yards from the tee box. The ball was hurtling up the fairway at speed x, the dogs were sprinting toward the fairway at speed y, and suddenly, as the two vectors approached each other, we were witnesses to a complicated math problem sprung horribly to life.

With what can only be described as a plaintive wail, one of the dogs collapsed. The rest of the team kept sprinting, dragging their fallen comrade behind the sled so that he resembled a tin can tied to the bumper of a newlywed couple's car. The driver glanced back at the dog and, with barely a shrug, continued to mush. Greenlandic sled drivers, in sealskin jackets and pants made of polar bear pelt, are not given to great displays of emotion, and the entire hallucinatory vision quickly disappeared into the white glare of an Arctic horizon.

Masters couldn't have anticipated this ludicrously improbable event, but a Danish woman following our foursome—she composed our entire gallery—repeatedly accused him of huskycide. "How could you?" she kept saying. "We are guests here." What the sled driver made of this act of God—a single optic-yellow hailstone falling from the sky and smiting his dog—is lost to history.

The very next hole was a right-hand dogleg—a word our foursome now studiously avoided using in Masters's presence—around an iceberg. I sliced consecutive tee shots on top of the berg and never recovered, especially as I had exhausted my one sleeve of optic-yellow Titleists and was now playing with the most garish range balls in my bag. Masters, shaken, carded a 40 on the front nine but recovered his composure to post a three-over-par 75 for the round.

At day's end Englishman Robert Bevan-Jones, whose record 31 on the back nine gave him a first-round 70, held a one-stroke lead over Scotsman Graeme Bissett. My first-round 99 left me in eighteenth place and in a powerful melancholia, especially considering that the tournament lasted but two days. We had come all this way, and it was already half over. Long after the round ended, I remained on the fjord, seasonal affective disorder setting in, and lost myself in the endless white.

I was wallowing in a profound silence, two miles from Uummannaq on the frozen fjord, when my driver, a Dane raised in Greenland, broke the spell. "*Uummannaq* means 'heart,'" said Christian Dyrlov while tracing a valentine in the air with his index finger. "Because the island is shaped like a heart, or like the back of a woman."

Hours later, back in my room, I unfolded a map and concluded that it would take the entire imaginative arsenal of a powerfully lonely man, in a frigid climate, at a far remove from the rest of the world, to see Uummannaq as even vaguely resembling a valentine. Or the tapering back of a beautiful woman.

It was beginning to look like both to me.

V.

Saturday night in Uummannaq began uneventfully enough. The dinner was verbally hijacked, as usual, by the speechifying representative of Drambuie, who kept urging us, somewhat salaciously, to nose his product. Two clowns performed. Then a few of us walked through the restaurant's kitchen. Which is to say, through the looking glass.

Behind the kitchen in the Hotel Uummannaq, should you ever find yourself there, is a disco. Greenland, I kid you not, is a hotbed of something called Arctic reggae. Alas, the headliners on this night were not Bob Marley and the Whalers. Rather, two aspiring rock stars from Moldavia took the stage, and they introduced themselves as Andy and Andreas. One played keyboards, the other guitar. "Our band is called Tandem," said Andy, or possibly Andreas. "You know, the bicycle with two seats?"

Andy and Andreas, singing from a notebook filled with handwritten lyrics to Western pop songs, performed phonetic covers of such unforgettable standards as "Unforgeteble" ("Like a song of love that clins to me / How a follow you that stins to me") and "Country Roads" ("Almost heaven, Vest Virginia / Blue Ridge Mountain, Shenandoah River"). A toothless woman forced me, at beerpoint, to dance with her, while leathery Inuit fishermen watched our group of golfing toffs and scrawny scribes pogo to the music and decided—for reasons known only to them—not to kill us with their bare hands.

"Why do you laugh during Mustang's Alley?" Andreas (or maybe it was Andy) asked as I flipped through his notebook at a set break.

"It's 'Mustang Sally,'" I replied, and a lightbulb buzzed to life above his head. "Ahh," he said, as if his world had finally begun to make sense. "Thank you." Forget love and Esperanto. The only two international languages are music and sports.

While Greenland has a home-rule government, it remains a province of Denmark, and just fourteen hours had elapsed since Denmark played Italy in a qualifying match for soccer's European Championship. The match had been broadcast live on Greenland's lone television network. This qualified as event programming; the fare on another day consisted principally of a travel agent riffling through brochures for tropical resorts.

I now understood why our gallery had been infinitesimal earlier in the day. Oblivious to golf, Greenlanders are soccer obsessives. The only permanent athletic facility visible in Uummannaq is a soccer pitch. Every fifth child wore a Manchester United ski cap. Man United's goalkeeper is Peter Schmeichel, who is also captain of the Danish national team. Additionally, England had played Poland that afternoon, and Man United star Paul Scholes scored all three goals for England.

So wired Uummannaqans were not ready to retire when the disco closed at 3 A.M., and we all repaired to a house party, which is when things began to get surreal. Just inside the door was a pair of size-twenty clown shoes. Fair enough. On a shelf were several impressive ivory souvenirs—swords, perhaps, or walking sticks—that are difficult to describe. An English photographer was twirling one like Mary Poppins's umbrella when the

Faroese hostess materialized to say, "I see you found my collection of walrus penis bones."

The clown shoes belonged to a thirty-one-year-old American named Joel Cole, who was visiting Uummannaq from his native Shakopee, Minnesota, a town nearly adjacent to the one I grew up in. The odds against us meeting near the North Pole were roughly six billion to one, but by this time I had come to expect anything in Uummannaq. Cole was once the national track and field coach for the Faroe Islands and led them to a respectable showing at the 1989 World Island Games, a kind of Olympics among Greenland, Iceland, the Isle of Wight, the Isle of Man, the Faroes, Shetlands, Gilligan's, and so forth. Cole now clowns—he used the word as a verb—in the world's underprivileged places for the real-life Patch Adams, whom Robin Williams portrayed in the film of that name. Indeed, Cole was the man who had clowned us at dinner just before we nosed our Drambuie. Said Cole, memorably, "I've clowned in Bosnia."

By 6:30 A.M. the evening was running out of steam, and I made my way back to the hotel with four journalists turned English soccer hooligans. As all twenty-nine-thousand of northeastern Greenland's sled dogs howled in unison, we strolled the streets— or, rather, street—of Uummannaq and sang (to the tune of "Kumbaya, My Lord"):

> He scores goals galore, he scores goals. He scores goals galore, he scores goals. He scores goals galore, he scores goals. Paul Scho-oles, he scores goals.

I was due to tee off in two hours.

VI.

I neglected to answer my wake-up call. I neglected to request a wake-up call. And I certainly neglected to "spring ahead" one hour in observance of daylight saving time. So I missed my tee time. Which is why in the final WIG results, listed in several international newspapers the next day—from the *New York Post* to the *Times* of London—my name would be followed by the ignominious notation WD. Which stands, I gather, for Was Drinking.

Having officially withdrawn from the WIG, I was free to follow the leaders. The gallery pursuing the final foursome on this soccer-free Sunday numbered several hundred townsfolk, whose mittened applause sounded like a million moth wings flapping.

Ronan Rafferty emerged from the hotel to watch the tournament play out. "You can cut the tension with a knife," someone said to him when three strokes separated the top three players with three holes to play. "Not really," said Rafferty. "You could maybe chip away at it a bit."

The improbable leader, by a single stroke, was Peter Masters, who had put his game and life back together after dropping a dog in the first round. When he finally holed a short putt to win the first WIG with a final round of 67, two under on the tournament, he was rushed by a jubilant gallery. An old woman thrust a napkin at him, and Masters, brand-new to Greenlandic fame, didn't know whether to blow his nose or sign his name. He signed with a felt-tip pen. "Being on the other side of that," said the journalist, more accustomed to interviewing golf champions than being one, "was surreal." There was that word again.

"What does Peter win?" asked Graeme Bissett, the Scotsman, who finished third, two strokes behind Masters.

"A ten-year exemption," I speculated.

Bissett chewed on this and said, "From coming back?"

On the contrary, returning is almost compulsory. Masters won an all-expenses-paid trip to defend his WIG title next year. Organizers were quite keen, really, to make this an annual event. Said a representative from Royal Greenland, the prawn-and-halibut concern that cosponsored the affair: "Bringing golf here shows we are not a static society." Imagine that. For the first time in recorded history, golf was a symbol of *un*stodginess: of forward-thinking, bridge-building multiculturalism.

Life is too often like the stomach of the reindeer, I reflected at dinner: neither delicious nor revolting, but somewhere in between. We had all come to the end of the earth to be delighted or revolted—to be anywhere but in the everlasting in-between of daily life. In that regard Greenland—without sunlight in winter, without moonlight in summer—succeeded on a grand scale.

"There are many difficulties here," said the mayor of Uummannaq. "The difficulties are darkness and harsh weather." He paused and added, "But there are also many beautiful times. The beautiful times are days like this."

The men, women, and children of the Uummannaq village choir appeared from nowhere and began to sing a cappella in their native tongue. One didn't have to speak Greenlandic to recognize the hymn. It was "Amazing Grace."

In that instant it occurred to me: Uummannaq is a Rorschach test. It really does resemble a human heart, for those willing to look long enough.

(May 17, 1999)

SUMMERY SUMMARY

This summer I will listen to baseball games on an AM radio while dozing in a hammock as a tall, sweating glass of lemonade rises and falls on my stomach with my breathing. The ice cubes will tinkle like wind chimes when I wake, with a start, to some ancient announcer shouting, "Tell Aunt Biddy to feed the kitty, 'cause that ball is gone!" Then I'll fall back to sleep.

I will buy one packet of Topps baseball cards this summer and peel open the wrapper, hoping to get an Ichiro Suzuki—only to find, instead, three Armando Almanzas, which I will clothespin to the front fork of the green Schwinn that I plan to buy this summer.

This summer I will play softball with my buddies in suburban parks with chain-link outfield fences, and we will drink Coors Light while getting ten-runned by lumberjacks. I will watch the games from right field through the airholes in the crown of my cap, which I will hold in front of my face to keep the gnats away. Then I will ride my Schwinn home with my mitt dangling from the handlebars, stopping at Dairy Queen for a Scrumpdillyishus bar, which I will eat in the parking lot, in full uniform, like a six-four Little Leaguer.

I will play pickup basketball games this summer on the baking asphalt of a brick-oven urban playground, and my sweet jump shot will make the chain net sway like the grass skirt on a hula dancer.

All the while, on my Samsonite-sized boom box, Earth Wind & Fire will sing "September."

This summer I will leave work at two o'clock on a Tuesday, citing a dental appointment, only to hit beautiful arcing draws and fades for three hours on a driving range out by the airport. Then on Saturday, full of hope, I will shoot 103 on some municipal goat track and pinch a nerve in my neck.

I will watch fat men sweat through gray T-shirts at an NFL training camp this summer while I sit comfortably in an aluminum-framed lawn chair. There I will drink beers kept cold by a foam-rubber can cozy and fan myself with a roster of rookies who just might—I will allow myself to believe—put the Vikings back in the Super Bowl.

I will fall off a skateboard sometime this summer and break my arm at a really cool angle. I will wear a cast that all my friends will sign and that women will find sexy. I will tell everyone that I broke it hang gliding.

This summer I will set my alarm on a Sunday morning to watch "Breakfast at Wimbledon" and see Bud Collins, in pants evidently cut from a Holiday Inn bedspread, interview a victorious Pete Sampras, a tradition that I always find comforting. Then, five hours after waking up, I will make several abortive efforts to get out of bed.

I will wait for the NBA Finals to conclude this summer in some oppressively hot city. As celebrating citizens light up the night with gunfire and blazing squad cars, I will watch the ten o'clock news and be glad that I don't live there. Because this summer I will have no greater concern than how to cut my lawn in those diagonal stripes of contrasting shades you see in major league stadiums. On that grass I will throw lawn darts and play croquet and make a Wiffle ball move like a moth in a maelstrom.

This summer I will buy live bait and sandwiches, served up by the same hands in a shack by the side of the road. Then I will fish from a dock with my feet in the water and my back resting on an Igloo cooler. In eight hours I will catch nothing but a buzz.

I will save seven hundred soda-pop proof-of-purchase labels this summer, and I will mail them to a P.O. box in Nebraska so that, sometime next December, I can giddily go to my mailbox and find inside a Tampa Bay Devil Rays souvenir key chain.

This summer I will spend all day at the beach throwing a football in flawless spirals and running tight post patterns around old men with metal detectors. I will never go into the water, and I will never make it past page 7 of James Michener's *Hawaii*.

I will stand on my front stoop this summer and watch kids plead "One more inning" when their mothers call them to wash up for dinner.

And when the sun goes down, I will park on the highest hill overlooking the city and tune in faraway, fifty-thousand-watt radio stations, and I will listen to ball games drifting in on a breeze from the West Coast. And when the games fade out, I will lie back on the hood of my car and look up at the stars and listen to the crickets.

(July 4, 2001)